AF568054

SRI BHAGVADGITA FOR MANAGERS

SRI BHAGVADGITA FOR MANAGERS

(A Managerial Interpretation of Sri Bhagvadgita)

With an Introductory Essay, Sanskrit Verses in Roman, English Translation and Comments

By

Dr. N.M. Khandelwal Ph.D.

Director

R.K. College of Business Management

Kasturba Dham, Rajkot – 360 020.

Bhavnagar Highway, Opp. Green Farm Hostel

(Gujarat - India)

Phone : 0281-2785114, Fax : 0281-2785114

E-mail : drmk65@gamil.

FIRST EDITION : 2011

Himalaya Publishing House

MUMBAI • NEW DELHI • NAGPUR • BENGALURU • HYDERABAD • CHENNAI • PUNE • LUCKNOW • AHMEDABAD • ERNAKULAM • BHUBANESWAR • INDORE

© **Author**

No part of this book shall be reproduced, reprinted or translated for any purpose whatsoever without permission of the author and publisher in writing.

First Edition : 2011 Edition : 2021

Published by : Mrs. Meena Pandey
for **HIMALAYA PUBLISHING HOUSE PVT. LTD.,**
"Ramdoot", Dr. Bhalerao Marg, Girgaon,
Mumbai - 400 004.
Phones: 2386 01 70/2386 38 63, Fax: 022-2387 71 78
Email: himpub@vsnl.com
Website: www.himpub.com

Branch Offices:

New Delhi : "Pooja Apartments", 4-B, Murari Lal Street, Ansari Road, Darya Ganj, **New Delhi - 110 002.**
Phones: 23270392, 23278631, Fax: 011-23256286

Nagpur : Kundanlal Chandak Industrial Estate, Ghat Road, **Nagpur - 440 018.**
Phones: 2738731, 3296733 Telefax : 0712-2721215

Bengalure : No. 16/1 (Old 12/1), 1st Floor, Next to Hotel Highlands, Madhava Nagar, Race Course Road, **Bengalure - 560 001.**
Phones : 22281541, 22385461, Telefax: 080-22286611

Hyderabad : No. 3-4-184, Lingampally, Besides Raghavendra Swamy Matham, **Hyderabad – 500 027.** Mobile: 09848130433

Chennai : No. 85/50, Bazullah Road, T. Nagar, **Chennai - 600 017.**
Phones: 044-28144004/28144005

Pune : First Floor, "Laksha" Apartment, No. 527, Mehunpura, Shaniwar Peth, (Near Prabhat Theatre), **Pune - 411 030.**
Phones: 020-24496323/24496333

Lucknow : C-43, Sector - C, Ali Gunj, **Lucknow - 226 024.**
Phone: 0522-2339329

Ahmedabad : 114, "SHAIL", 1st Floor, Opp. Madhu Sudan House, C.G. Road, Navrang Pura, **Ahmedabad – 380 009.**
Phone: 079-26560126,
Mobile: 09327324149,09314679413

Ernakulam : 39/104 A, Lakshmi Apartment, Karikkamuri Cross Rd., Ernakulam, **Cochin – 622011**.
Phones: 0484-2378012, 2378016, Mobile: 09344199799

Bhubaneswar : 5 Station Square, **Bhubaneswar - 751 001.**
Mobile: 9861046007, E-mail: orissa@himpub.com

Indore : Kesardeep Avenue Extension, 73, Narayan Bagh, Flat No. 302, IIIrd Floor, Near Humpty Dumpty School, Narayan Bagh, **Indore (M.P.)** Mobile: 09301386468

DTP by : Prerana Enterprises, Mumbai.

Printed by : A to Z Printers, New Delhi.

DEDICATED

TO

THE SACRED MEMORY

OF

SHRI MUKESH GUPTA, ACA

(MY ELDEST SON-B. 31-5-64

D. 10-9-90)

INTRODUCTORY ESSAY

Why Managerial Interpretation?

"History poses our problems, and if we restate old principles in new ways, it is not because we will do so but because we must. Such a restatement of the truths of eternity in the accents of our time is the only way in which a great Scripture can be of living value to mankind." – Dr. S. Radhakrishnan.

The book is intended for students and practitioners of management who desire to draw inspiration from spiritualism rather than for the specialist (philosophers). Scholarly differences on interpretation of the Gita find only minimum passing references in this book.

No translation of the Gita can bring out the dignity and grace of the original. Therefore, original sanskrit slokas have been given in Roman script. English translation is based on 'The Bhagwadgita' by Late Dr. S. Radhakrishnan. It is given under each sloka along with glossary of technical terms in order to help general reader to understand its meaning. Managerial interpretation is added by the author.

The current scene is full of failure of leadership, falling productivity, indiscipline. Corruption has become a global issue. It appears that people in general have been overtaken by materialism and attachment to lower sensory objects. In view of this, it is high time to go back to our roots and find a solution to contemporary managerial problems in '**celestial song**' the Srimadbhagvadgita.

The Bhagvadgita

The Bhagvadgita is celestial song which is not meant for esoteric only but is meant for all children of God for drawing solace, peace, tranquillity, equanimity and inspiration to perform duty successfully in the face of dilemma about goal. It offers a holistic integration of three essential ingredients of effectiveness — knowledge, devotion and action, called as *janan yoga*, *bhakti yoga* and *karma yoga*, respectively.

The Gita has provided great inspiration to several people all around the world when men struggle, fail and finally triumph. *Late Mahatma Gandhi* wrote, thus, "When disappointment stares me in the face and all alone I see not one ray of light, I go back to the Bhagvadgita. I find a verse here and a verse there and I immediately begin to smile in the midst of overwhelming tragedies — and my life has been full of external tragedies — and if they left no visible, no indelible scar on me, I owe it all to the teachings of *the Bhagvadgita*." [M.K. Gandhi, young India (1925), pp. 1078-79] *Jagadguru Samkaracharya* stated, "This famous Gita Sastra is an epitome of the essential of the whole *vedant* teaching. Its knowledge leads to the realisation of all human aspirations." (From introduction to Samkara's Commentary on Bhagvadgita). According to Late Dr. S. Radhakrishnan, the Gita has exercised an influence that extended in early times to China and Japan and latterly to the lands of the West. The two chief works of Mahayana Buddhism, *Mahayanasradhopatti* and *Saddharmapundarika* are deeply indebted to the teaching of the Gita. *J.W. Hauer*, the official exponent of the German faith and a Sanskrit Scholar gives to the Gita a central place in the German faith. He calls it, "*A work of imperishable significance*." He declares that the book, "gives us not only profound insights that are valid for all times and for all religious life, but it contains as well the classical presentation of the one of the most significant phases of Indo-Germanic religious history..." [From Introductory Essay to The Bhagvadgita by S. Radhakrishnan, Balckie & Son (India) Ltd., Bombay, (1977) p. 11]

The Gita inspires us to master the riddle of life through detached excellent performance of duty. Its message of action is rooted in the philosophy of life and philosophy of spirit. Healthy body and controlled mind are two preconditions of detached performance of duty leading to the realisation of the supreme goal of human life-emancipation or freedom from bondage of desires and cycle of rebirth. According to *Adi Samkara*, "The essential purpose of the Gita is to teach us a way – out of bondage and not merely enjoin action."

The **Gita** is the most systematic spiritual statement of the Perennial Philosophy meant for the whole mankind without any limitation of time and space. (Aldous Huxley, Swami Prabhavnanda and Christopher Isherwood, quoted by Dr. S. Radhakrishnan, p. 12). The Colophon indicates that Gita is a synthesis of metaphysics and ethics, *brahmavidya* and *yogshastra*, the science of reality and the art of union with reality. It is meant for practice by individuals with knowledge and devotion. First, mind should be cleared of all distractions (desire, attachment, aversion, anger, etc.), heart should be freed from all corruption in order to acquire spiritual wisdom. This will renew our life. We would be able to see the truth — what is our duty — power to discriminate between right and wrong. Second, we should perform our duty in a detached manner. Detachment may be based on 'Work of God' concept or 'offering to God' concept — freedom from selfishness. Then all actions will be free from bondage. No stress and strain will arise from action because equanimity of mind will give eternal bliss of peace. No sin will come to the performer of duty in this manner. In short, this is the Gita way of performing duty which combines realm of Spirit with the realm of life (duty). The transcendent (spirit) is combined with the empirical. The Gita shows us the way how can we live in the Highest Self (self–realised and free from bondage) and yet continue to perform our duty in this mortal world — A happy combination of immortality with mortality.

The Gita is called *Upanisad* because its main source of inspiration is *Upanisadas*. Thus, the Gita represents the best practical exposition of essential Vedantic philosophy. It is restatement of the Ancient Wisdom as revealed by the famous verse from the '*Vaisnaviya Tantrasara* —

sarvopanisado gava dogdha gopalanandanah
partho vatsah sudhir bhokta dugdham Gitamrtam mahai.

(The Upanisadas are the cows and the cowherd's son Krsna is the milker; Arjuna is the calf, the wise man is the drinker and the nectar–like Gita is the excellent milk).

The Gita presents a comprehensive synthesis of different currents of thought, the Vedic Cult of Sacrifice, the Upanisad teaching of the transcendent Brahman, the Bhagavata theism and tender piety, the Samkhya dualism and the yoga meditation. A unique convergence of various thoughts has been achieved by Lord Kṛsna (teacher in Gita) resulting into a unique model of inspirational motivation which led to willing (not forced) acceptance of duty by Arjuna (disciple). Detached willing performance led to victory as well as emancipation of Arjuna. It is stated in verse 73 ch. 18 of Gita —

nasto mohah smrtir labdha
tvatprasadan maya' cyuta
sthito' smi gatasamdehah
karisye vacanam tava.

(My delusion is destroyed and I have regained memory (recognition of truth or duty) by Thy grace, O Acyuta (Kṛsna). My doubts are dispelled. I stand firm. I shall act according to thy word.)

Finally, the ultimate secret of effective management has been revealed in last verse of the Gita (78 ch. 18) which is reproduced hereunder:

samjaya says:
yatra yogesvarah Krsno
yatra partho dhanurdharah
tatra s'rir vijayo bhutir
dhruva nitir matir mama

[Wherever there is Kṛsna, the Lord of yoga (as leader) and Partha (Arjuna), the archer (as executive), I think, there will surely be fortune, victory, welfare and morality.]

Thus, fortune, victory, welfare and ethics — prosperity and peace come through a combination of inspirational democratic leadership model of Kṛsna and devoted, detached and excellent executive model of Arjuna.

According to Dr. S. Radhakrishnan, the Gita is definitely a work of the pre – Christian era. Its date may be assigned to the fifth century B.C; though the text might have received many alterations in subsequent times. The author of the Gita is Ved Vyasa, the legendary compiler of the great epic *The Mahabharata*. The *Gita* is part of the *Bhishma parva* of the *The Mahabharata* from Chapters XXIII to XL. It contains 700 verses in Sanskrit. The *The Mahabharata* is called 'Fifth Veda' due to its comprehensive exposition of knowledge of four Vedas — Rig, Yajur, Sam, Atharva Vedas. Since Krsna is incarnation of Lord Vis'nu, the Gita — a part of Vedantic literature became adapted to *vais'navite cult*. Chief commentaries of Gita are by Adi Samkara (A.D. 788-820), Ramanuja (A.D. 1100), Madhava (A.D. 1199-1276), Nimbarka (A.D. 1162), Vallabhacharya (A.D. 1479). B.G. Tilak, Sri Aurobindo, Dr. S. Radhakrishnan, Mahatma Gandhi, Jaidayal Goenka, Swami Ramsukhdas, A.C. Bhaktivedantaswami and Swami Rangnathacharya have given recent/modern commentaries. Of late, management thinkers and practitioners have found the Gita of contemporary relevance for management. M.B. Athreya, S.K. Chakravarti, Maharishi Mahesh Yogi, Swami Chinmayananda, V.R. Panchmukhi, Rohit Mehta, Dr. Kirit Joshi are a few persons who have made notable contributions in this direction.

Being a student of commerce and management, the present author doesn't consider himself competent to talk about, *Advait*, *dvait*, *Shuddhadvait* and *Vis'isthadvait* philosophies of great classical commentators of Gita as stated above. For him, the Gita is a convergence of various philosophies. A practical guide to excellent performance. A great inspirational motivation model of democratic leadership and dedicated excellent detached performance. It provides practical solutions to the contemporary managerial problems of strategic management, executive health — stress and strain, failure of leadership, poor performance, etc. It shows the way to excellent performance coupled with eternal bliss of detached action. Putting the teachings of the Gita in actual practice can attain prosperity, peace and final emancipation of soul. Yajna, yoga, action, as redefined by Lord Krsna will make our society happy, prosperous and peaceful. The message of the Gita represents a secular socialist managerial model meant for the whole mankind. It is of universal character and is free from limitations of time and space.

The Gita assumes world as an arena where a constant struggle between good and evil, ethics and unethics, performance of duty and evading duty is going on. God Krsna is a leader who leads through example, conversation, psychological inspiration based on detached action, devotion and knowledge. He exhorts Arjuna, the executive, to perform his higher level of duty excellently without any attachment to action and its fruits. Through persuasive dialogue and clarification of doubts, he seeks willing consent to do duty. Lord Krsna is a democratic leader and not a dictator and converter. He doesn't advise to renounce the world but he is leading through example/practice, deliberation, trust, willing consent and detached action. He talks about mundane matters like enterprise, co-operation, meditation, regulated food and sleep for good executive health. He condemns procrastinators, idlers of time; pseudo renouncers, ritualist vedantins, observers of extreme fasts and excessive consumers. Regulated physical health, self-controlled and purified mind and detached action based on knowledge and devotion are the main ingredients of recipe of executive effectiveness according to him. He is our friend, philosopher, guide and protector. He is personal god or Is'vara. He is above/higher than Kshar (perishable physical body), akshar (imperishable soul) which is His part. He is self–illuminated '*Purshottama*' (Best of soul or creator of all, omnipotent and omnipresent, all pervading.) He controls *Maya* (illusion) which is his own creation. He is the creator of Vedic gods like Indra, Varuna, agni, vayu, yama, kuber, etc. He grants freedom to *Jeevatman* to be good or bad. He advises to be good but he does not dictate. Leader of Gita, Krsna is the Supreme Lord — Purshottama, Vishnu, Madhav, Madhusudan, Keshav, Devkinandan, Yasodanandan, Nandnandan, Vasudeva, Govind, Hrishikesha, Damodara. He is the creator of Brahma and Shiva. He is neither born nor dead. He is eternal. The Supreme Lord manifested Himself to save the world from decline of ethics, to protect good against evil and to reestablish ethical order. He reveals this truth to Arjuna as under:

yada–yada hi dharmasya
glanir bhavati bharata
abhyutthanam adhrmasya
ada'tmanam srjamy–aham.

(Ch. IV Verse 7 Gita)

(Whenever there is decline of righteousness and rise of unrighteousness, O Bharata (Arjuna), then I create my incarnation).

Object of incarnation is stated in next verse:

paritranaya sadhunam
vinasaya ca duskrtam
dharmasansthapa–narthaya
sambhavami yuge– yuge

(For the protection of the good, the destruction of the wicked and for the establishment of righteousness, I come into being from age to age).

When wrong prevails, Lord comes to reestablish right, not by force but by exemplary conduct and persuasive dialogue. He unifies practice and preaching of ethics.

Maya is illusion. It is created by the Supreme Lord. It is controlled by Him. It is rooted in trinity of *gunas* or attributes — *Sattva*, *rajas* and *tamogunas*. Those who are bound and blinded by Maya, they can't see the Lord manifest in this world as human being. Maya is ignorance in the Gita. Whole material and physical world is Maya of the Supreme Lord. Those who can overcome Maya/ignorance, they can realise God/Soul/Self.

Gita says that Supreme Lord resides in our heart as *atman* or *akshara* and at the same time he resides in the whole universe — micro and macro forms of the Supreme Lord. This knowledge grants us freedom from bondage. S. Radhakrishnan rightly observes, "By developing our inner spiritual nature, we gain a new kind of relatedness to the world and grow into freedom, where the integrity of the self is not compromised. We then become aware of ourselves as active creative individuals, living, not by the discipline of external authority but by the inward rule of free devotion to truth." (From introductory essay to Bhagvadgita, pp. 44-45). Gita propounds a principle that the best performance comes from spiritual power leading to self-control and self-management. External control is not sustainable. Thus, good managers must be good human beings first — self-controlled and self-managed, free from selfishness and other vices like desires, greed, lust, affection, aversion, jealousy, etc., Thus, who are spiritual and self-managed are liberated and excellent performers. Those who are enslaved to the object world, to desires, etc. they are not excellent performers. They can't enjoy sense of self-fulfilment and external bliss. They suffer from several ailments in spite of material success.

Karma is a condition, not a destiny. It is our natural duty. It is only one of five factors involved in the accomplishment of any act. One is *adhisthana* or workplace or organisation and management, *Karta* or doer, *Karma*, instrumentation, *Cesta* or effort and *daiva* or chance factor or luck. (Out of five factors, weightage of each successive factor is higher). It is our past *Karma* that determines our ancestry, heredity and environment. But subject to these limitations, we have freedom of choice. **Dr. S. Radhakrishnan again beautifully states, "Life is like a game of bridge. We did not invent the game or design the cards. We did not frame the rules and we can't control the dealing. The cards are dealt out to us, whether they be good or bad. To that extent determinism rules. But we have a choice to play well or play it badly. A skilful player may have a poor hand yet win the game."** (Introductory essay to the Bhagvadgita p.49). When we unite our–self with the Supreme Lord, we become *trigunatita*– free from bondage of the world. We win the game of life.

The *Gita* is yoga–sastra—a harmonious integration of knowledge, bhakti and karma yogas. It is the basis of best performance with a sense of enjoyment of bliss. Lord protects what is and unites with what is lacking. '*Yoga–Kshema vahamyahum*.' The Janana is reverse of ignorance. Ignorance is not intellectual error. It is spiritual blindness. Jnana illuminates and purifies your spirit and makes you an excellent performer. This may be called '*management through wisdom*' or '*wisdom management*.' An individual can become master of his life through '*self–realisation*' or '*spiritual reengineering*.' Body, life and mind must be integrated. We should avoid extremism and fundamentalism in our life. Best is to surrender to the Lord and put his preachings into actual practice. When we are emptied of 'I' or ego-related vices, God will take possession of us. We must do our duty to the best of our ability and share fruits as His *prasadam*. Offer our deeds to Him. This is the best '*puja*' of the Lord.

Wisdom will give us liberty and strength to perform excellently. The Gita is a treatise on '*Wisdom Management*.' It will grant us *Bhukti* (consumption) and *Mukti* (freedom from bondage of rebirth) both. The Supreme Lord will not allow His devotee to 'Perish.' It is His Supreme Sovereign Guarantee. The Gita will help us to prepare wisdom leaders like Krsna and devoted expert executives like Arjuna which will make world full of prosperity and peace.

Criticism of Gita

Although Gita is the most admired book, yet it is not free from criticism, mainly by leftist authors. Grifith has called ethical and moral aspects of Gita teachings as unclear and impractical. However, he has appreciated Yoga doctrine of Gita. Humboldt has crticised Gita on the ground that it promotes fatalism by saying that actions are predetermined. It gives speculation but does not reveal the solution. Mr. Risley has condemned Gita as a gospal of terrorism. Sri Aurobindo has effectively refuted this blatant charge by saying that if violence is not permitted to protect ethics then there is no moral basis for the State, Army and capital punishment. Pt. Jawaharlal Nehru has considered religion as personal matter. There is no place for organised communal form, according to him. Nishcam Karma theory is also not accepted by Pt. Nehru. He has considered plan and measurement, counting of fruits essential. Prem Nath Bajaj has called Gita as a Brahminism scripture. He has no knowledge of the concept of Brahmin used in our scriptures. Karl Marx has accepted socialism of Gita sans God. V.R. Narla has bitterly criticised Gita as supreme gospel of Nathuram Godse. D.D. Cosambi has called Gita as the Bible of bondage.

Conclusion

Srimadbhagvadgita provided great inspiration to eminent leaders of freedom movement of India. Mahatma Gandhi, Bal Gangadhar Tilak, Maharishi Aurobindo, Annie Bessant, Vinobha Bhave, Dr. S. Radhakrishnan, K.M. Munshi, C. Rajagopalachari, Pt. Madan Mohan Malviya and Morarji Desai who had deep faith in Gita and put its philosophy into practice successfully. Let the managers in this new millennium be enabled to solve the contemporary managerial problems through proper understanding and sincere practice of Gita as interpreted in this managerial commentary.

ability and share fruits as His *prasadam*. Offer our deeds to Him. This is the best '*puja*' of the Lord.

Wisdom will give us liberty and strength to perform excellently. The Gita is a treatise on '*Wisdom Management*.' It will grant us *Bhukti* (consumption) and *Mukti* (freedom from bondage of rebirth) both. The Supreme Lord will not allow His devotee to 'Perish.' It is His Supreme Sovereign Guarantee. The Gita will help us to prepare wisdom leaders like Krsna and devoted expert executives like Arjuna which will make world full of prosperity and peace.

Criticism of Gita

Although Gita is the most admired book, yet it is not free from criticism, mainly by leftist authors. Grifith has called ethical and moral aspects of Gita teachings as unclear and impractical. However, he has appreciated Yoga doctrine of Gita. Humboldt has crticised Gita on the ground that it promotes fatalism by saying that actions are predetermined. It gives speculation but does not reveal the solution. Mr. Risley has condemned Gita as a gospal of terrorism. Sri Aurobindo has effectively refuted this blatant charge by saying that if violence is not permitted to protect ethics then there is no moral basis for the State, Army and capital punishment. Pt. Jawaharlal Nehru has considered religion as personal matter. There is no place for organised communal form, according to him. Nishcam Karma theory is also not accepted by Pt. Nehru. He has considered plan and measurement, counting of fruits essential. Prem Nath Bajaj has called Gita as a Brahminism scripture. He has no knowledge of the concept of Brahmin used in our scriptures. Karl Marx has accepted socialism of Gita sans God. V.R. Narla has bitterly criticised Gita as supreme gospel of Nathuram Godse. D.D. Cosambi has called Gita as the Bible of bondage.

Conclusion

Srimadbhagvadgita provided great inspiration to eminent leaders of freedom movement of India. Mahatma Gandhi, Bal Gangadhar Tilak, Maharishi Aurobindo, Annie Bessant, Vinobha Bhave, Dr. S. Radhakrishnan, K.M. Munshi, C. Rajagopalachari, Pt. Madan Mohan Malviya and Morarji Desai who had deep faith in Gita and put its philosophy into practice successfully. Let the managers in this new millennium be enabled to solve the contemporary managerial problems through proper understanding and sincere practice of Gita as interpreted in this managerial commentary.

Instructional Notes For Teachers In Indian Ethos & Values for Managers

The University Grant Commission, New Delhi has published a model curriculum for MBA. It is available on its website also. Several Indian Universities have already introduced it and others are in the process of doing so. The UGC Model Curriculum contains a compulsory paper on ***'Indian Ethos & Values for Managers'.*** *Srimadbhagvadgita is a recommended book for this paper. However, existing commentaries on Gita are by experts in philosophy, Sanskrit literature and religion. None from management field was available. The present work is intended to fill–up this gap in management literature. The following instructional notes will prove to be of immense help to Faculty Members teaching this paper:*

(1) The topic **'Indian Work Ethos'** should be taught with the help of the following verses of Srimadbhagvadgita:

Chapter of Gita	Verses	Head or Subhead
2	47 – 53	Detached Karma or Karma with evenness of mind for attaining excellence.
3	04 – 16	Karma inescapable. Yagna concept of Karma co-operation and fair distribution. The principle of yagnaavashistha bhokta.
	19 – 43	Motivate others to do their duty by setting best example. Karma Yoga – Types of Karmas. Theory of sins. (36–43)
4	1 – 3	History of Indian Work Ethos
	7 – 8	God as protector of Ethics
	12 – 24	Karma Yoga in detail. Division of labour.
	31	Yagnaavashistha bhokta principle.
	37	Gyan – Karma Nexus

Chapter of Gita	Verses	Head/Subhead
5	4 – 16	Surrender Karma to God
	19 – 29	Karma and devotion
10	41	Excellence is my reflection
11	55	Devoted Karma
13	29	Karma as per nature
14	16 – 27	Effect of three gunas Theory on Karma
17	11 – 13	Three Types of Yagna (enterprise).
18	6 – 35	Karma Sanyasa
	41 – 48	Division of Labour
	57 – 66	Karma Theory Reviewed

(2) The topic **'Total Quality of Mind and Stress Management'** should be taught with the help of the following verses from 'Srimadbhagvadgita':

Chapter of Gita	Verses	Head/Subhead
2	55 – 72	Quality of person with evenness of mind. (Free from stress)
3	36 – 43	Control of desires to avoid sins.
4	33 – 42	Control Mind by gyana
6	1 – 10	Mind is a friend and an enemy.
	11 – 32	Meditation
	33 – 36	Control of Mind
	40 – 47	Destiny of a failed yogi.
8	7	Devotion and Action
18	51 – 53	Summary

(3) The topic **'Values for Leaders'** may be taught with the help of Chapter 3 Verses 21-26 on Leadership and Motivation by best example by a Leader.

(4) The topic **'Ethics and protection of Ethics'** may be taught with the help of Chapter 4 Verses 7-8 and Chapter 16 Verses 21-24.

(5) The topic **'Human Values'** Ethics may be taught with the help of the following verses:

Chapter of Gita	Verses	Head/Subhead
12	13 – 20	Qualities of a devotee.
13	7 – 10	Human values
14	21 – 27	Qualities of a 'gunateeta'
16	1 – 4	Divinity
	7 – 21	Demonic qualities

This may be used for Personality Development sessions also.

(6) Key to effective management is provided by Verse 78 of Chapter 18 of Srimadbhagvadgita.

Lord Shri Krishna is guru of the whole universe (Vande Krishnam Jagadgurum). His celestial song (Srimadbhagvadgita) is purely secular and spiritual being addressed to the whole humanity on Duty as Dharma and detached action as a way to emancipation. It is part of heritage of the whole humanity. It provides effectiveness in Management with eternal bliss, free from conflicts, stress, strain, anxiety, etc. Duty is propagated as Dharma.

The author firmly believes that the knowledge of management will be not fully effective without understanding and putting into practice the message of Jagatguru Lord Krishna contained in Gita. It is a unique case in inspirational leadership through best conduct, persuasive dialogue, freedom of expression and freedom of decision–making. It is an example of effective mentoring, coaching and counselling by a selfless/detached democratic leader to a devoted executive who is depressed due to lack of clarity of mission and duty due to attachment to own Kith and Kin. All doubts were clarified, memory was restored and freedom to take final decision was given. The decision with commitment was taken by the executive (Arjuna). It was executed under continued guidance and depression was converted into victory. Leader (Lord Krishna) was credible and transparent. He practised what He preached. Sacred knowledge of Gita – Duty as Dharma, if put into practise, will lead to improvement of productivity with happiness. It offers unique solution to the problem of stress and conflicts. Several leading companies have already put into practise with great success. Others may be tempted to do so after going through this maiden managerial commentary of Srimadbhagvadgita.

Constructive suggestions from indulgent readers are invited for further improvement in this work.

Prof. N. M. Khandelwal

EMINENT OPINIONS

"The Bhagvadgita is a valuable aid for the understanding of the supreme ends of life."

Dr. S. Radhakrishnan

"It (Bhagvadgita) is the spring of all wisdom. It contains the divine nectar. Just as the dark, unfathomed depth of the ocean contains most precious pearls, so also the Gita contains spiritual gems of incalculable value. One will have to dive deep into the depths of the Gita with sincere attitude of reverence and faith only then one can collect the spiritual pearls of Bhagvadgita."

Swami Sivananda

"In Bhagvadgita our modern world and its literature seems puny and trivial."

Henry David Thoreau

"Gita is our chief national heritage, our hope for the future, our great force for the purification of the moral weaknesses that stain and hamper our people."

Sri Aurobindo

"The Gita is God's Heart and man's breath, God's assurance and man's promise. .... Journey towards Immortality."

"If Avtar of Srikṛsna is the most complicated Door, the Gita, His song, is the most effective key."

"The West says that she has something special offer to the East: The New Testament. The East accept the offer with deepest gratitude and offers her greatest pride, the Bhagvadgita in return."

Chinmay

"One of the most revolutionary concepts enunciated in the Gita is that man is his saviour. Its salvation is not outside him, not in following the external authority. The Gita says, *let a man raise himself by himself.*"

Rohit Mehta

"Gita is my life's breath."

Vinoba Bhave

"I regret that the young men and women of our universities knew less about the Gita. .... than the undergraduates of the European universities knew about the Bible.

C. Rajagopalachari

“Often I indulge in what I call the Gita wash. I recite it for a number of days over and over again, doing nothing else. I gorge myself with it. At the end, I feel a new man. I find my mind reintegrated. Old problems assumes new shapes.”

Sri K.M. Munshi

“The Gita is the most beautiful, perhaps the only true philosophical song, existing in any known tongue.”

William Von Humboldt

“I believe that in all living laguages of the world, there is no book so full of knowledge, the purest love and the most luminious action. It teaches self–control, three fold yogas, non–violence, truth, compassion, obedience to the call of duty and putting up a fight against unricheousness or Adharma.”

Pandit Madan Mohan Malviya

“As I began to apply teachings of the Gita to the problems of my life, my doubts got resolved. Today my faith in teachings of the Gita is absolute and all doubts have disappeared.”

Morarji Desai

“Above all the Gita provides an exquisite technique of decision– making and which is valid and useful for us today as it was for Arjuna.”

I.P. Singh

“It (Gita) is a practical manual for daily living in any age. ....though the Bhagvadgita is timeless, it too must be interpreted in accordance with the needs of the time—The Yug Dharma.”

Eknath Iswarana

“Gita is the deepest and loftiest thing the world has to show.”

William Von Humbol

“Every Scripture has two sides, one temporary and perishable, belonging to the ideas of the people of the period and the country in which it is produced and, the other eternal and imperishable, and applicable to all ages and all countries.”

“The intellectual expression and the psychological idiom are the products of time while the permanent truths are capable of being lived and seen by a higher than intellectual vision at all times.”

Dr. S. Radhakrishnan

Contents

DILEMMA AND STRATEGIC MANAGEMENT

Contents

1. The Dilemma

The Eternal Question

dharmakṣetre Kurukṣetre
samaveta yuyutsavah
mamakah pandvas' cai'va
kim akurvata samjaya (1)

धृतराष्ट्र उवाच
धर्मक्षेत्रे कुरुक्षेत्रे समवेता युयुत्सवः ।
मामकाः पाण्डवाश्चैव किमकुर्वत सञ्जय ॥ (१ । १)

Dhritarastra said:

In the field of ethics and action, when my people and pandavas assembled for battle, what did they do, O Samjaya?

Dharmaksetre

The whole world is *dharmaksetre*, the battleground for ethics or moral struggle. This struggle goes on constantly in the hearts of people who are blinded by selfish motives and partiality like king Dhritarastra. The way to heaven passes through the path of dharma or ethics or duties.

Kuruksetre

The whole world is also a field of action or duty. Here we work out our karma and fulfil the mission of our birth as a human—emancipation or freedom from bondage of rebirth, self–realisation, etc.

The Gita is a scripture, which talks about ethics or values of action or practice. Its aim is to promote material prosperity with spiritualism—*bhukti* and *mukti* both simultaneously. Life has to be taken as a battle against evils, inaction/pseudo sanyas or renunciation. This type of war for ethics is a retributory judgement as well as an act of discipline or restoration of order. It is an act of creative destruction or innovation.

Mamakah

My people or own people. This sense of mine and not mine is the sign of partiality which is the result of *ahmkara* and cause of decisions with partiality.

Samjaya

He was the charioteer of king Dhrtarastra and also his management information system manager and expert advisor. He performed duty of reporting events of the war to the king.

The root cause of dilemma is role conflict. King Dhrtarastra is failing in his role as a king. He could not deliver justice to Pandavas because of his role conflict as king and as father to a son (Duryodhana). He is not impartial. He is attached to his son. This becomes the root cause of the Mahabharata war. Another role conflict is faced by Duryodhana who has no respect for the opinion of his seniors. He is seeking advice of Guru Dronacharya with a closed mind. He has pre–judged the issues. It was just a strategic move on his part. Third role conflict surfaces when Arjuna is in a bind due to lack of clarity about mission. He is stuck by his lower level role as a member of family which stops him from performing his higher role as a *kshatriya* or administrator is Gita offers remedy to dilemma about duty arising out of role conflict. "Arena of duty is arena of dharma." If this basic truth is understood clearly, then such role conflicts will not arise. No dilemma would be faced and excellent performance is guaranteed.

2. Strategic Management by Duryodhana

Analysis of strength, weaknesses, opportunities and threats (called as SWOT analysis) was carried out by Duryodhana just before the commencement of the

Mahabharata war. He approaches his teacher Dronacharya for advice on strategic and tactical planning of the Great War.

Duryodhana was the eldest son of king Dhritarastra. He was crown prince of the great kingdom of Hastinapur. Although he was a good administrator, yet he lacked in moral values. The Mahabharata war was a result of his selfishness, anger, jealousy and adamancy, which prevented him from heeding to the advice given by his seniors. He acted under motivated mis–guidance given by his maternal uncle Shakuni.

Now Samjaya communicates an eyewitness account of the war to the king.

dhratrastra uvaca
drstva tu pandavanikam
vyudham duryodhanas tada
acaryam upasamgamya
raja vacanam abravit (2)

दृष्ट्वा तु पाण्डवानीकं व्यूढं दुर्योधनस्तदा।
आचार्यमुपसङ्गम्य राजा वचनमब्रवीत्॥ (१।२)

Samjaya said:

Then, Duryodhana the prince, having seen the army of Pandavas , drawn up in battle order, approached his teacher and spoke this word:

Acharya:

A teacher, who has knowledge of scriptures, practices it and teaches it is called acharya. Dronacharya was the teacher of the Kauravas and the Pandavas both.

pa'syai'tam panduputranam
acarya mahatim camum
vyudham drupadaputrena
tava sisyena dhimata (3)

पश्यैतां पाण्डुपुत्राणामाचार्य महतीं चमूम्।
व्यूढां द्रुपदपुत्रेण तव शिष्येण धीमता॥ (१।३)

Behold, O Teacher, this strong army of the sons of Pandu (Pandavas) organised by your wise pupil, Drupadas' son.

Duryodhana is playing the psychological card to remind acharya Drona about his old enmity with king Drupada whose son Dhrstdhumna was a sworn enemy of acharya. He was born out of fire to kill acharya and fulfil the vow of king Drupada, his father, to finish Dronacharya.

First, he narrates the names of the chief warriors on the side of rival army.

atra sura mahesvasa
bhimarjunasma yudhi
yuyudhana viratas'ca
drupadas'ca maharathah (4)

अत्र शूरा महेष्वासा भीमार्जुनसमा युधि ।
युयुधानो विराटश्च द्रुपदश्च महारथ: ॥ (१ । ४)

Here are heroes, great bowmen equal to in battle to Bhima and Arjuna—

Yuyudhana, Virata and Drupada, a mighty warrior.

Bhima is Yudhisthira's commander in chief, though nominally Dhrstradyumna holds this office.

Arjuna is a friend of Kṛsna and the great hero on Pandava side.

Yuyudhana is Kṛsna's charioteer. He is also called as 'Satyaki.'

Virata is king of Viratnagar kingdom and father-in-law of Arjuna's son Abhimanyu.

Drupada is king of Drupad, father of Draupadi and Dhrstdhumna. A sworn enemy of Dronacharya.

dhrstaketus' cekitanah
kasirajas ca viryavan
purujit kuntibhojas' ca
saibyas'ca narapungavah (5)

धृष्टकेतुश्चेकितान: काशिराजश्च वीर्यवान् ।
पुरुजित्कुन्तिभोजश्च शैब्यश्च नरपुङ्गव: ॥ (१ । ५)

Dhrstaketu, Cekitana and the valiant king of Kasi, also Purujit, Kuntibhoja and Saibya, the foremost of men.

Dhrstaketu is the king of Cedis.

Cekitana is famous warrior in Pandavas army.

Purjit and *Kuntibhoja* are two brothers of Kunti–royal mother of Pandavas.

Saibya is a tribal king of the Sibi tribe.

yudhamanyus'ca vikranta
uttamaujaṣ' ca viryavan

saubhadro draupadeyas'ca
sarva eva maharathah (6)

युधामन्युश्च विक्रान्त उत्तमौजाश्च वीर्यवान्।
सौभद्रो द्रोपदेयाश्च सर्व एव महारथा:॥ (१।६)

Yudhamanyu is strong, Uttamouja is brave, son of Subhadra (Abhimanyu) and sons of Draupadi are all great warriors.

It should be noted carefully that before undertaking a big complex task, we must seek advice from a senior/expert. We must request him to advise with due respect. SWOT analysis must start with honest evaluation of strength of rival side. No mean expressions be used while doing this.

ama_kam tu visista ye
tam nibodha dvijottama
nayaka sainyasa
samjnartham tan bravimite (7)

अस्माकं तु विशिष्टा ये तान्निबोध द्विजोत्तम।
नायका मम सैन्यस्य सञ्ज्ञार्थं तान ब्रवीमि ते॥ (१।७)

O Best of twice born (cultured), know the leaders of my army. I will name them for thy information.

Dvijottama:

First, we are physically born in the world of nature. Our second birth occurs when we are initiated into the world of 'spirit'. Then we become cultured and illuminated self. Such self–realised and cultured persons are called twice born or *dvij*. The best amongst them is '*dvijottama*'. This word of respect has been used by Duryodhana for his teacher 'Dronacarya'.

Now main warriors in Kaurava army are mentioned to Dronacharya:

bhavan Bhishmas' ca Karnas' ca
krpas'ca samitimyayah
asvatthama vikranas'ca
saumadattis tathai'va ca (8)

भवान् भीष्मश्च कर्णश्च कृपश्च समितिञ्जय:।
अश्वत्थामा विकर्णश्च सौमदत्तिस्तथैव च॥ (१।८)

Thyself (Dronacharya), Bhishma, and Karna and Krpa (Krpacharya) are ever victorious in battle; Asvatthaman, Vikarna, and also the son of Somdatta.

anye ca bahavah sura
madrathe tayaktcjivitah
nanas'astrapraprahаranah
sarve yudhhavisardah (9)

अन्ये च बहवः शूरा मदर्थे त्यक्तजीविताः ।
नानाशस्त्रप्रहरणाः सर्वे युद्धविशारदाः ॥ (१।९)

And many other heroes who have risked their lives for my sake. They bear many kinds of weapons and are skilled in war.

Duryodhana has first highlighted the high quality of his army chiefs. Now he talks about quantitative balance of two armies.

aparyapatam tad asmakam
balam Bhishmabhirksitam
paryaptam tv idam estesam
balam bhimabhiraksitam (10)

अपर्याप्तं तदस्माकं बलं भीष्माभिरक्षितम् ।
पर्याप्तं त्विदमेतेषां बलं भीमाभिरक्षितम् ॥ (१।१०)

Our army is unlimited and is guarded by Bhishma, while Bhima guards the limited army of Pandavas.

The ratio was 11:7.

Bhishma is the grandfather of Kauravas and Pandavas both. He brought–up three brothers—Pandu, Dhrtrashtra and Vidur. Pandu had five sons—Yudhisthir, Bhim, Arjuna (from Kunti) and Nakul and Sahdeva (from Madri). He was the king. When Pandu died of liver trouble, blind Dhritarastra became king. Vidur was Prime Minister of the State. *Karna* is the eldest son of Kunti. He was born before marriage. He was reared by Radha. Therefore, he is also called Radheya. He was an expert archer and the main challenger to Arjuna.

Krpa is the brother–in–law of Dronacharya.
Asvatthaman is son of Dronacharya.
Vikarna is third of the 100 sons of Dhritarastra.
Somadatti is the son of Somdatta, the king of Bahikas.

After informing Dronacharya about comparative quality and quantity of two armies, Duryodhana now comes to the key factor — Protect Bhishma from all sides. Kauravas can't be defeated till Bhishma is safe.

ayanesu ca sarvesu
yathabhagam avasthitah

Bhishmam eva' bhiraksantu
bhavantah sarva eva hi (11)

अयनेषु च सर्वेषु यथाभागमवस्थिता:।
भीष्ममेवाभिरक्षन्तु भवन्त: सर्व एव हि॥ (१।११)

Therefore, all of you support Bhishma, standing firm in all the fronts, in your respective ranks.

By saying this to Dronacharya, Duryodhana wants to ensure full support of Dronacharya to Bhishma. It was a strategic move. Karna had already refused to come to battlefield till Bhishma was the chief of Kaurava army. Karna had a strained relationship with Bhishma and Dronacharya could have also developed cold rift on account of Drona being serious contender for the position of the Chief of Army. Duryodhana wanted to prevent such a disastrous cool conflict. *He has ordered to his teacher under the garb of seeking advice.* The teacher has not opened his mouth at all. It was a great strategic move on the part of Duryodhana.However, he has not waited for advice. He has a closed selfish and suspicious mind but well informed and has clear understanding of environment and time. He has knowledge and action both but lacks devotion and ethics. He knew that his seniors were sympathetic to Pandavas. That is why he resorted to tactical announcement of his decision.

3. Confirmation of Loyalties/ Morale

When Duryodhana gave order/direction, no warrior had any option but to confirm his loyalty/morale to the crown by blowing his conch. First Kaurava army chiefs did it followed by Pandava Army Chiefs.

tasya samjanayan harsain
kuruvrddhah pitamahah
simhanadam vinadyo' ccaih
sankham dadhmau pratapavan (12)

तस्य सञ्जनयन्हर्षं कुरुवृद्ध: पितामह:।
सिंहनादं विनद्योच्चै: शङ्खं दध्मौ प्रतापवान्॥ (१।१२)

In order to cheer–up him (Duryodhana), the aged Guru (Bhishma) roared like a lion and blew his conch.

tatah sankhas ca bheryas'ca
panavankagomukah
sahasi'va'bhyahanyanta
sa sabdastumule' bhavat (13)

तत: शङ्खाश्च भेर्यश्च पणवानकगोमुखा: ।
सहसैवाभ्यहन्यन्त स शब्दस्तुमुलोऽभवत् ॥ (१ । १३)

Then conches and kettledrums, tabors and drums and horns were struck suddenly which made tumultous noise.

tatah svetair hayair yukte
mahati syandane sthitan
madhvah pandvas' cai' va
divyan sankhau pradhmatuh (14)

तत: श्वेतैर्हयैर्युक्ते महति स्यन्दने स्थितौ ।
माधव: पाण्डवश्चैव दिव्यौ शङ्खौ प्रदध्मतु: ॥ (१ । १४)

Stationed in their great chariot yoked to white horses, Kṛsna and Arjuna blew their celestial conches.

pancajanyam hrsikeso
devadattam dhanamjayah
paundram dadhman mahasankham
bhimakarma v r kodarah (15)

पाञ्चजन्यं हृषीकेशो देवदत्तं धनञ्जय: ।
पौण्ड्रं दध्मौ महाशङ्खं भीमकर्मा वृकोदर: ॥ (१ । १५)

Kṛsna blew his Pancajanya conch and Arjuna his Devadatta conch. Bhima, who had great appetite and terrific deeds, blew his mighty conch called Paundra.

anantavijayam raja
kuntiputro yudhisthirah
nakulah sahadevas' ca
sughosamanipuspakau (16)

अनन्ताविजयं राजा कुन्तीपुत्रो युधिष्ठिर: ।
नकुल: सहदेवश्च सुघोषमणिपुष्पकौ ॥ (१ । १६)

Son of Kunti, Yudhistirah blew his conch named 'Anantavijaya'; Nakula and Sahadeva blew their conches named Sughosa and Manipuspaka respectively.

kasyas'ca paramesvasah
shikhandi ca maharathah

dhrsh–tadhyumne virata'ca
satyakis' ca' parajtah (17)

काश्यश्च परमेष्वास: शिखण्डी च महारथ: ।
धृष्टद्युम्नो विराटश्च सात्यकिश्चापराजित: ॥ (१ । १७)

drupado draupadeyas' ca
sarvas'ah prithvipate
saubhadras'ca mahabahuh
sankhan dadhmuh prthak–prthak (18)

द्रुपदो द्रौपदेयाश्च सर्वश: पृथिवीपते ।
सौभद्रश्च महाबाहु: शङ्खान्दध्मु पृथक् पृथक् ॥ (१ । १८)

King of Kasi, the chief of archers, Sikhandin, the great warrior, Dhristadhymna and Virata and the invincible Satyaki; Drupada and the sons of Draupadi and Subhadra blew their respective conches from all sides.

sa ghoso dhartarastranam
brdayani vyadarayat
nabhas'ca prthvim cai'va
tumulo vyanunadayn (19)

स घोषो धार्तराष्ट्राणां हृदयानि व्यदारयत् ।
नभश्च पृथिवीं चैव तुमुलो व्यनुनादयान् ॥ (१ । १९)

The tumultous uproar resounding through earth and sky rent the hearts of Dhritarastra's sons.

Thus, Pandavas Army Chiefs responded to Kaurva Army Chiefs in a befitting manner. This was indication of 'ready' position on the battlefield.

4. Faulty SWOT Analysis by Arjuna

Having declared his loyalty and morale through blewing devdatta conch by Arjuna, there was no point in his asking Krsna to take his chariot between the two armies for SWOT analysis through observation. The attack was already started by Kauravas. Therefore, decision to undertake SWOT analysis was belated or untimely on the part of Arjuna.

atha vyavasthitan drstva
dhartarastran kapidhvjah
pravrtte s'astrasampate
dhenur udyamya pandavah (20)

अथ व्यवस्थितान्दृष्ट्वा धार्तराष्ट्रान् कपिध्वजः ।
प्रवृत्ते शस्त्रसम्पाते धनुरुद्यम्य पाण्डवः ॥ (१ । २०)

Then Arjuna, whose flag bore the crest of Hanuman, looked at the sons of Dhritarastra drawn up in battle order; and as the fight of missiles just started, he took up his bow.

hrsikes'am tada vakyam
idam aha mahipate
senayor ubhayor madhye
ratham sthapaya me' cyuta (21)

हृषीकेशं तदा वाक्यमिदमाह महीपते ।
अर्जुन उवाच
सेनयोरुभयोर्मध्ये रथं स्थापय मेऽच्युत ॥ (१ । २१)

yavad etan nirikse' ham
yoddhukaman avasthitan
kair maya saha yoddhavyam
asmin ranasa mudyame (22)

यावदेतान्निरीक्षेऽहं योद्धुकामानवस्थितान् ।
कैर्मया सह योद्धव्यमस्मिन्रणसमुद्यमे ॥ (१ । २२)

O king! Arjuna spoke this word to Hrsikes'a (Krsna): O Acyuta! Draw up my chariot between the two armies, so that I may observe these men standing with whom I have to fight.

Hrsikesa and Acyuta are other names of Krsna .

yotsyamanan avekse' ham
ya ete' tra samagatah
dhartarastrasya durbuddher
yuddhe priyacikirsvah (23)

योत्स्यमानानवेक्षेऽहं य एतेऽत्र समागताः ।
धार्तराष्ट्रस्य दुर्बुद्धेर्युद्धे प्रियचिकीर्षवः ॥ (१ । २३)

I wish to look at those who are assembled here ready to fight and eager to attain in the battle what is dear to the evil–minded son of Dhrtarastra (Duryodhana).

If we compare action by Duryodhana and Arjuna, it becomes clear that Strategic Management of Duryodhana was better. He was well informed about chief warriors on both the sides. He made strategic moves very timely.

He could prevent any indifference or revolt by Dronacharya and he appointed Bhishma as Chief of his Army knowing fully well that Arjuna would not be able to adjust psychologically while fighting with his own grandfather who loved him the most. Both his strategic moves were successful, for Arjuna developed cold feet when he saw Bhishma ready to fight with him. Arjuna tries to collect information about Kaurava army very late when war was almost on. His lack of information and choice of wrong time were indicators of his poor strategic management. Even mission of war is not clear to him. He is bound by social ties, blood relations, etc., even at the cost of his duty as *Kshatriya* to fight a war for re-establishment of ethical order. Lack of clarity about mission causes delusion, affection and attachment leading to depression and nervousness. The major defect of Arjuna from management viewpoint was his utter lack of advance planning by a careful analysis of implications of war. Some commentators feel that Arjuna's ego is displayed by saying, "I want to see who have come to fight with me in this war."

samjay uvac
evam ukto hrsikeso
gudakes'ena bharata
senayor ubhayor madhye
sthapayitva rathottamam (24)

सञ्जय उवाच
एवमुक्तो हृषीकेशो गुडाकेशेन भारत।
सेनयोरुभयोर्मध्ये स्थापयित्वा रथोत्तमम्॥ (१।२४)

O Bharata! (king Dhrtarastra)! Hrsikes'a (Krsna) stationed the best of chariots between the two armies, as told by *Gudakesa* (Arjuna).

Now what Arjuna observes which causes depression in him—

Bhishmadronapramukhtah
sarvesam ca mahiksitam
uvaca partha pasyai' tan
samavetan kurum iti (25)

भीष्मद्रोणप्रमुखत: सर्वोषां च महीक्षिताम्।
उवाच पार्थ पश्यैतान् समवेतान्कुरुनिति॥ (१।२५)

tatra' pas'yat sthitan parthah
pitrn atha pitamahan
acaryan matulan bhratrn
putran pautran sakhims tatha (26)

तत्रापश्यत्स्थितान् पार्थः पितॄनथ पितामहान्।
आचार्यन्मातुलान्भ्रातॄन्पुत्रान्पौत्रान्सखींस्तथा ॥ (१ । २६)

s'vas'uran suhradas'cai' va
senayor ubhayor api
tan samiksya sa kaunteyah
sarvan bandhun avasthitam (27)

श्वशुरान् सुहृदश्चैव सेनयोरुभयोरपि।
तान्समीक्ष्य स कौन्तेयः सर्वान्बन्धूनवस्थितान् ॥ (१ । २७)

krpaya paraya' visto
visidann idam abravit
arjun uvac
drstve' mam svajanam Krsna
yuyutsam samupasthitam (28)

कृपया परयाविष्टो विषीदन्निदमब्रवीत्।
अर्जुन उवाच
दृष्टेमं स्वजनं कृष्ण युयुत्सुं समुपस्थितम् ॥ (१ । २८)

Krsna asked Arjuna in front of Bhishma, Drona and all chiefs to see who were standing there. Arjuna saw fathers, grandfathers, teachers, uncles, brothers, sons, grandsons and friends/companions standing there. He also saw father–in–law and friends standing in both the armies. When he saw all these kinsmen thus arrayed, he was overtaken by grief and uttered with sadness.

sidanti mama gatrani
mukham ca parisusyati
vepathus' ca saritre me
romaharsas' ca jayate (29)

सीदन्ति मम गात्राणि मुखं च परिशुष्यति।
वेपथुश्च शरीरे मे रोमहर्षश्च जायते ॥ (१ । २९)

gandivam sramsate hastat
tvak cai' va paridahyate
na ca s'aknomy avasthatum
bhramati' va ca me manah (30)

गाण्डीवं स्रंसते हस्तात्त्वक्चैव परिदह्यते ।
न च शक्नोम्यवस्थातुं भ्रमतीव च मे मन: ॥ (१ । ३०)

nimittani ca pas'yami
viparitani kes'ava
na ca s'reyo' nupas'yami
hatva svajanam ahave (31)

निमित्तानि च पश्यामि विपरीतानि केशव ।
न च श्रेयोऽनुपश्यामि हत्त्वा स्वजनमाहवे ॥ (१ । ३१)

O Kṛsna ! My limbs quail, my mouth goes dry, my body shakes and my hair stands on end. The Gandiva bow slips from my hand and my skin too is burning all over. I am not able to stand steady. My mind is reeling. I see evil omens. I don't see any good by slaying my own people in the fighting. (He must have known this much before.)

Now this is the usual dilemma faced by every manager. They fail to take objective stand when their own relatives and friends are involved in any decision.

Attachment to my and mine is the cause of the war on the part of King Dhritarastra. The same element becomes a cause of depression and nervousness for Arjuna. ***Thus, a manager must avoid element of I, my, mine–others while taking a decision***. All these subjective considerations must be avoided in order to decide objectively.

Let us see now the excuses found by such managers in support of their inaction/wrong decisions to avoid their duty.

5. Excuses—Escape Routes of Depressed

na kankse vijayam Kṛsna
na ca rajyam sukhani ca
kim no rajeyena govinda
kim bhogair jivitena va (32)

न काङ्क्षे विजयं कृष्ण न च राज्यं सुखानि च ।
किं नो राज्येन गोविन्द किं भोगैर्जीवितेन वा ॥ (१ । ३२)

(After seeing bad omen and sin in killing own people (not others, of course). Arjuna says 0 Govinda (Kṛsna)! I don't want victory, nor kingdom, nor pleasures. Of what use is kingdom, enjoyment, or even life for us?

Thus, those who want to run away from duty due to sense of attachment, they find a pet excuse in '*sanyas*' or renouncement. This type of renouncement is not genuine but it is an escape route from facing the harsh realities of life.

yesam arthe kanksitam no
rajyam bhogah sukhani ca
ta ime' vasthita yuddhe
pranams tyktva dhanani ca (33)

येषामर्थे काङ्क्षितं नो राज्यं भोगा: सुखानि च ।
त इमेऽवस्थिता युद्धे प्राणांस्तक्त्वा धनानि च ॥ (१ । ३३)

Those for whose sake we desire kingdom, enjoyments and pleasures, they stand here in battle renouncing their lives and riches. (Therefore, victory for what when they are to be killed.)

Another escape route is family or relations interest. One pretends to be living for others.

acaryah pitarah putras
tathai' va pitamah
matulah svasurah pautrah
syalah sambandhinas tatha (34)

आचार्या: पितर: पुत्रास्तथैव च पितामहा: ।
मातुला: श्वशुरा: पौत्रा: श्याला: सम्बन्धिनस्तथा ॥ (१ । ३४)

etan na hantum icchami
ghnato' pi madhusudana
api trailkyarajyasya
hetoh kim nu mahikrte (35)

एतान्न हन्तुमिच्छामि घ्नतोऽपि मधुसूदन ।
अपि त्रैलोक्यराज्यस्य हेतो: किं नु महीकृते ॥ (१ । ३५)

nihatya dhartarastran nah
ka pritih syaj janardana
papam eva s'rayed asman
hatvai'tan atatayinah (36)

निहत्य धार्तराष्ट्रान्न: का प्रीति: स्याज्जनार्दन ।
पापमेवाश्रयेदस्मान्हत्वैतानाततायिन: ॥ (१ । ३६)

tasman na' rha vayam
hantumdhartarastran svabandhavan
svajanam hi katham hatva
sukhinah syama madhava (37)

तस्मान्नार्हा वयं हन्तुं धार्तराष्ट्रन् स्वबान्धवान् ।
स्वजनं हि कथं हत्वा सुखिन: स्याम माधव ॥ (१ । ३७)

I will not consent to kill teachers, fathers, sons, grandfathers, uncles, fathers-inlaw, grandsons, brother-in-laws (loosers) and kinsmen. O Madhusudana (Krsna)! I will not do so even for the kingdom of the three worlds so why for the sake of this earth? O Madhva (Krsna)! We can't derive any pleasure after slaining our own cousins (sons' of Dhritrashtra). Only sin will accrue to us by killing these sinners.

(Thus, Arjuna wants to take refuge under false concern for the welfare of his own relations. If he had so much love and affection for them, then why he had come to the battlefield.)

Trailokya: Earth, heaven and atmosphere.

Now he projects himself **as holier than thou**.

yadav apy ete na pasyanti
lobho pahatacetasah
kulaksayakrtam dosam
mitradrohe ca patkam (38)

यद्यप्येते न पश्यन्ति लोभोपहतचेतस: ।
कुलक्षयकृतं दोषं मित्रद्रोहे च पातकम् ॥ (१ । ३८)

katham na jneyam asmabhih
papad asman nivarititum
kulaksayakrtam dosam
prapasyadbhir janardana (39)

कथं न ज्ञेयमस्माभि: पापादस्मान्निवर्तितुम् ।
कुलक्षयकृतं दोषं प्रपश्यद्भिर्जनार्दन ॥ (१ । ३९)

Even if their (Kauravas) minds are overpowered by greed and they see no wrong in the destruction of the family and no crime in treachery to friends, why should we not have the wisdom to turn away from this sin (of war)? O Janardana (Krsna)! We should see the wrong in the destruction of the family.

Arjuna talks about his duty to family ignoring a higher level duty to the nation, society and humanity to save it from the unethical rule of Kauravas.

kulaksaye pranasyanti
kuladharmah sanatanah
dharme naste kulam krtsnam
adhermo' bhibhavaty uta (40)

कुलक्षये प्रणश्यन्ति कुलधर्माः सनातनाः ।
धर्मे नष्टे कुलं कृत्स्नमधर्मोऽभिभवत्युत ॥ (१।४०)

adharmabhibhavat Krsna
pradhusyanti kulastriyah
strisu dustansu varsneya
jayate varnasamkarah (41)

अधर्माभिभवात् कृष्णा प्रदुष्यन्ति कुलस्त्रियः ।
स्त्रीषुदृष्टासु वार्ष्णेय जायते वर्णसंकरः ॥ (१।४१)

samkaro narkayai' va
kulaghnanam kulasya ca
patenti pitaro hy esam
- luptapindodakakriyah (42)

संकरो नरकायैव कुलघ्नानां कुलस्य च ।
पतन्ति पितरो ह्येषां लुप्तपिण्डोदकक्रिया: ॥ (१।४२)

dosair etaih kulaghnanam
varnasamkarakaih
utsadyante jatidharmah
kuladharmas' ca sasvatah (43)

दोषैरेतैः कुलघ्नानां वर्णसंकरकारकैः ।
उत्साद्यन्ते जातिधर्माः कुलधर्माश्च शाश्वताः ॥ (१।४३)

utsannakuladharmanam
manusyanam janardana
narake niyatam vaso
bhavati' ty anususruma (44)

उत्सन्नकुलधर्माणां मनुष्याणां जनार्दन ।
नरकेऽनियतं वासो भवतीत्यनुशुश्रुम ॥ (१।४४)

aho bata mahat papam
kartum vyavasita vayam
yad rajyasukhalobhena
hantum svajanam udyatah (45)

अहो बत महत्पापं कर्तुं व्यवसिता वयम् ।
यद्राज्यसुखलोभेन हन्तुं स्वजनमुद्यताः ॥ (१ । ४५)

yadi mam apratikarma
asastram sastrapanayah
dhartarastra rane hanyus
tan me ksemataram bhavet (46)

यदि मामप्रतीकारमशस्त्रं शस्त्रपाणयः ।
धार्तराष्ट्रा रणे हन्युस्तन्मे क्षेमतरं भवेत् ॥ (१ । ४६)

When family is ruined in a war, its content laws are also destroyed. When laws perish, family becomes lawless. O Vars'neya (Krṣna) Women of such families become corrupted. Then confusion of caste arises. The family and its destroyer, both go to hell. The spirits of ancestors fall for the want of offerings of rice and water (because these spirits don't accept offerings from child born of corrupt ladies). This results into destruction of laws of the caste and family. Man of such corrupt family lives in hell. Alas, we have resolved to commit what a great sin by killing our own people out of our greed for the pleasures of kingdom! Better it would be for me if the cousins (sons of Dhritarastra) bearing weapons in their hand kill me unresisting and unarmed.

samjay uvaca
evam uktva' rjunah samkhye
rathopastha upavisat
visrjya sa'aram capam
sokasamvignamanasah (47)

सञ्जय उवाच
एवमुक्त्वार्जुनः सङ्ख्ये रथोपस्थ उपाविशत् ।
विसृज्य सशरं चापं शोकसंविग्नमानसः ॥ (१ । ४७)

Having spoken this on the battlefield, Arjuna sank down on the seat of his chariot, casting away his bow and arrow, his spirit overwhemed by sorrow.

This is the perpetual recurring dilemma of the whole mankind, especially of decision–makers. They lack objectivity due to attachment to kiths and kins and care for lower level objectives. They lack in clarity of mission. They want to run–away from their duty by advancing all such arguments to justify their inaction. A leader like Lord Kṛsna can advise them correctly in such a complicated situation.

Effective strategic management requires good management information system, timely SWOT analysis, clarity of mission and advice of mature objective leaders/experts. A respectful but frank communication is also needed between seeker of advice and giver of advice. Seek advice with open mind, trust, devotion and respect.

Colophon: *ity srimad bhagwadgitasupanisastu brahma vidyayam yogas'astre srikrsnarjunasamvade arjunavisadayoga nama prathmo' dhyayah.*

Upanisad: There are 108 upanisadas. Srimadbhagvadgita (celestial song) is essence of all upanisadas. It is the best exposition of vedantic philosophy.

Brahm vidya: Science of the Absolute; Knowledge of the God/ Soul/ Self.

Yoga sastra: The scripture of yoga. Union of man with spirit. Self–improvement is the best way to social betterment.

Kṛsna–arjuna samvada: This is a dialogue between a great leader and his disciple and companion or devoted executive Arjuna. Kṛsna resides in our hearts. If we become pure hearted, pure intellect and regulated mind, we can also have a dialogue with Him. He is very close to us. (Rig. Veda speaks of two birds who live together on a tree. One of them is witness.)

Visad Yoga: Depression. It is the starting point for moving towards light of knowledge.

Celestial song shows us light of knowledge to remove darkness of depression/ ignorance/ inaction or non–performance. The use of the term **visad yoga** is very intelligent. It indicates that depression can also be converted into an opportunity **to learn and unlearn** by seeking advice of competent expert.

SUMMARY

In management, dilemma arises due to role conflicts and lack of clarity about mission. Duty is Dharma. *Advice of seniors should be sought with humility/ submissiveness, open mind and full trust. Depression arises due to attachments to kiths and kins rather than commitment to duty, i.e.–Dharma. Strategic Management requires up to date timely information, impartial analysis, competent advice, timely decision and execution, independence of mind and approach. Non–attachment to selfish motives or holistic approach.*

BUDDHI YOGA

Contents

1. Counselling by the Leader

Samjaya uvaca
tam tatha krapaya' vistam
as'rupurnakuleksanam
visidantam idam vakyam
uvacha madusudanah (1)

संजय उवाच
तं तथा कृपयाविष्टमश्रुपूर्णाकुलेक्षणम् ।
विषीदन्तमिदं वाक्यमुवाच मधुसूदन: ॥ (२।१)

Sribhagwan uvaca
kutas tva kas'malam idam
visame sampupasthitam

anaryajustam asvargyam
akirtikarma arjuna (2)

श्रीभगवानुवाच
कुतस्त्वा कश्मलमिदं विषमे समुपस्थितम् ।
अनार्यजुष्टमस्वर्ग्यमकीर्तिकरमर्जुन ॥ (२।२)

Samjaya said, "Madhusudan (Kṛsna) spoke to Arjuna who was overcome by pity, whose eyes were filled with tears and who was much depressed in mind. He told that why he (Arjuna) has developed dejection of spirit in this hour of crisis? It is not liked by Aryans; it does not lead to heaven and it causes disgrace (on earth), O Arjuna."

Anaryajustam: Un–aryan. Aryan means a person of good conduct consisting of courage, courtesy, nobility and straight dealing; emotional stability, firmness in critical moments.

In fact, these qualities are essential for good leader/ manager.

Thus, Kṛsna mildly chides (rebukes) Arjuna for his unaryan conduct or misconduct as a manager by displaying lack of emotional stability at a critical juncture.

klaibyam ma sma gamah partha
nai' tat tvayy upapadyate
ksudram hrdayadaurbalyam
tyakvo' ttistha paramtapa (3)

क्लैब्यं मा स्म गमः पार्थ नैतत्त्वय्युपपद्यते ।
क्षुद्रं हृदयदौर्बल्यं त्यक्त्वोत्तिष्ठ परन्तप ॥ (२।३)

Kṛsna continued to rebuke Arjuna. Don't yield to unmanliness, O Partha (Arjuna). It is not befitting for him to show pettiness, weakness of heart. Give it up and arise, O oppressor of foes (Arjuna).

Paramtapa: Oppressor of foes—a honourable title given to a great warrior.

Partha: Son of '*pratha*' (Kunti).

Here Lord Kṛsna reminds Arjuna of his great strength as compared to enemies and also his celebrated parentage. This is psycho–social therapy used by Kṛsna.

2. Revelation of Doubts/causes of depression

This mild rebuke and psycho–social treatment led to disclosure of doubts or causes of depression by Arjuna to Kṛsna. Proper counselling is possible only when a counsellor motivates sufferer to reveal causes of depression/ problem transparently.

Arjuna uvaca
katham Bhishmam aham samkhye
dronam ca madhusudana
isubhih pratiyotsyami
pujarhav arisudana (4)

अर्जुन उवाच
कथं भीष्ममहं सङ्ख्ये द्रोणंच मधुसूदन।
इषुभिः प्रति योत्स्यामि पूजार्हावरिसूदन॥ (२।४)

gurun ahatva hi mahanubhavan
s'reyo bhoktum bhaik'sam api'ha loke
hatva' rthakamams tu gurun ihai' va
bhunjiya bhogan rudhirapradigdhan (5)

गुरुनहत्वा हि महानुभावान् श्रेयो भोक्तुं भैक्ष्यमपीह लोके।
हत्वार्थकामांत्सु गुरुनिहैव भुञ्जीय भोगान् रुधिरप्रदिग्धान्॥ (२।५)

na cai' tad vidmah kataram no gariyo
yadva jayema yadi va no jayeyuh
yan eva hatva na jijivisamas
te' vasthitah pramukhe dhartarstrah (6)

न चैतद्विद्मः कतरन्नो गरीयो–
यद्वा जयेम यदि वा नो जयेयुः।
यानेव हत्वा न जिजीविषाम–
स्तेऽवस्थिताः प्रमुखे धार्तराष्ट्राः॥ (२।६)

karpanyadosopahatasvabhavah
precchami tvam dharmasammudhace tah
yac chreyah syan niscitam bruhi tan me
sisyas te' ham sadhi mam tvam prapanam (7)

कापर्णदोषोपहतस्वभावः
पृच्छामि त्वां धर्मसम्मूढचेताः।
यच्छ्रेयः स्यान्निश्चितं ब्रूहि तन्मे
शिष्यस्तेऽहं शाधि मां त्वां प्रपन्नम्॥ (२।७)

na hi prapasyami mama'panudyad
yac chokam ucchosanam indriyanam
avapya bhumav asapatnam rddham
rajyam suraanam api ca' dhipatyam (8)

न हि प्रपश्यामि ममापनुद्याद्
यच्छोकमुच्छोषणमिन्द्रियाणाम् ।
अवाप्य भूमावसपत्नमृद्धं–
राज्यं सुरणामपि चाधिपत्यम् ॥ (२।८)

Arjuna said, "O slayer of foes (Kṛsna)! How shall I strike Bhishma (my grandfather) and Dronacharya (my teacher) with arrows in battle?" It is better to live in this world even by begging than to slay these honoured seniors. Although they are selfish, yet I would enjoy delights smeared with blood by slaying them. Further, we don't know which one is better for us—whether we conquer them or they conquer us. The sons of Dhritarastra, without whom we don't care to live, are standing before us in battle array. I am stricken with the weakness of pity. My mind is bewildered about my duty. I ask you. Tell me, for certain, which is better for me. I am your pupil; teach me, I seek refuge in you. My sorrow dries up my senses even if I should attain rich and unrivalled kingdom on earth or even the sovereignty of the gods. I don't see what will drive away my sorrow.

A seeker of advice must be transparent, free from ego and respectful before a leader/adviser like Arjuna. Only then proper advice can be given by an adviser. He admits the existence of attachment to seniors, lack of clarity towards duty, objectives and absence of power of discrimination between right and wrong. He candidly confesses that his mind was bewildered about duty. He surrenders before Kṛsna and seeks his instruction/ advice. Every executive must seek advice of competent expert/senior whenever he is faced with such dilemma about duty.

Samjaya uvaca
evam uktva hrsikesam
gudakesah paramtapah
na yotsya iti govindam
uktva tusinim babhuva ha (9)

सञ्जय उवाच
एवमुक्त्वा हृषीकेष गुडाकेश: परन्तप ।
न योत्स्य इति गोविन्दमुक्त्वा तूष्णीं बभूव ह ॥ (२।९)

Samjaya said to Dhritarastra, "Having thus addressed Hrisikesa (Kṛsna), the mighty Gudakesha (Arjuna) said to Govinda (Kṛsna), "I will not fight" and became silent.

The inaction and silence by Arjuna at this point indicates his preparation to listen the advice of Kṛsna.

tam uvaca hriskesah
prahasann iva bharata
senayor ubhayor madhye
visidanatam idam vacah (10)

तमुवाच हृषीकेशः प्रहसन्निव भारत।
सेनयोरुभयोर्मध्ये विषीदन्तमिदं वचः॥ (२।१०)

Samjaya continued, "O Bharata (Dhritarastra)! Hrisrikesa (Kṛsna) smilingly spoke this word to Arjuna who was depressed in the midst of the two armies."

Smile on face of Kṛsna indicates that he could see through the underlying causes of dilemma of Arjuna.

3. First Advice: Understand what you are —Immortal Soul, Not Mortal Body

Sribhagvan uvaca
asocyan anvasocas tvam
prajnavadams' ca bhasase
gatasun agatasums ca
na' nus'canti pandtah (11)

श्रीभगवानुवाच
अशोच्यानन्वाशोचस्त्वं प्रज्ञावादांश्च भाषसे।
गतासूनगतासूंश्च नानुशोचन्ति पण्डिताः॥ (२।११)

na tv eva'ham jatu na' sam
na tvam ne' me janadhipah
na cai' va na bhavisyamah
sarve vayam atah param (12)

न त्वेवाहं जातु नासं न त्वं नेमे जनाधिपा: ।
न चैव न भविष्याम: सर्वे वयमत: परम् ॥ (२ । १२)

dehino' smin yatha dehe
kaumaram yauvanam jara
tatha dehantrapraptir
dhiras tatra na muhyati (13)

देहिनोऽस्मिन्यथा देहे कौमारं यौवनं जरा ।
तथा देहान्तरप्राप्तिर्धीरस्तत्र न मुह्यति ॥ (२ । १३)

matrasparsas tu kaunteya
sitosnasukhaduhkhadah
agamapayino' nityas
ams titiksasva bharata (14)

मात्ररस्पर्शास्तु कौन्तेय शीतोष्णसुखदु:खदा: ।
आगमापायिनोऽनित्यास्तांस्तितिक्षस्व भारत ॥ (२ । १४)

yam hi na vyathayanty ete
purusam purusarsabha
samaduhkhasukham dhiram
so' mrt tvaya kalpate (15)

यं हि न व्यथयन्त्येते पुरुषं पुरुषर्षभ ।
समदु:खसुखं धीरं सोऽमृतत्वाय कल्पते ॥ (२ । १५)

na' sato vidyate bhavo
na' bhavo vidyate satah
ubhayor api drsto' ntas tv
anayos tattvadarsbhih (16)

नासतो विद्यते भावो नाभावो विद्यते सत: ।
उभयोरपि दृष्टोऽन्तस्त्वनयोस्तत्त्वदर्शिभि: ॥ (२ । १६)

avinasi tu tad viddhi
yena sarvam idam tatam
vinasam avyayasya' sya
na kascilt kartum arhati (17)

अविनाशि तु तद्विद्धि येन सर्वमिदं ततम्।
विनाशमव्ययस्यास्य न कश्चित्कर्तुमर्हति॥ (२।१७)

antavanta ime deha
mityasyo' ktah s'aririnah
anasno' prameyasya
tasmad yudhyasva bharata (18)

अन्तवन्त इमे देहा नित्यस्योक्ताः शरीरिणः।
अनाशिनोऽप्रमेयस्य तस्माद्युध्यस्व भारत॥ (२।१८)

ya enam vetti hantaram
yas'cai'nam manyate hatam
ubhau tau na vijanito
na' yam hanti na hanyate (19)

य एनं वेत्ति हन्तारं यश्चैनं मन्यते हतम्।
उभौ तौ न विजानीतो नायं हन्ति न हन्यते॥ (२।१९)

na jayate mriyate va kadacin
na' yam bhutva bhavita vana bhuyah
ajo nityah sasvato' yam purano
na hanyate hanyamane sarire (20)

न जायते म्रियते वा कदाचि–
न्नायं भूत्वा भविता वा न भूयः।
अजो नित्यः शाश्वतोऽयं पुराणो
न हन्यते हन्यमाने शरीरे॥ (२।२०)

vedavinasinam nityam
ya enam ajam aryayam
katham sa purusah partha
kam ghatayati hanti kam (21)

वेदाविनाशिनं नित्य य एनमजव्ययम्।
कथं स पुरुषः पार्थ कं घातयति हन्ति कम्॥ (२।२१)

vasamsi jirnani yatha vihaya
navani grhnati naro' parani

tatha sarirani vihaya jirnany
anyani samyati navam dehi (22)

वासांसि जीर्णानि यथा विहाय
नवानि गृह्णाति नरोऽपराणि।
तथा शरीराणि विहाय जीर्णा–
न्यन्यानि संयाति नवानि देही॥ (२।२२)

nainam chindanti sastrani
nainam dahati pavakah
na cainam kledayanty apo
na sosayati marutah (23)

नैनं छिन्दन्ति शस्त्राणि नैनं दहति पावकः।
न चैनं क्लेदयन्त्यापो न शोषयति मारुतः॥ (२।२३)

acchedyo' yam adahyo' yam
akledyo' sosyo eva ca
nityah sarvagatah sthanur
acalo' yam sanatanah (24)

अच्छेद्योऽयमदाह्योऽयमक्लेद्योऽशोष्य एव च।
नित्यः सर्वगतः स्थाणुरचलोऽयं सनातनः॥ (२।२४)

avyakto' yam acintyo' yam
avikaryo' yam ucyate
tasmad evam viditvai' nam
na' nusocitum arhasi (25)

अव्यक्तोऽयमचिन्त्योऽयमविकार्योऽयमुच्यते।
तस्मादेवं विदित्वैनं नानुशोचितुमर्हसि॥ (२।२५)

Srikṛsna said, "Arjuna! You grieve for those whom you should not. You don't speak as an intelligent man. Never was a time when I was not, nor you, nor these kings were not; nor there will be a time hereafter we all shall cease to be. As the soul passes in this body through childhood, youth and old age, even so it is taking on of another body, the sage is not perplexed by this. Contacts with their objects give rise to duals like cold and heat, pleasure and pain. They come and go and don't last for ever. The man who is not troubled by these (duals) is wise. He makes himself fit for eternal life. (Eternal life is the transcendence of life and death). The unreal is body and the real is the soul.

Soul is all–prevading and indestructible. Bodies of the soul come to an end. Therefore, you should fight. Neither anybody slays (soul) nor is (soul) slain. Soul is never born, nor does he ever dies, having come, he (soul) will never cease. He is unborn, eternal, permanent and primeval. He is never slain when body is slain.

(Soul derives its existence from God). One who knows that soul is indestructible and eternal, how can such a person slays one or causes anyone to slay? A person casts off wornout garments and puts on new ones. In the same way, soul casts off wornout bodies and take on new bodies. Weapons do not cleave this self (soul), fire does not burn him; waters do not wet him; nor does the wind make him dry. He is uncleavable. He can't be burnt. He can be neither wetted nor dried. He is eternal, all–pervading, unchanging and immovable. He is the same for ever. He is unmanifest, unthinkable and unchanging. Knowing this (unpanishadic or vedantic philosophy of 'Samkhya'), you should not grieve.

4. Second Advice (alternative argument): Don't grieve over what is perishable (i.e., body)

atha cai'nain nityajatam
nityam va manyase mrtam
tatha' pi tvam mahabaho
nai' nam s'ocitum arhasi (25)

अथ चैनं नित्यजातं नित्यं वा मन्यसे मृतम् ।
तथापि त्वं महाबाहो नैवं शोचितुमर्हसि ॥ (२ । २६)

jatsaya hi dhruvo mrtyur
dhruvam janma mrtasya ca
tasmad apariharye' rthe
na tvam socitum arhasi (27)

जातस्य हि ध्रुवो मृत्युर्ध्रुवं जन्म मृतस्य च ।
तस्मादनरिहार्येऽर्थे न त्वं शोचितुमर्हसि ॥ (२ । २७)

avyaktadini bhutam
vyaktamadhyani bharata
avyaktanidhanay eva
taitra ka paridevana (28)

अव्यक्तदीनि भूतानि व्यक्तमध्यानि भारत ।
अव्यक्तनिधनान्येव तत्र का परिदेवना ॥ (२ । २८)

ascaryavat pasyanti kascid enam
ascaryavad vadati tathai' va ca' nyah
ascaryavae cai' nam anyah s'rnoti
srutva' py enam veda na cai' va kascit (29)

आश्चर्यवत्पश्यति कश्चिदेनं-
आश्चर्यवद्वदति तथैव चान्यः ।
आश्चर्यवच्चैनमन्यः शृणोति
श्रुत्वाप्येनं वेद न चैव कश्चित् ॥ (२ । २९)

dehi nityam avadhyo' yam
dehe sarvasya bharata
tasmat sarvani bhutani
na tvam socitum arhasi (30)

देही नित्यमवध्योऽयं देहे सर्वस्य भारत ।
तस्मात्सर्वाणि भूतानि न त्वं शोचितुमर्हसि ॥ (२ । ३०)

Srikṛsna said, "O Arjuna! Even if you think that the self is perpetually born and perpetually died, then also you should not grieve, for one who is born is bound to die and that birth is certain for those who die. *Therefore, what is unavoidable should not be grieved*. Beings are unmanifest in their beginning, manifest in the middle and unmanifest again in their ends. Then what is there in this for lamentation? One looks upon him (soul) as a marvel; another speaks of him as a marvel; another hears him as a marvel but none has known him (through sensuary organs). The dweller in the body of everyone (soul) is eternal and cannot be slain. Therefore, you should not grieve for any creature.

5. Third Advice: Realise your own duty

An excellent executive will be one who is free from grief, fear, nervousness, indecision, attachment, etc., and knows well what is his duty. Knowledge of Vedantic Samkhya will make him free from grief. Then he will be in a position to realise what is his duty in a given circumstance.

svadharmam api ca'veksya
na vikampitum arhasi

dharmayad dhi yuddhac chreyo' nyat
ksatriyasya na vidyate (31)

स्वधर्ममपि चावेक्ष्य न विकम्पितुमर्हसि।
धर्म्याद्धि युद्धाच्छ्रेयोऽन्यत्क्षत्रियस्य न विद्यते॥ (२।३१)

yadrcchaya co' papannam
svargadvaram apavrtam
sukhinah ksatriyah partha
labhante yuddham idrs'am (32)

यद्दृच्छया चोपपन्नं स्वर्गद्वारमपावृतम्।
सुखिन: क्षत्रिया: पार्थ लभन्ते युद्धमीदृशम्॥ (२।३२)

atha cet tvam imam dharmyam
samgramam na karisyasi
tatah svadharmam na kirtim ca
hitva papam avapsyai (33)

अथ चेत्त्वमिमं धर्म्यं सङ्ग्रामं न करिष्यसि।
तत: स्वधर्मं कीर्तिं च हित्वा पापमवाप्स्यसि॥ (२।३३)

akirtim ca' pi bhutani
kathayisyanti te' vyayam
sambhavitasya ca' kirtir
maranad atiricyate (34)

अकीर्तिं चापि भूतानि कथायिष्यन्ति तेऽव्ययाम्
सम्भावितस्य चाकीर्ति–र्मरणादतिरिच्यते॥ (२।३४)

bhayad ranad uparatam
mamsyante tvam maharathah
yesam ca tvam bahumato
bhutva yasyasi laghavam (35)

भयाद्रणादुपरतं मस्यन्ते त्वां महारथा:।
येषां च त्वं बहुमतो भूत्वा यास्यसि लाघवम्॥ (२।३५)

avacyavadams ca bahun
vadisyanti tava samarthyam
tato duhkhataram nu kim (36)

अवाच्यवादांश्च बहून्वदिष्यन्ति तवाहिताः ।
निन्दन्तस्तव सामर्थ्यं ततो दुःखतरं नु किम् ॥ (२ । ३६)

hato va prapsyasi svargam
jitva va bhoksyasi mahim
tasmad uttistha kaunteya
yuddhaya krtaniscayah (37)

हतो वा प्राप्स्यसि स्वर्गं जित्वा वा भोक्ष्यसे महीम् ।
तस्मादुत्तिष्ठ कौन्तेय युद्धाय कृतनिश्चयः ॥ (२ । ३७)

sukhadukhe same krtva
labhalabbau jayajayau
tato yuddhaya yujyasva
nai' vam papam avapsyasi (38)

सुखदुःखे समे कृत्वा लाभालाभौ जयाजयौ ।
ततो युद्धाय युज्यस्व नैवं पापमवाप्स्यसि ॥ (२ । ३८)

Srikrsna said to Arjuna, "Having regard to your duty, you must not falter. There is no greater good for a Ksatriya (administrator) than a battle enjoined by duty. O Arjuna! Happy are those who get such opportunity (to do own duty) which is an open door to heaven. (Happiness of an administrator lies in fighting for the right cause—to maintain order by force). If you fail to perform your lawful duty, then you will loose your glory and incur sin. (It will amount to serious misconduct). People will recount your ill–fame. For an honourable person (administrator), ill–fame is worse than death. The warriors who hold you in high esteem will make light of you or condemn you (for this misconduct). Many unseemly words your enemies will utter, slandering your strength. Could anything be sadder than that? If you are slain you will go to heaven, if you win you will enjoy the kingdom. Therefore, arise, O son of Kunti (Arjuna), resolved on duty. Treat alike pleasure and pain, gain and loss, victory and defeat, then be ready to perform your duty. Thus, no sin will come to you.

Performing duty has worldly considerations—compliance with law, ethics/code of conduct, discipline, reputation, etc., but a higher level of inspiration comes from self–control and self–discipline. Duty is duty. One must perform it with equanimity. Emotional stability, freedom from stress and strain will come through maintaining balance between dualities of pleasure and pain, gain and loss, victory and defeat, etc. Gain inward freedom from duals in order to be the best performer of duty. Dr. S. Radhakrishnan has commented on this verse as follows: –

"Without yielding to the restless desire for change, without being at the mercy of emotional ups and downs, let us do the work assigned to us in the situation in which we are placed. When we acquire faith in the Eternal and experience His reality, the sorrows of the world do not disturb us." (p.114)

This is the secret of becoming good performer—excellent executive.

6. Fourth Advice—Practice yoga to be an excellent executive

esa te' bhihita samkhye
buddhir yoge tv imam srnu
buddhye yukto yaya partha
karmabandhan prahasyasi (39)

एषा तेऽभिहिता साङ्ख्ये
बुद्धिर्योगे त्विमां शृणु।
बुद्ध्या युक्तो यया पार्थ
कर्मबन्धं प्रहास्यसि ॥ (२।३९)

ne' ha' bhikramanaso' sti
pratyavayo na vidyate
svalpam apy asya dharmasya
trayate mahato bhayat (40)

नेहाभिक्रमनाशोऽस्ति प्रत्यवायो न विद्यते।
स्वल्पमप्यस्य धर्मस्य त्रायते महतो भयात् ॥ (२।४०)

vyavasayatmika buddhir
eke' ha kurunandana
bahusakha hy anantas'ca
buddhayo' vyavasayinam (41)

व्यवसायात्मिका बुद्धिरेकेह कुरुनन्दन।
बहुशाखा ह्यनन्ताश्च बुद्धयोऽव्यवसायिनाम् ॥ (२।४१)

Srikṛsna continued, "O Partha (Arjuna)! I have given you wisdom of samkhya of upanisads to you. Now you listen to the wisdom of yoga of knowledge. If your intelligence accepts it, you shall cast away the bondage of work. (Yoga of knowledge is *buddhi yoga*. *Buddhi* is not merely the capacity to formulate concepts or theory but it has the function of recognition and discrimination. Budhhi must be trained to attain insight, constancy, *samta* or equal–mindedness. The mind should be guided by buddhi or intellect which is higher than mind rather than being united to the senses. Thus, union of mind with intellect is buddhi or knowledge yoga. *Purusa* is inactive. Bondage and liberation are functions of *buddhi*. *Prakrati* evolves five *mahabhuta* – matter, ether, fire, water and earth, **five properties of matter**—sound, touch, form, taste and smell, buddhi or mahatatva, ahamkara and mind with ten sense functions—five of knowledge and five of action. Liberation is achieved when *buddhi* discriminates between *purusa* and *prakrati*. *Buddhi* is the driver of the chariot of the body drawn by the horses of senses which are controlled by reins of mind. The self is superior to *buddhi* but it is a passive witness. If *buddhi* is illuminated by the light of the consciousness of the self and makes it the master–light of its life, its guidance will be in harmony with the cosmic purpose. If *buddhi* is cleansed of desire, lust, greed, anger, jealousy/attachment, etc., the light of the self will be undistorted. Then *buddhi* will be in union with the spirit. The sense of ego and separatedness will be replaced by the vision of harmony in which one is all and all is one. Thus, samkhya and yoga may have different approaches but have the same objective.

"In *buddhi* yoga, no effort is ever lost and no obstacle prevails. Even a little of this Dharma (duty) saves from great fear." (Every effort in performance of duty will be counted as merit. It is never lost). The understanding of resolute (decided) is one but the thoughts of irresolute (undecided) are many and endless.

Be concentrated and single–minded or the resolute to be the best performer. Conversely, poor performance comes due to indecision coupled with many and endless thoughts and lack of concentration.

7. Fifth Advice—Be free from worldly attachments

yam imam puspitam vacam
pravadanty avipascitah
vedavadartah partha
na' nyad asti'ti vadinah (42)

यामिमां पुष्पितां वाचं प्रवदन्त्यविपश्चित: ।
वेदवादरता: पार्थ नान्यदस्तीति वादिन: ॥ (२।४२)

kamatmanah svargapara
janmakarmaphalapradam
kriyavisesabahulam
bhogaisvaryagatim prati (43)

कामांत्मान: स्वर्गपरा जन्मकर्मफलप्रदाम् ।
क्रियाविशेषबहुलां भोगैश्वर्यगतिं प्रति ॥ (२ । ४३)

Those who are undiscerning; who rejoice in Vedic *Karmakandas* (rituals) to attain heaven, enjoyment, power, etc. — *istapurtam* those who use intelligence in discrimating between right and wrong (but not action) can't be well–established in 'self' or concentration. (They can't be the best performers).

bhogais'varya–prasaktanam
tayapahrta–cetasam
vyavasayatmika buddhih
samadhau na vidhiyate (44)

भोगैश्वर्यप्रसक्तनां तयापहृतचेतसाम् ।
व्यवसायत्मिका बुद्धि: समाधौ न विधीयते ॥ (२ । ४४)

traigunyavisaya veda
nistraigunyo bhava' rjuna
nirdvando nityasattvastho
niryogaksema atmavan (45)

त्रैगुण्यविषया वेदा निस्त्रैगुण्यो भवार्जुन ।
निर्द्वन्द्वो नित्यसत्त्वस्थो निर्योगक्षेम आत्मावान् ॥ (२ । ४५)

The action of three–fold modes—*satva–raja, tamas*—is the subject matter of veda; O Arjuna! You be free from this three–fold nature; be free from dualities; be firmly fixed in purity; do not care for acquisition and preservation and be possessed of the "self". (Outward conduct of *Satvaguni* performer and a detached performer may be the same. But, however, the vedic ritualistic or *Karmakandi* will be attached to fruits of action, whereas the knowledge of yoga person will have no interest in the fruits of action).

Nityasattva: stand above/ beyond trinity of *gunas*.

Yogaksema: acquisition of the new and preservation of the existing.

Atmavan: possessed of 'self', ever vigillant.

(Be a detached but single–minded, concentrated performer. Never bother about fruits).

Yavan artha udapane
Sarvatah samplutodake
Tavan sarvesu vedesu
Brahmansaya vijanatah (46)

यावानर्थ उदपाने सर्वत: सम्प्लुतोदके।
तावान्सर्वेषुब्राह्मणस्य विजानत:॥ (२।४६)

Vedic rituals of worldly objectives have no utility for a 'self–realised' person because pond is of no use when a place is flooded with water.

8. Sixth Advice: Work without Concern for Fruits

karmany eva'dhikaraste
ma phalesu kadacana
ma karmaphalahetur bhur
ma te' sango' stva akarmani (47)

कर्मण्येवाधिकारस्ते मा फलेषु कदाचन।
मा कर्मफलहेतुर्भूर्मा तेसङ्गोऽस्त्वकर्मणि॥ (२।४७)

Your right is solely in action and never in its fruits; let not fruits of action be your motive; nor let there be any attachment of yours to inaction.

This famous verse is a key verse of Gita. It makes it clear that everybody has a right in action alone. It is duty. No right in fruits does not mean deprivation of remuneration or exploitation. It does not mean that action should not be planned and cost and benefit analysis be not done. It merely warns against attachment to selfish motives. Let us take a mundane example. If a batsman concentrates on score board, then he can't play well. He must concentrate on batting. Whether he will score or will be out is not within his hands exclusively. Nobody should have any attachment to in action due to pre-occupation with imaginary fears of serious implications and loss of lower level selfish motives. Duty must by performed as 'Dharma.'

yogasthah kuru karmami
sangam tyaktva dhanamjaya
siddhyasiddhyoh samo bhutva
samatvam yoga ucyate (48)

योगस्थ: कुरु कर्माणि सङ्गं त्यक्त्वा धनञ्जय।
सिद्ध्यसिद्ध्यो: समो भूत्वा समत्वं योग उच्यते ॥ (२।४८)

"O Dhanamjaya (Arjuna)! Be fixed in yoga and perform your duty without attachment, with an even mind in success and failure. This evenness of mind is called yoga."

Yogasthah: steadfast in inner composure.

Samatvam: inner poise, self–control, equanimity. Absence of anger, ego, pride, ambitions.

Best performance comes when one is working with a pure intellect united with 'self' and without attachment to fruits. A vehicle can be started when gear is in neutral.

9. Equanimity of Mind or Yoga

durena hy avaram karma
buddhiyogad dhanamjaya
buddhau s'arnam anivaccha
krpanah phalahetavah (49)

दूरेण ह्यवरं कर्म बुद्धियोगाद्धनञ्जय।
बुद्धौ शरणमन्विच्छ कृपणा: फलहेतव: ॥ (२।४९)

Mere action is far inferior to buddhi yoga. O Dhanamjaya (Arjuna)! Seek refuge in buddhi yoga (intelligence). Pitiful are those who seek for the fruits (of their actions).

buddhiyukto jahati'ha
ubhe sukrtaduskrte
tasmad yogaya yujyasva
yogah karmasu kausalam (50)

बुद्धियुक्तो जहातीह उभे सुकृतदुष्कृते।
तस्माद्योगाय युज्यस्व योग: कर्मसु कौशल्यम् ॥ (२।५०)

One who has united (yoked) his buddhi with the divine casts away even here both good and evil deeds. Therefore, strive for yoga because it gives skill (excellence) in action.

(Yoga is evenness of mind in success or failure, possessed by one who is engaged in the performance of his proper duties, while his mind rests in God—*Samkara*).

karmajain buddhiyukta hi
phalam tyaktva manisinah
janamabandhavinirmuktah
padam gacchanty anamayam (51)

कर्मजं बुद्धियुक्ता हि फलं त्यक्त्वामनीषिणः।
जन्मबन्धविनिर्मुक्ताः पदं गच्छन्त्यनामयम्॥ (२।५१)

yada te mohakalilam
buddhir vyatitarisyati
tada gantasi nirvedam
s'rotavyasya s'rutasya ca (52)

यदा ते मोहकलिलं बुद्धिर्व्यतितरिष्यति।
तदा गन्तासि निर्वेदं श्रोतव्यस्य श्रुतस्य च॥ (२।५२)

srutivipratipanna te
yada sthasyati nisc'ala
samadhav acala buddhis
tada yogam avapsyavi (53)

श्रुतिविप्रतिपन्ना ते यदा स्थास्यति निश्चला।
समाधावचला बुद्धिस्तदा योगमवाप्स्यसि॥ (२।५३)

The wise who have united their buddhi (with the divine) renouncing the fruits of their action and freed from the bonds of birth reach the state where there is no sorrow.

(Budhhi yoga is emancipated and free from any sorrow. This is the secret of his excellent performance. They are free from bondage of life even when alive—*jeevanmuktah*).

When your buddhi shall cross the turbidity of delusion, you will become indifferent to what has been heard and what is yet to be heard. (He does not care for hearsay. He reaches beyond the range of *Vedas* and *Upanisada* or *Shruti*).

Then your buddhi will become stable—free from bewilderment due to Vedic texts. You will attain *samadhi* and will attain insight (yoga).

S'rutivipratipanna: One becomes bewildered or confused due to various schools of thought in *Shrutis* (Veda, Upanaisadas).

Samadhi: Highest kind of consciousness—concentrate itself into 'self'. Mind is united with divine self. Duty is done with equanimity and detachment to its fruits.

It is not material what we do, but how we do. The quality of spirit of action is important.

10. Qualities of a Buddhi Yoga

Every executive must strive to develop the qualities/ characteristics of a buddhi yoga as stated by Kṛsna to Arjuna in the following verses. This will make them excellent executives.

Arjuna uvaca
sthita–prajnasya ka bhasa
samadhisthasya kes'ava
Sthitadhih Kim prabhaseta
Kim asita vrajeta Kim (54)

अर्जुन उवाच
स्थितप्रज्ञस्य का भाषा समाधिस्थस्य केशव ।
स्थितधी: किं प्रभाषेत किमासीत व्रजेत किम् ॥ (२।५४)

Arjuna asked Kṛsna, "What is the description of a buddhiyogi (*sthitaprajana*, *samadhistha*)? How does he speak, sit and walk?

Sribhagavan uvaca
Sri–bhagavan uvaca
prajahati yada kaman
sarvan partha mano–gatan
atmany eva' tmana tustah
sthitaprajnas tado' cyate (55)

प्रजहाति यदा कामान्सर्वान्पार्थ मनोगतान् ।
आत्मन्येवात्मना तुष्ट: स्थितप्रज्ञस्तदोच्यते ॥ (२।५५)

Kṛsna said, "He is free from selfish desires, his spirit is content in itself. He is called '*Sthitaprajna*' (Stable in buddhi, full of concentration).

duhkhesv anudvigna–manah
sukhesu vigata–sprah
vita–raga–bhaya–krodhah
sthitadhir munir ucayate (56)

दुःखेष्वनुद्विग्नमनाः सुखेषु विगतस्पृहः ।
वीतरागभयक्रोधः स्थितधीर्मुनिरुच्यते ॥ (२।५६)

His mind is not perturbed amid sorrows; he is free from eager desire amid pleasures; he is free from passion, fear and rage. Therefore, he is called a '*muni*' (Sage).

yah sarvatranabhisnehas
tat tat prapya subhasubham
nabhinandati na dvesti
tasya prajna pratisthita (57)

यः सर्वत्रानभिस्नेहस्तत्तत्प्राप्य शुभाशुभम् ।
नाभिनन्दति न द्वेष्टि तस्य प्रज्ञा प्रतिष्ठिता ॥ (२।५७)

He has no affection on any side (independent or impartial). He maintains equanimity of mind in success or failure (good or bad). His buddhi is firmly set in wisdom.

(We must receive whatever comes our way without excitement, pain or revolt.—Dr. S. Radhakrishnan, p. 124).

yada samharate cayam
kurmo' nganiva sarvasah
indriyanindriyarthebhyas
tasya prajna pratisthita (58)

यदा संयरते चायं कूर्मोऽङ्गानीव सर्वशः ।
इन्द्रियाणीन्द्रियार्थेभ्यस्तस्य प्रज्ञा प्रतिष्ठिता ॥ (२।५८)

He has withdrawn from the objects of senses like a tortoise draws in his limbs. His intellect is firmly set in wisdom.

visaya vinivartante
niraharasya dehinah
rasavarjam raso'py asya
param drstva nivartate (59)

विषया विनिवर्तन्ते निराहारस्य देहिनः ।
रसवर्जं रसोऽप्यस्य परं दृष्टा निवर्तते ॥ (२।५९)

Sometimes objects of sense are renounced but still taste for them remains. But even the taste is gone when the Supreme is seen. (*Buddhi yoga* has both outward abstention and inner renunciation of objects of sense. He has control over body and mind both).

(Truly brave are those whose minds are not disturbed when the sources of disturbance are present.—Kalidasa in *Kumarasambhava*, I, 59).

yatato hy api Kaunteya
purusasya vipascitah
indriyani pramathini
haranti prasabham manah (60)

यतते ह्यपि कौन्तेय पुरुषस्य विपश्चितः ।
इन्द्रियाणि प्रमाथीनि हरन्ति प्रसभं मनः ॥ (२ । ६०)

O Kaunteya (Arjuna), "Even though a man may ever strive (for perfection) and be ever so discerning, his impetuous senses will carry off his mind by force."

(This is word of caution. Never trust your sensuary organs. Be always vigillant).

tani sarvani samyamaya
yukta asita matparah
vas'e hi yasye' ndriyani
tasya prajna pratisthita (61)

तानि सर्वाणि संयम्य युक्त आसीत मत्परः ।
वशे हि यस्येन्द्रियाणि तस्य प्रज्ञा प्रतिष्ठिता ॥ (२ ।६१)

He should remain firm in yoga intent on Me (God) after bringing all senses under control. His buddhi is firmly set whose senses are under control.

(Self–discipline or self–control comes through will and emotions rather than intelligence).

dhyayato visayan pumsah
sangas tesu' pajayate
sangat samjayate kamah
kamat krodho' bhijayate (62)

ध्यायतो विषयान्पुंसः सङ्गस्तेषूपजायते ।
सङ्गात्सञ्जायते कामः कामात्क्रोधोऽभिजायते ॥ (२ । ६२)

krodhad bhavati sammohah
sammohat smrtivibhramah
smrti–bhramsad buddhi–naso
buddhi–nasat pranasyati (63)

क्रोधाद्भवति सम्मोहः समोहात्स्मृतिविभ्रमः ।
स्मृतिभ्रंशाद् बुद्धिनाशो बुद्धिनाशात्प्रणश्यति ॥(२।६३)

(Causes of stress and poor performance).

When a man dwells in his mind on objects of sense, attachment comes desire and from desire (unsatisfied) comes anger. From anger arises bewilderment, loss of memory; from loss of memory arises the destruction of intellect and from this man perishes.

Buddhinasa: Failure to discriminate between right and wrong.

(Such a state leads to stress and poor performance. The remedy lies in inward withdrawal rather than forced isolation. Control senses by the reins of mind rather than hating them).

raga–dvesa–viyuktais tu
visayan indriyas' caran
atma–vasyair vidheyatma
prasadam adhigacchati (64)

रागद्वेषवियुक्तैस्तु विषयानिन्द्रियैश्चरन् ।
आत्मवश्यैर्विधेयात्मा प्रसादमधिगच्छति ॥ (२ । ६४)

prasade sarva–duhkhanam
hanir asyopajayate
prasanna–cetaso hy as'u
buddhih paryavatisthate (65)

प्रसादे सर्वदुःखानां हानिरस्योपजायते ।
प्रसन्नचेतसो ह्येशु बुद्धिः पर्यवतिष्ठते ॥ (२ । ६५)

nasti buddhir ayuktasya
na cayuktasya bhavana
na cabhavayatah santir
asantasya kutah sukham (66)

नास्ति बुद्धिरयुक्तस्य न चायुक्तस्य भावना ।
न चाभा वयतः शान्तिरशान्तस्य कुतः सुखाम् ॥ (२ । ६६)

indriyanam hi caratani
yan mano' nuvidhiyate
tad asya harati prajnam
vayur navam iva' mbhasi (67)

इन्द्रियाणां हि चरतां यन्मनोऽनुविधीयते ।
तदस्य हरति प्रज्ञा वायुर्नावमिवाम्भसि ॥ (२ । ६७)

tasmad yasya maha–baho
nigrhitani sarvas'ah
indriyani ndriyarthebhyas
tasya prajna pratisthita (68)

तस्माद्यस्य महाबाहो निगृहीतानि सर्वशः ।
इन्द्रियाणीन्द्रियार्थेभ्यस्तस्य प्रज्ञा प्रतिष्ठिता ॥ (२ । ६८)

ya nis'a sarvabhutanam
tasyam jagrati samyami
vasyam jagrati bhutani
sa nis'a pas'yato munch (69)

या निशा सर्वभूतानां तस्यां जागर्ति संयमी ।
यस्यां जाग्रति भूतानि सा निशा पश्यतो मुनेः ॥ (२ । ६९)

apuryamanam acala–pratistham'
samudram a pah pravisanti yadvat
tadvat kama yani pravis'anti sarve
so santim apnoti na kama–kami (70)

आपूर्यमाणमचलप्रतिष्ठ–
समुद्रमापः प्रविशन्ति यद्वत् ।
तद्वत्कामा यं प्रविशन्ति सर्वे
स शांन्तिमाप्नोति न कामकामी ॥ (२ । ७०)

vihaye kaman yah sarvan
pumams' carati nihsprhah
nirmano nirahamkarah
sa santim adhigacchanti (71)

विहाय कामान्यः सर्वान्पुमांश्चरति निःस्पृहः ।
निर्ममो निरहङ्कार स शान्तिमधिगच्छति ॥ (२ । ७१)

esa brahmi sthitih partha
nai' nam prapya vimuhyati
sthitvasyam anta–kale' pi
brahmanir vanam rcchati (72)

एषा ब्राह्मी स्थितिः पार्थ नैना प्राप्य विमुह्यति ।
स्थित्वास्यामन्तकालेऽपि ब्रह्मनिर्वाणमृच्छति ॥ (२ । ७२)

A man of disciplined (controlled) mind, who moves among the objects of sense, with the senses under control and free from attachment and aversion, he attains purity of spirit. (He is real brave person). This purity of spirit gives end of all sorrow; the *buddhi* (intelligence) of such a man of pure spirit is soon established (in the peace of self). But for the uncontrolled, there is no intelligence; no power of concentration, no peace. For unpeaceful, how can there be happiness? When mind runs after roving senses, it takes away understanding just like wind carries away ship on the waters. Therefore, O Mighty armed (Arjuna)! Intelligence is firmly set of those only whose senses are withdrawn from their objects. What is night for all beings is the time of waking for the disciplined Soul and what is the time of waking for all beings is night for the sage who sees (visionary sage). All desires enter as waters enter into the sea which remains ever motionless though ever filled. Such a person attains peace and not the one who is disturbed by desires. One who abandons all desires and acts without longing, without any sense of I/ mine (ego), he attains peace. This is the divine state. O Arjuna, then you will not be bewildered. Fixed in that state (*brahmisthiti*) even at the end, you can attain to the bliss of God (*brahmanirvana*). (This gives perfection, excellence in performance).

Carati: acts.

S'antim: peace.

Brahmisthiti: Life eternal.

Nirvanam: moksam or state of perfection, excellence.

(Wisdom is supreme means of liberation/discharge of duties excellently—without stress and bondage).

This is yoga of knowledge—union of intellect with Spirit/ Self/ God.

(Be a good human being (yogi) before you can be a good executive/ manager.)

SUMMARY

A good manager/leader must be Aryan—courageous, courteous, noble, straight–dealer, emotionally stable and firm at critical moments. A good counsellor or adviser should motivate a client to reveal underlying causes of his problem. Then various pieces of advice be given in proper sequence. First, tell the client what is he. Avoid grief for what is beyond control is another advice. Thirdly, make his duty clear. Fourthly, advise him to perform duty with yoga (union of regulated mind and pure intellect with Self/God). Duty has to be taken as Dharma, free from worldly attachments. Then advise him to be detached from fruits (selfish motives). Then tell him what are the qualities of a knowledge yogi or buddhi yogi. Ask him to do self-appraisal and then develop these qualities in him in order to become an excellent executive. He must become a good human being (buddhi yogi) before he can be an good executive. This is the ideal process of counselling which Srikṛsna adopted to inspire his disciple and companion Arjuna in his hour of great depression. Qualities of a buddhi yogi *executive are enumerated here which every executive must strive to develop:*

1. *Free from selfish desires.*
2. *Emotionally stable and full of concentration.*
3. *Mind is not perturbed amid sorrows (setbacks/ failures).*
4. *Mind is not overwhelmed amid pleasures.*
5. *He is free from passion, fear and rage.*
6. *He is independent/impartial.*
7. *His* buddhi *is firmly set in wisdom.*
8. *He has withdrawn from the objects of senses.*
9. *He has control over body and mind both.*
10. *He is always vigillant. He has strong will and emotion to exercise self–control.*
11. *He has intellectual power to discriminate between right and wrong.*
12. *He is at peace in his inner–self.*

He will discharge his duty as *Dharma* without any stress and attachment. This will make him an effective/ excellent executive.

KARMA YOGA

Contents

1. Why to work?

arjuna uvaca
jyayasi cet karmanas te
mata buddhir janardana
tat kim karmani ghore mam
niyojayasi keshava (1)

अर्जुन उवाच
ज्यायसी चेत्कर्मणस्ते मता बुद्धिर्जनार्दन ।
तत्किं कर्मणि घोरे मां नियोजयसि केशव ॥ (३ । १)

Arjuna said, "O Janardana (Kṛsna)! O Kesava (Kṛsna)! If you deem path of knowledge/understanding is better than action, then why do you urge me to do this savage deed (war)?"

vyamis'rene 'va vakyena
buddhim mohayasi' va me
tad ekam vada nis'citya
yena s'reyo' ham apunyam (2)

व्यामिश्रेणेव वाक्येन बुद्धिं मोहयसीव मे।
तदेकं वद निश्चित्य येन श्रेयोऽहमाप्नुयाम्॥ (३।२)

With apparently confusing utterances, you seem to bewilder my intelligence. Tell me with certainty/ decisively the one thing by which I can attain to the highest good.

(Arjuna reveals his confusion clearly that whether knowledge without action is better than action. In fact, he is confused. He is seeking clarification of his doubt/confusion in a honest and transparent manner.)

2. Life is Work or Action

Sribhagvan uvaca
loke' smin dvividha nistha
pura prokta maya' nagha
jnanayogena samkhyanam
karmayogena yoginam (3)

श्रीभगवानुवाच
लोकेऽस्मिन्द्विविधा निष्ठा पुरा प्रोक्ता मयानघ।
ज्ञानयोगेन साङ्ख्यानां कर्मयोगेन योगिनाम्॥ (३।३)

na karmanam anarambhan
naiskarmyam puruso' s'nute
na ca samnyasanad eva
siddhim samadhigacchati (4)

न कर्मणामनारम्भान्नैष्कर्म्यं पुरुषोऽश्नुते।
न च सन्न्यासनादेव सिद्धिं समधिगच्छति॥ (३।४)

na hi kas'cit ksanam api
jatu tisthaty akarmakrat
karayate hy avas'ah karma
sarvah prakritijair gunaih (5)

न हि कश्चित्क्षणमपि जातु तिष्ठत्यकर्मकृत् ।
कार्यते ह्यवशः कर्म सर्वः प्रकृतिजैर्गुणैः ॥ (३ । ५)

karmendriyam samyamya
ya aste manasa smaran
indriyarthan vimudhatma
mithyacarah sa ucayate (6)

कर्मेन्द्रियाणि संयम्य य आस्ते मानसा स्मरन् ।
इन्द्रियार्थान्विमूढात्मा मिथ्याचारः स उच्यते ॥ (३ । ६)

yas tv indriyani manasa
niyamya' rabhate' rjuna
karmendriyaih karmayogam
asaktah sa vis'isyate (7)

यस्त्विन्द्रियाणि मनसा नियम्यारभतेऽर्जुन ।
कर्मेन्द्रियैः कर्मयोगमसक्तः स विशिष्यते ॥ (३ ।७)

Srikṛsna said:

O blameless (Arjuna)! A two-fold way of life has been taught by me to you in this world. The path of knowledge for men of contemplation and the path of work for men of action.

[Manager is man of knowledge as well as action. There are some exceptional people who are introvert. They take inner flights of deep spiritual contemplation and avoid external actions. Then there are people who are so much involved in action that they have hardly any time to do spiritual contemplation. They suffer from stress and strain. They remain subject to dualities — pains and pleasures, etc. Dr. S. Radhakrishnan has observed that this division is not ultimate, for all men are introvert and extrovert in different degrees. (The Bhagvadgita p.132).

Both modes of life are supported by Vedas. (Mahabharata S'antiparva, 240-6.)

[However, Srikṛsna points out that wisdom and action are compatible. Samkara also supports the view that work is compatible with enlightenment. (SBG. II, 11.) In the action of buddhi yogi, the ego and attachment to fruits are absent. This is the real source of excellence without stress and strain.]

Not by abstaining from work does a man attain freedom from action; nor by mere renunciation he will attain perfection.

(What is required is renunciation of attachment to selfish motives or fruits rather than renunciation/abstention from work or action itself. *Nis'karma* is recommended and not the '*Ni'karma* (inaction) or '*Nis'karma phalc*' (fruits without action or theft of wages).

None can remain without doing work even for a moment in this world. Everyone is made to act helplessly by the natural impulses.

(We can't live embodied life without action. Life can't be sustained without work. One who has no control over body and mind, he is driven to action by the *gunas*. But a *buddhi yogi* will act as per the direction of Self/God in a detached manner).

One who restrains his organs of action but continues in his mind thought of the objects of senses is deluded and called a 'hypocrite'. (a man of false conduct).

One who controls the senses by the mind and acts without attachment, he is superior, O. Arjuna.

(To develop this non-attachment and control of mind, contemplation is necessary).

3. Sacrifice

niyatam kuru karma tvam
karma jyayo hy akarmanah
s'arirayatra' pi ca te
na prasidhyed akarmanah (8)

नियतं कुरु कर्म त्वं कर्म ज्यायो ह्यकर्मणः ।
शरीरयात्रापि च ते न प्रसिद्ध्येदकर्मणः ॥ (३।८)

yajnarthat karmano' nyatra
loko' yam karmabandhanah
tadartham karma kaunteya
muktasangah samacara (9)

यज्ञार्थात्कर्मणोऽन्यत्र लोकोऽयं कर्मबन्धनः ।
तदर्थं कर्म कौन्तेय मुक्तसङ्गः समाचर ॥ (३।९)

sahayajnah prajah srstva
puro' vaca prajapatih
anena parasavisyadhvani
esa vo' stv istakamadhuk (10)

सहयज्ञा: प्रजा: सृष्ट्वा पुरोवाच प्रजापति: ।
अनेन प्रसविष्यध्वमेष वोऽस्त्विष्टकामधुक् ॥ (३ । १०)

devan bhavayata' nena
te deva bhavayantu vah
parasparam bhavantah
s'reyah param avapasyatha (11)

देवान्भावयतानेन ते देवा भावयन्तु व: ।
परस्परं भावयन्त श्रेय: परमवाप्स्यथ ॥ (३ । ११)

istan bhogan hi vo deva
dasyante yajnabhavitah
tair dattan apradayai' bhyo
yo bhunkte stena eva sah (12)

इष्टान्भोगान्हि वो देवा दास्यन्ते यज्ञभाविता: ।
तैर्दत्तानप्रदायैभ्यो यो भुङ्क्ते स्तेन एव स: ॥ (३ । १२)

yajnas' istasinah santo
mucyante sarvakilbisaih
bhunjate te tv aghain papa
ye pacanty atmakaranat (13)

यज्ञशिष्टाशिन: सन्तो मुच्यन्ते सर्वकिल्बिषै: ।
भुञ्जते ते त्वघं पापा ये पचन्त्यात्मकारणात् ॥ (३ । १३)

annad bhavanti bhutani
prajanyad annasambhavat
yajnad bhavati prajanyo
yajnah karmasamudbhavah (14)

अन्नाद्भवन्ति भूतानि पर्जन्यादन्नसम्भव: ।
यज्ञाद्भवति पर्जन्यो यज्ञ: कर्मसमुद्भव: ॥ (३ । १४)

karma brahmodbhavam viddhi
brahma ' ksarasamudbhavam
tasmat sarvagatam brahma
nityam yajne pratisthitam (15)

कर्म ब्रह्योद्भवं विद्धि ब्रह्माक्षरसमुद्भवम् ।
तस्मात्सर्वगतं ब्रह्म नित्यं यज्ञे प्रतिष्ठितम् ॥ (३ । १५)

evam parvartitam cakram
na' nuvartayati ' ha yah
agharyur indriyaramo
mogham partha sa jivati (16)

एवं प्रवर्तितं चक्रं नानुवर्तयतीह यः ।
अघायुरिन्द्रियारामो मोघंपार्थ स जीवति ॥ (३ । १६)

Do your allotted work. Action is better than inaction. Even physical life can't be maintained without action. Do your work as a 'Sacrifice', becoming free from all attachment (selfish motives).

Yajna: Sacrifice; enterprise; divine duty.

(Sacrifice attachment to fruits. Sacrifice lower order goals for higher level mission. Work as sacrifice can't bring any sin. It has no bondage power).

Lord (God) created men along with sacrifice and said, "By this, you will bring forth and this will yield the milk of your desires."

Kamadhuk: The mythical cow of Indra from which all desires can be fulfilled. Doing allotted work in a spirit of sacrifice gives you *kamdhenu*. It will fulfil all your desires.

By doing duty as 'Sacrifice', you will foster the gods (owners or leaders) and they will bring the supreme good. Fostered by your sacrifice, the gods (owners or leaders) will give you the enjoyment you desire. One who enjoys without making contribution to the gods (owners, leaders) is verily a thief.

(Here community of interest of owners and employees is advocated. Doing duty as Dharma, making contribution to the enterprise/organisation and fair sharing of gains of action are the fundamental principles of '**Gita economy**' advocated by Srikṛsna. He has condemned work–shirkers or '*Ni'karma* wage earners as thieves. Those who do not do fair and equitable distribution are all thieves — whether they are employers or employees. Thus, there is no place for inaction and exploitation in 'Gita model of economic system).

The good people eat what is left from sacrifice — they fairly and equitably distribute amongst all claimants and then consume the remainder as 'residual claimants'. Such people are released from all sins (stress, conflicts, etc.). But those wicked people who cook food for their own sake — verily they eat sin. They face stress, strain, conflicts, attacks, etc.

(Here it is clear that Gita model of economy is based on Social Responsibility Concept. It has no place for unfair distribution, exploitation, selfish work and self-centred consumption. Thus, Srikṛsna has advocated 'Socialistic economy model'.)

Food gives life to creatures; food is born of rain; from sacrifice (tapa of Lord sun) rain comes into being and sacrifice is born of work or action. The origin of karma is in Brahma (knowledge). The Brahma springs from imperishable (Soul). Therefore, the Brahma, which comprehends all, always centres round the sacrifice. (Action of the supreme saves this world from ruin. Action is a moral as well as physical necessity to maintain human world).

O Partha (Arjuna)! He lives in vain who does not do duty as sacrifice. Such a person is evil in his nature and sensual in his delight.

4. Self–Contentment

yas tv atmartir eva syad
atmatrptas' ca manavah
atmany eva ca samtustas
tasya karyam na vidyate (17)

यस्त्वात्मरतिरेव स्यादात्मतृप्तश्च मानव: ।
आत्मन्येव च सन्तुष्टस्तस्य कार्यं न विद्यते ॥ (३ । १७)

One who is self–delighted and self-contented, for him there is no work to be done. (It does not mean that he is inactive. In fact, he does not work under pressure of duty but he works spontaneously).

naiva tasya krtenartho
nakretena ' ha kascana
na casya sarvabhutesu
kascid artha–yapasrayah (18)

नैव तस्य कृतेनार्थो नाकृतेनेह कश्चनं ।
न चास्य सर्वभूतेषु कश्चिदर्थव्यपाश्रय: ॥ (३ । १८)

He has no interest in gains by action or inaction. He does not depend on all beings for any self-interest. (He works independently for the well–being/ welfare of the humanity).

tasmad askatah satatam
karyam karma samacara
asakto hy acaran karma
param apnoti purusah (19)

तस्मादसक्त: सततं कार्यं कर्म समाचर ।
असक्तो ह्याचरन्कर्म परमाप्नोति पूरुष: ॥ (३ । १९)

Therefore, perform your duty always without attachment (to fruits), for you will attain to the highest (excellence) by doing work without attachment. (Perfection/ excellence is attained by action with pure mind).

5. Lead others by good conduct

karmanai' va hi samsiddhim
asthita janakadayah
lokasamgraham eva' pi
sampasyan kartum arhasi (20)

कर्मणैव हि संसिद्धिमास्थिता जनकादय: ।
लोकसङ्ग्रहमेवापि सम्पश्यन्कर्तुमर्हसि ॥ (३ । २०)

King Janaka and others attained to perfection by doing their duty. You should do your duty in order to set good example before others to be emulated. (You should work with a view to maintain this world).

yad–yad acarati S'resthas
tad–tad eve' taro janah
sa yat pramanam kurute
lokas tad anuvartate (21)

यद्यदाचारति श्रेष्ठस्तत्तदेवेतरो जन: ।
स यत्प्रमाणं कुरुते लोकस्तदनुवर्तते ॥ (३ । २१)

Whatsoever a great man (leader) does, the same is done by people. It becomes a standard or norm, the people follow.

(Leaders must lead people through their exemplary work/ conduct. *Yatha Raja tatha praja* — As is king or leader as will become public Quality of governance of any organisation can't be better than quality of its Leader/ CEO/Head. A leader can't be effective merely by orders passed by him. People will respect his orders/words willingly when his own conduct is worth–emulating and in conformity with orders given for others).

S'resthas: Leaders, chiefs, heads, highly placed people in organisations/society.

Janah/ Lokas: People, subordinates.

Pramanam: Norm/Standard.

Anuvartate: Follow.

na me partha 'sti kartavyain
trisu lokesu kimacana
na 'mavaptam avaptavyam
varta eva ca karmani (22)

न मे पार्थास्ति कर्तव्यं त्रिषु लोकेषु किञ्चन।
नानवाप्तमवाप्तव्यं वर्त एवं च कर्मणि॥ (३।२२)

'O Partha (Arjuna)! In all the three worlds, there is no work which has to be done nor anything to be obtained which is not obtained by me. Yet I am engaged in work (as your charioteer and teacher/ adviser).

yadi hy ahain na varteyam
jatu karmany atandritah
mama vartma ' nuvartante
manusyah partha sarvasah (23)

यदि ह्यहं न वर्तेयं जातु कर्मण्यतन्द्रितः।
मम वर्त्मानुवर्तन्ते मनुष्याः पार्थ सर्वशः॥ (३।२३)

For if I do not engage myself in work unwearied, O Partha (Arjuna), men in every way will follow my path. (They will also avoid work).

(Thus, the *Gita* concept of leader is of a playing captain of a team. He must set good examples before his followers/people through his own performance. If he is inactive or corrupt, he will loose moral authority to direct and control. He can't motivate others. He must be a role model for others to be followed).

utsideyur ime loka
na karyam karna ced aham
samkarasya ca karte syam
upahanyam imah prajah (24)

उत्सीदेयुरिमे लोका न कुर्यां कर्म चेदहम्।
सङ्करस्य च कर्ता स्यामुपहन्यामिमाः प्रजाः॥ (३।२४)

If I should cease to work, these worlds would fall in ruin and I would become the creator of disordered life and destroy these people.

(Organisation/ Societies are ruined by corrupt, inactive people placed in key positions. The main cause of ruin in any organisation or country is crisis of leadership).

saktak karmany avidvaniso
yatha kurvanti bharata

kuryad vidvams tatha saktas
tikirsur lokasamg raham (25)

सक्ता: कर्मण्यविद्वांसो यथा कुर्वन्ति भारत ।
कुर्याद्विद्वांस्तथासक्तश्चिकीर्षुर्लोकसङ्ग्रहम् ॥ (३ । २५)

The learned (jnanin) must not unsettle (confuse) the minds of unlearned (ignorant) who are attached to action. He should work in a spirit of yoga and set (inspire) others to act (as well).

Here a word of caution for learned in the society is given by Srikrsna. Experts of various schools of thought should not confuse the minds of ignorant people through their philosophical preachings. They must act with purity of mind and inspire others to work through their good deeds. But, however, the tragedy of situation in *Kaliyuga* is there are lot of preachers but very few doers—*Par updesh kus'hal bahutere je acarahi te hoi na ghanere*—Tulsidas in *Ramcharitmanas*. This is another root cause of anarchy and poor performance).

6. Be Free from Ego

na buddhi–bhedam janayed
ajnanam karma–sanginam
josayet sarva–karmani
vidvan yuktah samacaran (26)

न बुद्धिभेदं जनयेदज्ञानां कर्मसंगिनाम् ।
जोषयेत्सर्वकर्माणि विद्वान् युक्त: समाचरन् ॥ (३ । २६)

prakrteh kriyaman ani
gunaih karmani sarvas'ah
ahmkaravimudhatma
karta'ham iti manyate (27)

प्रकृते: क्रियमाणानि गुणै: कर्माणि सर्वश: ।
अहङ्कारविमूढात्मा कर्ताहमिति मन्यते ॥ (३ । २७)

All kinds of work are done by (three) modes of nature (satva, raja, tam) but an egoist will say "I am the doer."

tattvavit tu mahabaho
guna karmavibhagayah

guna gunesu vartanta
iti matva na sajjate (28)

तत्त्ववित्तु महाबाहो गुणकर्मविभागयो: ।
गुणा गुणेषु वर्तन्त इति मत्वा न सज्जते ॥ (३ । २८)

But who knows the true character of the two distinctions—Soul is distinct from the modes of nature and their work; understanding that it is the modes (of nature) which are acting on the modes, he does not get attached (to ego of I am doer).

(*Prakrati* and its three modes represent the limits of human freedom through the force of heredity and the pressure of environment. The empirical self and self–sense (ego) are the products of works even as the whole cosmic process is the result of the operation of causes. To a certain extent ego and stress motivate people to work but finally they result into bondage, sin, etc.).

prakrster gunasaminudhah
sajjante gunakarmasu
tan akrtsnavide mandan
krtsnavin na vicalayet (29)

प्रकृतेर्गुणसम्मूढा: सज्जन्ते गुणकर्मसु ।
तानकृत्स्नविदो मन्दान्कृत्स्नविन्न विचालयेत् ॥ (३ । २९)

Those who are misled by the modes of nature get attached to the work done by them. But knowledgeable (learned) persons who know the whole must not confuse (unsettle) the minds of the ignorant who have partial knowledge.

(*Jannani* or learned must not disturb those who are working under the impulse of nature. They should be gradually trained to know the 'self' and be free from ego, stress and attachment. But they must not be advised to renounce duties and go to seclusion—escape from duties. Thus, Gita does not support the *samkhya* view of the withdrawal of *purusa* from prakrati by complete inaction.–See Dr.S. Radhakrishnan's The Bhagwadgita p.144).

mayi sarvani karmani
samnyasya ' dhyatmaeesta
nirasir nirmano bhutva
yudhyasva vigatajvarah (30)

मयि सर्वाणि कर्माणि सन्न्यस्याध्यात्मचेतसा ।
निराशीर्निर्ममो भूत्वा युध्यस्व विगतज्वर: ॥ (३ । ३०)

Surrender 'self' to me, fix your consciousness in the 'self' be free from desire and egoism then act (fight) delivered from your fever (stress).

(We must do duty as Dharma, as direction of Supreme Lord and offer our work as *pooja* to Him. It is His work which we do as per his desire. We should work as His servants. This should be our attitude towards work. This will release us from all fevers—worry, anxiety, pre-occupation, fear leading to stress and strain).

ye me matan idam nityam
anutisthanti manvah
s'raddhavanto ' nasuyanto
mucyante te' pi karmabhih (31)

ये मे मतमिदं नित्यमनुतिष्ठन्ति मानवा: ।
श्रद्धावन्तोऽनसूयन्तो मुच्यन्तेतेऽपि कर्मभि: ॥ (३ । ३१)

ye tv etad abhyasuyanto
na' nutisthanti me matam
sarvajnanavimudhanis tan
viddhi nastan acetasah (32)

सद्दशं चेष्टते स्वस्या: प्रकृतेर्ज्ञानवानपि ।
प्रकृतिं यान्ति भूतानि निग्रह: किं करिष्यति ॥ (३ । ३२)

My devotees, who are full of faith and free from cavil, and follow this teaching of mine are released from (bondage) of works. But those who ignore this teaching of mine are blind to all wisdom and are lost and senseless.

7. Mind your own Duty only

sadrasam cestate svasyah
prakrter jnanavan api
prakrtim yanti bhutani
nigrahah kim karisyati (33)

सद्दशं चेष्टते स्वस्या: प्रकृतेर्ज्ञानवानपि ।
प्रकृतिं यान्ति भूतानि निग्रह: किं करिष्यति ॥ (३ । ३३)

Even the man of knowledge acts in accordance with his own nature. All beings follow their nature. Then why repression be applied?

(As the result of past deeds, everyone is born with nature or *prakrati* as mental equipment. Even God can't prevent its operation. Restraint is of no avail because actions flow inevitably from the workings of the nature. Self is an impartial witness. Nature overpours soul. This is the law of our being. But, it does not mean that we must indulge in every impulse. We must strive to find our true 'self' and strengthen it to regulate nature. Nature suppressed and violated may take its revenge. It is just like a 'Spring'. More you pressurise it more it will jump.)

indriyase ' ndriyasa' rthe
ragadvesau vyavasthitau
tayor na vasam agacchet
tau hy asya paripanthinau (34)

इन्द्रियस्येन्द्रियस्यार्थे रागद्वेषौ व्यवस्थितौ ।
तयोर्न वशमागच्छेत्तौ ह्यस्य परिपन्थिनौ ॥ (३ । ३४)

For (every) sense attachment and aversion are fixed to the objects of that sense. No one should be swayed by them, for they are his waylayers.

(Normally people act as per impulse of nature. But *buddhi* and understanding can save us from being fallen victims of our impulses. Without knowledge and understanding, we fall victim of our impulses and behave/act like animals. Our personal likes and dislikes—attachment and aversion for certain actions will create bondage. But if we use our *buddhi* and understanding to overcome these impulses and do our duty as Dharma, we are free from bondage of nature. The human freedom is conditioned but not annulled by the needs of nature. Practice makes a man perfect.

However, *prarabhadha* (destiny) arising out of bondage of past deeds can't be overcome. *Buddhi*, understanding, power of discrimination—power to decide what is right and what is wrong—makes man better decision–maker and performer).

s'reyan svadharma vigunah
pardharmat svanusthitat
savadharme nidhanam s'reyah
pardharmo bhayavah (35)

श्रेयान्स्वधर्मो विगुण: परधर्मात्स्वनुष्ठितात् ।
स्वधर्मे निधनं श्रेय: परधर्मो भयावह: ॥ (३ । ३५)

It is in your interest to mind your own duty. It is better to do own duty even imperfectly than doing other's duty perfectly. Even death is better in performing one's duty as *Dharma*. It is perilous to follow/do other's duty.

(Understand own nature (psychological make–up) and accept duty accordingly. Do not get lured by charm of other's duty for which your nature is not fit. Most important thing is not what we do but how we do. Do your duty with full sense of responsibility. We must be faithful and committed to our duty till our death. Mind your own duty is an important *mantra* for attaining excellence).

8. Know your Real (inner) Enemies

arjuna uvaca
atha kena prayukto 'yam
papam carati purusah
anicchann api varsneya
balad iva niyojitah (36)

अर्जुन उवाच
अथ केन प्रयुक्तोऽयं पापं चरति पूरुषः ।
अनिच्छन्नपि वार्ष्णेय बलादिव नियोजितः ॥ (३ । ३६)

Arjuna asked, "O Varsneya (Krsna)! By what is a man is impelled to commit sin, as if by force, even against his own will?

Anicchannapi: against own will.

(It is the feeling of Arjuna. However, it is not true. Man tacitly gives his consent. If a wrong is done unintentionally, then it does not come into the category of a sin. *Prakrati* creates fire when it is fuelled by desire, attachment, aversion, greed, ego, anger, etc. Next verse makes this point clear. These are real inner enemies which we must identify and be always cautious).

sribhagwan uvaca
kama esa krodha esa
rajogunasamudbhavah
mahas'ano mahapapma
viddhy enam iha vairinam (37)

श्रीभगवानुवाच
काम एष क्रोध एष रजोगुणसमुद्भवः ।
महाशनो महापाप्मा विद्ध्येनमिह वैरिणम् ॥ (३ । ३७)

Srikṛsna said:

You real (inner) enemy is carving/desire, anger, born of or made of passion/action (rajoguna). Know it.

dhumena ' vriyate vahnir
yatha ' drso malena ca
yatha ' 1 bena ' vrto garbha
tatha tene ' dam avrtam (38)

धूमनाव्रियते वह्निर्यथादर्शो मलेन च ।
यथोल्बेनावृतो गर्भस्तथा तेनेदमावृकम् ॥ (३ । ३८)

As fire is covered by smoke, as mirror is covered by dust, as an embryo is enveloped by the womb, so wisdom is covered by passion or desire.

(Control your desires, if you want to avoid sins).

avrtam jnanam etena
jnanino nityavairina
kamarupena kaunteya
duspurena ' nalena ca (39)

आवृतं ज्ञानमेतेन ज्ञानिनो नित्यवैरिणा ।
कामरूपेण कौन्तेय दुष्पूरेणानलेन च ॥ (३ । ३९)

"O Kaunteya (Arjuna)! Wisdom is enveloped by insatiable fire of desire. It is the consent enemy of the wise."

(Desire is a fire which will grow–up more as we add fuel of consumption to it. It can be controlled through its elimination by wisdom of self or inner satisfaction).

indriyani mano buddhir
asya ' dhisthanam ucyate
etair vimohayaty esa
jnanam avrtya dehinam (40)

इन्द्रियाणि मनो बुद्धिरस्याधिष्ठानमुच्यते ।
एतैर्विमोहयत्येष ज्ञानमावृत्य देहिनम् ॥ (३ । ४०)

tasmat tvam indriyany adan
niyamya bharatsabha

papmanam prajabi hy enam
jna navijnanasanam (41)

तस्मात्त्वमिन्द्रियाण्यादौ नियम्य भरतर्षभ ।
पाप्मानं प्रजहि ह्येनं ज्ञानविज्ञाननाशनम् ॥ (३।४१)

indriyani parany ahur
indriyebhyah param manah
manasas tu para buddhir
yo buddheh paratas tu sah (42)

इन्द्रियाणि पराण्याहुरिन्दियेभ्य: परं मन: ।
मनसस्तु परा बुद्धिर्यो बुद्धे: बरतस्तु स: ॥ (३।४२)

evam buddheh param buddhva
samstabhya ' tmanam atmana
jahi satrum mahabaho
kamarupam durasadam (43)

एवं बुद्धे: परं बुद्ध्वा संस्तभ्यात्मानमात्मना ।
जहि शत्रुं महाबाहो कामरूपं दुरासदम् ॥ (३।४३)

The senses, the mind and the intelligence are said to be seats of this enemy (passion). Veiling wisdom by these, it deludes the embodied (soul). Control your senses from the very beginning and slay this sinful destroyer of wisdom and discrimination. (This enemy is passion).

Jnana: Knowledge of self and other things acquired through scriptures and teachers.

Vijnana: The personal experiment/experience—based knowledge—*atma–viveka*.

Jnana is taken as 'spiritual wisdom' and *vijnana* as logical knowledge in our translation.

Senses are great; greater than senses is the mind; greater than mind is the intellect but greater than intellect is Soul/God. (This hierarchy indicates that the best situation comes when our acts are determined by *buddhi* illuminated by the light of 'self'/God. We are liberated then).

Know Him who is beyond intellect. Make steady the lower 'Self' by the Self/God.

O Mighty Arjuna! The enemy is desire, so hard to get at.(Control the restless ego by the light of eternal 'Spiritual Self'. Be independent of desires and attachments and seek guidance from inner light only).

The third chapter 'Karma Yoga' is over.

Summary

Manager is man of knowledge as well as action. Wisdom and action are compatible. Attachment to selfish motives should be renounced but action can't be and should not be renounced. None can remain without doing work in this world. One who renounces action but thinks about it in mind is a 'hypocrite'. Control senses by mind and do your duty without attachment. Sacrifice attachment to fruits and do your duty as a sacrifice. Gains of activity/enterprise must be shared fairly and equitably between employers or owners and employees. There is no place for exploitation by any party. Community of interest in enterprise is essential. Wages without work and consumption without fair and equitable distribution are forms of thefts. Both must be avoided. Action is a moral as well as physical necessity to maintain this world. His life is useless who does not do duty as sacrifice. Self–controlled person does his duty spontaneously and independently for the well–being of the humanity. Such action detached from fruits will bring excellence in performance. There is great responsibility on leaders. They must lead people by their exemplary conduct. Quality of leadership determines organisational effectiveness. As are leaders so are their people (subordinates). Leaders be role models for their people. Corrupt and inactive leaders ruin organisations/societies. More knowledgeable people should not confuse the mind of ignorant/ less knowledgeable people by controversial philosophical preaching. They must act with purity of mind and inspire others to do their duties. Those who merely preach but not practise cause poor performance. Be free from ego of doer. Three modes of nature cause action. Regulate impulses by purity of mind and act without attachment. Surrender self-sense to Self/God, concentrate on action and be detached from fruits. This will bring out excellent performance. Training of mind improves performance but repression is of no use. Nature may react, if suppressed or violated. Apply buddhi and understanding to regulate natural impulses. Everyone must mind his own work (duty) and avoid thinking about or doing duty of others. Desire is our inner real enemy. It leads to attachment, aversion, anger, etc., which cause stress and strain and poor performance. Knowledge is covered by desires or passions. It is the destroyer of wisdom and power to discriminate between good and bad. Actions must be determined (decided) by buddhi illuminated by the light of Self/God. Then excellent performance without any bondage will come.

BE FREE FROM DESIRES, EGO AND ATTACHMENT TO FRUITS. SEEK GUIDANCE FROM 'SELF'. DO YOUR DUTY AS DHARMA OR SACRIFICE FOR GOOD OF HUMANITY.

THE PATH OF KNOWLEDGE

–JANANA YOGA

Contents

1. The Tradition of Janana Yoga

Sribhgwan uvaca
imam vivasvate yogam
proktavan aham avyayam
vivasvan manave prabha
manur Iksvakave 'bravit (1)

इमं विवस्वते योगं प्रोक्तवानहमव्ययम् ।
विवस्वान्मनवे प्राह मनुरिक्ष्वाकवेऽब्रवीत् ॥ (४ । १)

Srikṛsna said:

I proclaimed imperishable Janana Yoga (The path of knowledge) to Vivasvan who told it to Manu and Manu told it to Iksavaku.

evam paramparapraptam
imam rajarsayo viduh
sa kalene ' ha mahata
yo go nastah paramtapa (2)

एवं परम्पराप्राप्तमिमं राजर्षयो विदुः ।
स कालेनेह महता योगो नष्टः परन्तप ॥ (४ । २)

"O Oppressor of foes (Arjuna)! Thus, handed down from one to another the Royal Sages but it was lost due to long lapse of time.

sa evayam maya te ' dya
yogah proktah puratanah
bhakto ' si me sakha ceti
rahasyam hy etad uttamam (3)

स एवायं मया तेऽद्य योगः प्रोक्तः पुरातनः ।
भक्तोऽसि मे सखा चेति रहस्यं ह्येतदुत्तमम् ॥ (४ । ३)

The same ancient yoga (Jnana Yoga) is today being taught to you by me because you are my devotee and my friend. This is the Supreme Secret (which is taught to only a devotee).

Rajars'ayah: Sages who were born in royal families, i.e., Rama, Janaka, Manu, Iks'vaku, etc., in the past. Later on, Buddha and Mahavira were also Royal Princes who taught path of knowledge to humanity.

Kalena mahata: By the great efflux of time. The teaching of Jnana Yoga became obscured due to lapse of long time. Then the path of knowledge was renovated and retold by teachers like Krsna, Buddha, Mahavira. Thus, faith was rekindled in different ages by different teachers.

Yogah puratanah: The ancient yoga. Path of knowledge was ancient which was retold by Krsna to Arjuna for rekindling his faith. Thus, Krsna honestly declared that he was not propounding any new doctrine but he was restoring the old tradition of path of knowledge (*jnanana yoga*). No teacher has claimed originality because this yoga is part of eternal dharma (*Sanatan Dharma*). Wisdom is never made. It is ever present and shall remain so. Teachers in different ages will rediscover and restore it.

Bhaktosi me sakha cesti: You are my devotee and my friend. It indicates that God will always disclose His secrets so long human heart has qualities of devotion and friendship. Divine inner communication or self–communication is possible only when heart is filled–up with devotion and friendship. It is right of all and not of any privileged class/person. None is barred or excluded.

arjuna uvaca

aparam bhavato janma
param janma vivasvatah
katham etad vijaniyam
tvam adam proktavan iti (4)

अर्जुन उवाच
अपरं भवतो जन्म परं जन्म विवस्वत: ।
कथमेतद्विजानीयां त्वमादौ प्रोक्तवानिति ॥ (४।४)

Arjuna said:

The birth of Vivasvat (sun) is very old and you (Kṛsna) are born recently. How is it possible that you gave this knowledge to him in the beginning?

(The question raised by Arjuna is quite relevant).

2. The Theory of Avatars (Incarnation)

Sribhagwan uvaca

bahuni me vyatitani
janmani tava ca' rjuna
tany aham veda sarvani
na tvam vettha paramtapa (5)

श्रीभगवानुवाच
बहूनि मे व्यतीतानि जन्मानि तव चार्जुन ।
तान्यहं वेद सर्वाणि न त्वं वेत्थ परन्तप ॥ (४।५)

Srikṛsna said:

Many are past lives of me as well as yours, O Arjuna; I know them all but you know not Paramtapa (Arjuna).

(Kṛsna claims jatsmruti).

ajo ' pi sann avyayatma
bhutanam is'varo ' pi san
prakrtim svam adhisthaya
samhavamy atmamayaya (6)

अजोऽपि सन्नव्ययात्मा भूतानामीश्वरोऽपि सन् ।
प्रकृतिं स्वामधिष्ठाय सम्भवाम्यात्ममायया ॥ (४।६)

Although I am unborn and my 'self' (is) not perishable, (I am) the Lord of all creatures, yet establishing Myself in My own nature, I come into (empiric) being through my own Maya (power).

(Kṛsna says he takes avatar in this world).

(The difference between birth of people and avatar or incarnation of God should be noted very carefully. People are born by force of desires and past actions, whereas avatar of God takes place at His sweet will to restore ethical order, to protect good people and to punish sinners).

yada–yada hi dharmasya
glanir bhavati bharata
abhyutthanam adharmasyat
ada' tmanam srjamy aham (7)

यदा यदा हि धर्मस्य ग्लानिर्भवति भारत ।
अभ्युत्थानमधर्मस्य तदात्मानं सृजाम्यहम् ॥ (४।७)

paritranaya sadhunam
vinasaya ca duskrtam
dharmasamsthapanarthaya
sambhavami yuge–yuge (8)

परित्राणाय साधूनां विनाशाय च दुष्कृताम् ।
धर्मसंस्थापनार्थाय सम्भवामि युगे युगे ॥ (४।८)

O Bharata (Arjuna)! I incarnate myself whenever there is a decline of righteousness (Dharma) and rise of Adharma. I come into being from age–to–age for the protection of the good, for the destruction of the wicked and for the establishment of righteousness (Dharma).

Kṛsna is a leader. He has given a hint about role of Leaders/CEOs. They must restore order and rule of Dharma (ethics/duty) in the organisations. They have duty to protect good people and punish/ eliminate wicked or non–performers.

janma karma ca me divyam
evam yo vetti tattvatah
tyaktva deham punarjanma
nai ' ti mam eti so 'rjuna (9)

जन्म कर्म च मे दिव्यमेवं यो वेत्ति तत्त्वत: ।
त्यक्त्वा देहं पुनर्जन्म नैति मामेति सोऽर्जुन ॥ (४।९)

He who knows this in its true nature My divine birth (incarnation) and its objective is emancipated.

vitaragabnayakradha
manmaya mam upasritah
b–havo jnantapasa
puta madbham agatah (10)

वीतरागभयक्रोधा मन्मया मामुपाश्रिता: ।
बहवो ज्ञानतपसा पूता मद्भावमागता: ॥ (४ । १०)

Freed from passion fear and anger absorbed in Me taking refuge in Me, many purified by the austerity of wisdom have attained to my state of being.

Incarnation has one more purpose of facilitating ascent of man into God hood or excellence. Avatar sets norms or standards to be followed by others. Purpose of leadership must be the development of subordinates).

ye yatha mami prapadyante
tams tathai va bhajamy aham
mama vartmanuvartante
manasyah partina sarvasah (11)

ये यथा मां प्रपद्यन्ते तांस्तथैव भजाम्यहम् ।
मम वर्त्मानुवर्तन्ते मनुष्या: पार्थ सर्वश: ॥ (४ । ११)

As people approach Me so I accept them; people on all sides follow my path.

(A leader should carry people with him. His order/direction/ instruction must be followed by all.

kankshatah *karmanam siddhini*

yajanta iha devtah
ksipraim be manuse loke
siddhir bharati karmaja. (12)

काङ्क्षन्त: कर्मणां सिद्धिं यजन्त इह देवता: ।
क्षिप्रं हि मानुषे लोके सिद्धिर्भवति कर्मजा ॥ (४ । १२)

Those who desire fruitition of their works on earth offer sacrifices to the Gods for the fruitition of works in this world of men is very quick. (This is vedic way of performing work. However, it does not give freedom from bondage stress and strain).

3. Nature of God's Work

caturvarnyam Maya shstam
guna Karma vibhagasah
tasyaKartaram api Mani
viddhy a Kartaram avyayam (13)

चातुर्वर्ण्यं मया सृष्टं गुणकर्मविभागशः ।
तस्य कर्तारमपि मां विद्ध्यकर्तारमव्ययम् ॥ (४ । १३)

The four–fold order (Chaturvarna, Brahmin, Kshtriya, Vaishya, Shudra has been created by Me according to division of Quality (aptitude) and work (action/function/duty). Though I am its Creator, know Me incapable of action or change.

(This is made very clear that the four–fold order division or four varnas are based on aptitude and function. It has nothing to do with caste, (birth) sex, breedings, etc. A class is determined by temperament. Vocation is not a caste determined by Birth and Heredity. In the *Mahabharata* also this fact is stated that in the beginning the whole world was of one class but later it became divided into four divisions on the basis of the specific duties. The distinction between caste and outcaste is artificial. Thus, leader in Gita (Srikrishna) talks about division based on aptitude and functions. He does not approve of caste system. Every leader should classify his people on the basis of aptitude and functions. There must be a matching of aptitude with the function for the creation of an effective organisation. The leader should remain unattached to it. He must remain independent (impartial) and never try to disturb matching of aptitude with functions. All functional classes are equally important for him– Intellectual or Knowledge resources, administrators. Businessmen and supportive services. No organisation can work if a leader starts interfering and showing bias in favour of a particular functional group as against other functional groups. Work should not affect his changeless being, though he is the unseen background of all works. There is no place for introducing caste, sex, region, community, language factors in this matching of aptitude with functions. In the light of this basic tenet of leadership function exposed by Srikrishna in the Gita, we should review the policy of job reservations based on caste and sex factors.)

4. Freedom from Bondage

na man karmani limpanti
na me karmaphale sprha
iti mam yo bhi a nati
karmabhir na sa badhyate (14)

न मां कर्माणि लिम्पन्ति न मे कर्मफले स्पृहा।
इति मां योऽभिजानाति कर्मभिर्न स बध्यते ॥ (४ । १४)

Works do not defile Me, nor do I have any yearning for their fruits. Those who know Me this is not bound by works. (He is free from bondage who is not attached to actions and their fruits).

evam jnatva krtam karma
purvair api mumuksubhih
kuru karmai va tasmat tvain
purvaih purvataram krtam (15)

एवं ज्ञात्वा कृतं कर्म पूर्वैरपि मुमुक्षुभिः।
कुरु कर्मैव तस्मात्त्वं पूर्वैः पूर्वतरं कृतम् ॥ (४ । १५)

In the past also work was done in this way (detached way) by ancient people who sought liberation. You follow their path.

(This verse establishes utility of following the best precedents. Ideal role models should be relived in management. The less knowledgeable persons perform action for self-purification but the wise do so for maintaining the world (organisation). The wise or wisdom manager should carry the pilgrimage of life for the good of the creatures and for the glory of God/ supreme leader).

5 Action – Inaction

kim karma kim akarma ti
kavaya py atra mohitah
tat tekarma pravaksyami
yau jnatva moksayse subhat (16)

किं कर्म किमकर्मेति कवयोऽप्यत्र मोहिताः।
तत्ते कर्म प्रवक्ष्यामि यज्ज्ञात्वा मोक्ष्यासेऽशुभात् ॥ (४ । १६)

Even the wise are bewildered (confused) on what is Karma and what is Akarma (Action and Inaction). I will tell you what is action(karma) knowing which you will be freed from evil.

karmano by api boddhavyam
boddhavyam ca vidarmanah
akarmanas ca boddhavyam
gahana karmana gathi (17)

कर्मणो ह्यपि बोद्धव्यं बोद्धव्यं च विकर्मण: ।
अकर्मणश्च बोद्धव्यं गहना कर्मरो गति: ॥ (४ । १७)

One has to understand what action is? (Karma). What is Prohibited or Wrong Action? (Vikarma) What is inaction? (akarma). It is very hard to understand the way of Karma.

(What is right course is generally not obvious. We are confused by mixing–up of the contemporary ideas, precedents of the tradition and voice of conscience. We must resolve this problem by reference to immutable truths with the insight of the highest reason).

karmany akarma yah pasyed
akarmani ca karma yah
sa buddhiman manusyesu
sa yuktah krtsnakarma krt (18)

कर्मण्यकर्म य: पश्येदकर्मणि च कर्म य: ।
स बुद्धिमान्मनुष्येषु स युक्त: कृत्स्नकर्मकृत् ॥ (४ । १८)

One who sees inaction in action and action in inaction is the wise man. He is yogin (karma yogi) and has accomplished all his work.

[When we work without any attachment to action and its fruits and we do it as our duty (Dharma) with our soul linked to the divine (With buddhi yoga), our mental balance is not disturbed. This is the state where we see inaction in action. This non–action preserves our equanimity of mind. Absence of bondage, stress and strain is called akarma. This is equal to renunciation of fruits of action (Karma Yoga). Thus, buddhi yoga and karma yoga go together and lead to the same resuts–excellence in performance without any bondage of pleasure and pain, success or failure, stress and strain, sin and good (*paap* and *punya*). Self is inactive but body is active with the feeling that it is God who works or I do the duty of God. Spirit brings excellence in performance.]

How to see action in inaction? Astavakragita explains that the turning away from action by tools due to perversity and ignorance amounts to action. This must be avoided.(15,3,61). People avoid work on the false pretext that it is petty work, it is difficult or hard to do. This is the root cause of poor performance/lower levels of effectiveness. Leaders must see through these excuses and explain the nature of action and inaction to their followers.

yasa sarve samarambhah
kamasamkalp–a varjitah.
jnanagnidaghhakarmanam
tam ahuh panditam budhah (19)

यस्य सर्वे समारंम्भा: कामसङ्कल्पवर्जिता: ।
ज्ञानाग्निदग्धकर्माणं तमाहु: पण्डितं बुधा: ॥ (४ । १९)

One whose undertakings are all free from the will of desires or passions whose works or actions are burned up in the fire of wisdom (detachment from fruits and freedom from ego) he is called by the wise as man of learning (Wisdom Manager).

tyakiva karmaphatasangam
nityatriptu nirasrayah
karmany abhipravrtto pi
nai va kimit karoti sah. (20)

त्यक्त्वा कर्मफलासङ्गं नित्यतृप्तो निराश्रय: ।
कर्मण्यभिप्रवृत्तोऽपि नैव किञ्चित्करोति स: ॥ (४ । २०)

One does nothing though he is ever engaged in work when he has given up attachment to the fruits of the works he is ever content and is independent he has no kind of dependence.

Such self–inspired worker does not require external supervision and control, external motivation. He deserves complete autonomy to give excellent performance. Astavakragita also says the same thing, " he who is devoid of existence and non–existence, who is wise, satisfied, free from desire, does nothing even if he may be acting in the eyes of the world . (XVIII,19)

nirasir yatacittatma
tyaktasarvaparigrahah
sariram kevalam karma
kurvan na, proti kilbisam (21)

निराशीर्यतचित्तात्मा त्यक्तसर्वपरिग्रह: ।
शारीरं केवलं कर्म कुर्वन्नप्नोति किल्बिषम् ॥ (४ । २१)

He commits no wrong who does duty with no desires with self–control of heart and body, giving up all possessions or possessiveness. He performs action by the body alone. (Virtue or vice mixes up with work not through body but by mind. If spirit is pure this is avoided automatically)

yadrcchalabhasamtusto
dvandvatito vimatsarah
samah sidhav asiddhau ca
krtva pi na nibadhyate (22)

यदृच्छालाभसन्तुष्टो द्वन्द्वातीतो विमत्सरः ।
समः सिद्धावसिद्धौ च कृत्वापि न निबध्येते ॥ (४ । २२)

He has no bondage in spite of doing work who is satisfied with whatever comes by chance, who has passed beyond the dualities (of pleasure and pain, gain and loss,etc.), who remains the same in success and failure.

(Action does not create any bondage. It is the spirit of attitude and motives which create bondage.)

6. Symbolic Value of Sacrifice

gatasangasya muktasya
jnanavasthitacetasah
yajnaya caratah karma
samagram praviliyate (23)

गतसङ्गस्य मुक्तस्य ज्ञानावस्थितचेतसः ।
यज्ञायाचरतः कर्म समग्रं प्रविलीयते ॥ (४ । २३)

brahma rpanam brahma havir
brahmagnau brahmana hutam
brahmai va tena gantavyam
brahmakarmasamadhina (24)

ब्रह्मार्पणं ब्रह्म हविर्ब्रह्मणा हुतम् ।
ब्रह्मैव तेन गन्तव्यं ब्रह्मकर्मसमाधिना ॥ (४ । २४)

daivam eva pare yajnam
yoginah paryupasate
brahmagnav apare yajnam
yajnenai vo pajuhvati (25)

दैवमेवापरे यज्ञं योगिनः पर्युपासते ।
ब्रह्माग्नावपरे यज्ञं यज्ञेनैवोपजुह्वति ॥ (४ । २५)

srotradini ndriyany anye
samyamagnisu juhvati
sabdadin visayan anya
indriyagnisu juhvati (26)

श्रोत्रादीनीन्द्रियाण्यन्ये संयमाग्निषु जुह्वति ।
शब्दादीतन्वषयानन्य इन्द्रियाग्निषु जुह्वति ॥ (४ । २६)

sarvani ndriyakarmani
pranakarmani ca pare
atmasmayamayogagnau
juhvati jnanadipite. (27)

सर्वाणीन्द्रियकर्माणि प्राणकर्माणि चापरे ।
आत्मसंयमयोगाग्नौ जुह्वति ज्ञानदीपिते ॥ (४ । २७)

dravyayajnas tapoyajna
yogayajnas taha pare .
svadhyayajnas ca
yatayah samsitavratah (28)

द्रव्ययज्ञास्तपोयज्ञा योगयज्ञास्तथापरे ।
स्वाध्यायज्ञानयज्ञाश्च यतय: संशितव्रता: ॥ (४ । २८)

apane juhvati pranam
prane panam tatha pare
pranapanagati ruddhva
pranayamaparayanah (29)

अपाने जुह्वति प्राणं प्राणेऽपानं तथापरे ।
प्राणापानगती रुद्ध्वा प्राणायामपरायणा: ॥ (४ । २९)

apare niyataharah
pranan pranesu juhvati
sarve py tc yajnavido
yajnaksapitakalmasah (30)

अपरे नियताहारा: प्राणान्प्राणेषु जुह्वति ।
सर्वेऽप्येते यज्ञविदो यज्ञक्षपितकल्मषा: ॥ (४ । ३०)

yajnasistamrtabhujo
yanti brahma sanatanam
na yam loko sty ayajnasya
kuto nyah kurusattama (31)

यज्ञशिष्टामृतभुजो यान्ति ब्रह्म सनातनम् ।
नायं लोकोऽस्त्ययज्ञस्य कुतोऽन्य: कुरुसवम ॥ (४ । ३१)

evam bahuvidha yajna
vitata brahmano mukhe
karmajan viddhi tan sarvan
evam jnatva vimoksyase (32)

एवं बहुविधा यज्ञा वितता ब्रह्मणो मुखे ।
कर्मजान्विद्धि तान्सर्वानेवं ज्ञात्वा विमोक्ष्यसे ॥ (४ । ३२)

sreyan dravyamayad yajnaj
jnanayajnah paramtapa
sarvam karma khilam partha
jnane parisamapyate (33)

श्रेयान्द्रव्यमयाद्यज्ञाज्ज्ञानयज्ञ: परन्तप ।
सर्वं कमाखिलं पार्थ ज्ञाने परिसमाप्यते ॥ (४ । ३३)

tad viddhi pranipatena
pariprasnena seyaya
upadeksyanti te jnanam
jnaninas tattvadarsinah (34)

तद्विद्धि प्रणिपातेन परिप्रश्नन सेवया ।
उपदेक्ष्यन्ति ते ज्ञानं ज्ञानिनस्तत्त्वदर्शिन: ॥ (४ । ३४)

The work of a man who has no attachments, who is liberated, whose mind is firmly set in wisdom, who does work as a sacrifice, is dissolved entirely. For him the act of offering is God, the oblation is God. It is offered by God to the fire of God, God is the objective of one who realizes God in his work/ deeds. Some yogis offer sacrifices to the Gods while others offer sacrifices by the sacrifice itself into the fire of the supreme.(Some seek divine favour by offering sacrifices, whereas other offers all works to the divine itself– *krsnarpanmastu*).

Some offer hearing and other senses into the fires of restraint– practice mental control and discipline of sensuary pleasures. The objects of sense are sacrificed in the fire of sense. For example, sacrifice of ego, anger, lust,greed. desires(lower impulses).

Some offer sacrifice in the form of material possessions, live a simple and austerious life, give donation while others of subdued minds and severe fasts offer their learning and knowledge (janana yoga).Some others offer sacrifice in the form of *pranayama*. Some others restrict their food (observe fast). All these sacrificers get their sins destroyed.

(All sacrifices lead to spiritual growth if mind is controlled).

The eternal absolute (God/Bliss) can be attained by those who consume as residual claimants–after offering sacrifice to all other claimants. The world is not for him who offers no sacrifice, then how the other world can be good for him, O Best of Kurus (Arjuna)? (Here the consumption after fair, just and equitable distribution is reiterated which is the basic tenet of socialism.)

These several sacrifices are spread out as various ways to attain the God. You must know that all these are born of duty/action/work. This knowledge will make you free or liberated. (Never avoid sacrifice/duty).

7. Role of Wisdom in Performance

yaj jnatva na punar moham
evam yasyasi pandava
yena bhutany asesena
draksyasy atmany asesena
draksyasy atmany atho mayi (35)

यज्ज्ञात्वा न पुनर्मोहमेवं यास्यसि पाण्डव ।
येन भूतान्यशेषेण द्रक्ष्यस्यात्मन्यथो मयि ॥ (४ । ३५)

api ced asi papebhyah
sarvebhyah papakrttamah
sarvam jnanaplavenai va
vrjinam samtarisyasi (36)

अपि चेदसि पापेभ्य: सर्वेभ्य: पापकृत्तम: ।
सर्वं ज्ञानप्लवेनैव वृजिनं सन्तरिष्यसि ॥ (४ । ३६)

yathai dhamsi samiddho gnir
bhasmasat kurute rjuna
jnanagnish sarvaarmani
bhasmasat kurute tatha (37)

यथैधांसि समिद्धोऽग्निर्भस्मसात्कुरुतेऽर्जुन ।
ज्ञानाग्नि: सर्वकर्माणि भस्मासात्कुरुते तथा ॥ (४ । ३७)

na hi jnanena sadram
pavitram iha vidyate
tat svaya yogasamsiddhah
kalena tmani vindati (38)

न हि ज्ञानेन सदृशं पवित्रमिह विद्यते ।
तत्स्वयं योगसंसिद्धः कालेनात्मनि विन्दति ॥ (४ । ३८)

Knowledge as sacrifice (Jnan dan/Yagna) is greater than any material sacrifice. O Arjuna, all works culminate in wisdom without any exception. Knowledge can be gained by humble reverence, by inquiry and by service (of wise persons) The men of wisdom who have seen truth (who have practised ethics) are entitled to preach.

(This verse indicates that in spiritual life, faith comes first then knowledge and then experience). This is the duty cast upon wisdom leaders to first practice Truth (ethics) and then preach it to their followers. They should not be self – centred but must actively spread knowledge to enable others to develop).

When you know it you will overcome your confusion . O Pandava (Arjuna)! By this knowledge you shall see all existences without exception in the self and then in Me (God). Even if you are the most sinful of all sinners you shall cross over all evil by the boat of wisdom alone. As the fire turns fuel to ashes, the fire of wisdom turns to ashes all work (deeds). (It means a man of wisdom will never develop ego of a doer). In this world, there is nothing equal in purity to wisdom. He who becomes perfected by yoga (Buddhi and karma yoga) will find this of himself in his self in course of time.

8. Role of Faith in Wisdom

sraddhavaml labhate jnanan
tatparah samyatendriyah
jnanam labdhva param santim
acirena dhigacchati (39)

श्रद्धावाँल्लभते ज्ञानं तत्परः संयतेन्द्रियः ।
ज्ञानं लब्ध्वा परां शान्तिमचिरेणाधिगच्छति ॥ (४ । ३९)

ajnas ca sraddadhanas ca
samsayatma vinasyati
na yam loko sti paro
na sukham samsayatmanah (40)

अज्ञश्चाश्रद्दधानश्च संशयात्मा विनश्यति ।
नायं लोकोऽस्ति न परो न सुखं संशयात्मनः ॥ (४ । ४०)

Yogasamnyastakarmanam
jnanasamchinnasamsayam
atmavantam na karmani
nibadhnanti dhanamjaya (41)

योगसन्न्यस्तकर्माणं ज्ञानसञ्छिन्नसंशयम् ।
आत्मावंन्त न कर्माणि निबध्नन्ति धनञ्जय ॥ (४ । ४१)

tasmad ajnanasambhutam
hrtstham jnanasina tmanah
chittvai nam samsayam yogam
atistho ttistha bharata (42)

तस्मादज्ञानसम्भूतं हृत्स्थं ज्ञानासिनात्मनः ।
छित्त्वैनं संशयं योगमातिष्ठोत्तिष्ठ भारत ॥ (४ । ४२)

He who has faith, who is absorbed in it (wisdom) and who has subdued his senses gains wisdom and having gained wisdom he quickly attains the supreme peace. (Faith is essential for gaining self-control, wisdom and peace.)

But the man who is ignorant, who has no faith, who is of doubting nature is bound to perish. He will not be happy in this world as well as in the other world.

Works do not bind a karma yogi–who has renounced all works as sacrifice or offering who has destroyed all doubts by wisdom and who ever possesses his soul.

Therefore, O Bharata (Arjuna)! You should cut your doubts born of ignorance by the sword of wisdom. Resort to Yoga (karma and buddhi yoga) and stand up (to perform your duty).

The fourth chapter titled the Janana yoga is over. (Sometimes it is titled as the Janana Karmasamnyasa Yoga – Yoga of Knowledge and renunciation of action.

SUMMARY

The tradition of Janana yoga (path of knowledge) is ancient. It has been handed down from ages by various Royal sages like Rama, Janaka, Ikswaku, Manu, etc. Srikrishna restated it to Arjuna. The objectives of incarnation of God from ages–to–ages has been to restore rule of ethics to protect good people and to punish wicked ones. This is the duty enjoined upon all leaders. Another duty of leader is to help people in their development to the level of excellence. He should carry people with him but his orders/direction must be obeyed by people.

Those who want fruits of duty in the world they make offerings to Gods (Middle level Management). But this way of performance does not give freedom from bondage, stress and strain. The leader must match functions with aptitude. No consideration of caste, sex, language, province, community be there in this matching. Top management should not be affected by division of labour. It must have unseen presence in all works (Its policy must prevail). In management the best precedents be followed and ideal role models be re–lived. Ordinary people work for their self-purification (compliance with orders) but wise people work for maintenance of the world order (organisation). Life is lived by them as pilgrimage for the good of people and glory of the God/top Management. Duty must be performed as Dharma without any attachment to desires, fruits and ego. In this way, action becomes non–action. It will not cause any stress and strain. Renouncement of action due to perversity and ignorance amounts to action. This is the root cause of poor performance. The leaders must see through such excuses and explain the true nature of action and inaction to such subordinates. Wise is one who performs duty free from desires and ego. No external supervision and control, no external motivation are required for such wise people. They require autonomy to give best performance. No sin comes to such people because of 'pure spirit' put in the work. All work done must be sacrificed/offered to the leader. But never avoid work and consider it to be sacrifice. Best sacrifice is knowledge. First practise it and then preach it to others for making them excellent performers and free from bondage. All evils can be overcome by wisdom.

Faith is essential for gaining self-control, wisdom and peace. He who has no faith is ignorant and of doubting nature (indecisive) will perish. He can't be happy in this world and in other world. But doubt must be overcome through wisdom and duty be performed as 'Yogin' (With full spirit, concentration, determination) detachment and equanimity of mind). This is mantra for excellent performance.

THE YOGA OF RENUNCIATION OF ACTION

Contents

1. The Common Goal of Samkhya and Yoga

arjuna uvaca
samnyasam karmanam krṣna
punar yogani ca samsasi
yac cnreya etayor ekam
tam me bruhi suniscitone (1)

अर्जुन उवाच
सन्न्यासं कर्मणां कृष्ण पुनर्योगं च शंससि ।
यच्छ्रेय एतयोरेकं तन्मे ब्रूहि सुनिश्चितम् ।। (५ । १)

Arjuna raises a query out of ignorance for clarification of his doubt about true meaning of Renunciation of Action.

" O Krṣna, you praise the renunciation of works and again their unselfish performance. Tell me for certain which one is better of the two."

Shribhagavan uvaca
samnyasah karmayogas ca
nihsreyaskarav ubhau
tagor tu karmasamn yasat
karmayogo visisyate (2)

सन्न्यास: कर्मयोगश्च नि:श्रेयसकरावुभौ ।
तयोस्तु कर्मसन्न्यासात्कर्मयोगो विशिष्यते ॥ (५ । २)

Srikrsna said:

"The renunciation of works and their unselfish performance both lead to the salvation of soul (from bondage). But of the two, the unselfish performance of work (duty) is better than renunciation.

(In a working society/organisation, people can't survive without work. No organisation can survive if people renounce work/duty. Therefore, the pragmatic choice is to perform duty with renunciation of selfish motives–passions, ego, attachment to fruits, etc. This is the practical way of attaining excellence in performance and salvation of soul).

jneyah sa nityasamnyasi
yo na dvesti na kanksati
nirdvandvo hi mahabaho
sukhami bandhat pramucyate (3)

ज्ञेय: स नित्यसन्नयासी यो न द्वेष्टि न कांक्षति ।
निर्द्वन्द्वो हि महाबाहो सुखं बन्धात्प्रमुच्यते ॥ (५ । ३)

"O Arjuna, know him as a man of ever spirit of renunciation who has no aversion and desires. Being free from dualities and desires, he is released from bondage very easily."

(One who does his work in a detached spirit is a true worker (Karmayogin) as well as the true renouncer (Nitya samnyasin). Gita does not support renunciation of duties but it stresses upon unselfish and detached performance of duty).

samikhyayogau prthag balah
pravadanti na panditah
ekam apy asthitah samyag
ubhayor vindate phalam (4)

साङ्ख्ययोगौ पृथग्बाला: प्रवदन्ति न पण्डिता: ।
एकमप्यास्थित: सम्यगुभयोर्विन्दते फलम् ।। (५।४)

Thus, ignorant speak of renunciation of duty (samkhya) and practice of work (karma yoga) as different. One who applies either of the two, gets the fruits of both (freedom from Bondage).

(In Shantiparva of the *Mahabharata* this fact is clearly stated that the true renouncer is not he who remains completely inactive but he who does work in the spirit of detachment (316,4). Thus, renunciation is a mental attitude rather than physical phenomenon. The physical body action is the same when work is being done by a wise or a fool. But, however, the spirit is different, attitude is different. This is the main cause of difference in level of excellence in performance between the work done by a wise person and a fool/ignorant.)

[What is told by Srikrsna in this verse applies to wise people only. For them the result of samkhya and karma yoga will be the same– freedom from bondage. But for ordinary mortals who lack wisdom the results will be vastly different. They will misuse samkhya as a tool to avoid work and invite disciplinany action. It will lead to poor performance. It is better to keep them engaged in work till they understand that renunciation is not physical but a mental and spiritual phenomenon].

uat samkhyaih prapyate sthanam
tad gogair api gamyate
ekami samkhyam ca yagam ca
yahj pasyati sa pasyati (5)

यत्साङ्ख्यै: प्राप्यते स्थानं तद्योगैरपि गम्यते ।
एकं साङ्ख्यं च योगं च य: पश्यति स पश्यति । (५।५)

The status which is obtained by man of renunciation is reached by man of action also. He who sees that the ways of renunciation and of action are identical, he sees truly.(This is true if both are persons of wisdom).

samnyasan tu mahabaho
dukam aptum ayogtah
yogayukto munir brahma
nacirena dhigacchati (6)

सन्न्यासस्तु महाबाहो दु:खमासुमयोगत: ।
योगयुक्तो मुनिर्ब्रह्म नचिरेणाधिगच्छति ।। (५।६)

"O Arjuna! It is difficult to do renunciation without yoga; the sage who is earnest in yoga (buddhi and karma yoga) attains soon to the absolute.

(Thus, Samkhya or Renunciation is not meant for ordinary mortals.)

yogauk to Visuddhatma
vijitatma Jitendriyah
sarvabhutatma bhutatma
kurvann api na lipyate (7)

योगयुक्तो विशुद्धात्मा विजितात्मा जितेन्द्रियः ।
सर्वभूतात्मभूतात्मा कुर्वन्नपि न लिप्यते ॥ (५ । ७)

One who is trained in the way of works. (karma yogi), and is pure in soul (buddhi yogi), who is master of his self (self–controlled), who has won the senses, whose soul becomes the self of all–beings, he is not tainted by works though he works.

(All actions are renounced inwardly, not outwardly by yogins. They are released from all bondage by such work).

naiva kimcit karomn ti
yukto manyeta tattvavit
pasyan srnvav sprsan jighrann
asnan gacchan svapan svasan (8)

नैव किञ्चित्करोमीति युक्तो मन्येत तत्त्ववित् ।
पश्यञ्शृण्वन्स्पृशञ्जिघ्रन्नश्नन्गच्छन्स्वपञ्श्वसन् ॥ (५ । ८)

pralapan visrjan grhnann
unmisan nimisann api
indriyam ndriyarthesu
vartanta iti dharayan (9)

प्रलपन्विसृजन्गृह्णन्नुन्मिषन्निमिषन्नपि ।
इन्द्रियाणीन्द्रियार्थेषु वर्तन्त इति धारयन् ॥ (५ । ९)

brahmany adhaya karmani
sangam tyaktva karoti yah
lipyate na sa papena
padmapattram iva mbhasa (10)

ब्रह्मण्याधाय कर्माणि सङ्गंत्यक्त्वा करोति यः ।
लिप्यते न स पापेन पद्मपत्रमिवाम्भसा ॥ (५ । १०)

kayena manasa buddhya
kevalair indriyair api
yoginah karma kurvanti
sangam tyaktva tmasuddhaye (11)

कायेन मनसा बुद्ध्या केवलैरिन्द्रियैरपि ।
योगिन: कर्म कुर्वन्ति सङ्गं त्यक्त्वात्मशुद्धये ॥ (५।११)

yuktah karmaphalam tyaktva
santim apnoti naisthikim
ayuktah kamakarena
phale sakto nibadhyate (12)

युक्त: कर्मफलं त्यक्त्वा शान्तिमाप्नोति नैष्ठिकीम् ।
अयुक्त: कामकारेण फले सक्तो निबध्यते ॥ (५।१२)

The man who is united with the divine (Janana Yogi) thinks that "I do nothing at all." Only senses are occupied with the objects of senses. He has no attachments and offers all his actions to God (Karma Yogi). He is not touched by sin, even as a lotus leaf (is untouched) by water.

(This is the way of true renunciation of action).

The yogin (Karma Yogi) does work with body, mind, understanding or merely with the senses, abandoning attachment, for self–purification.

(Karma yoga purifies soul through detached work).

Such a pure soul (of Karma Yogi) will attain peace by abandoning attachment to the fruits of action. But, however, peace and freedom from bondage do not come to those whose soul is not united with the Divine (Janana yoga). It is impelled by desire and attached to the fruits.

2. The Enlightened Self

sarvakarmani manasa
samnyasya ste sukham vasi
navadvare pure dehi
nai va kurvan na karayan (13)

सर्वकर्माणि मनसा सन्न्यस्यास्ते सुखं वशी ।
नवद्वारे पुरे देही नैव कुर्वन्न कारयन् ॥ (५।१३)

na kartrtvm na karmani
lokasya srjati prabhuh
na karmaphalasamyogam
svabhavas tu pravartate (14)

न कर्तुत्वं न कर्माणि लोकस्य सृजति प्रभु: ।
न कर्मफलसंयोगं स्वभावस्तु प्रवर्तते ॥ (५।१४)

na datte kasyacit papam
na cai va sukrtam vibhuh
ajnanena vrtam jnanam
tena muhyanti jantavah (15)

नादत्ते कस्यचित्पापं न चैव सुकृतं विभु: ।
अज्ञानेनावृतं ज्ञानं तेन मुह्यन्ति जन्तव: ॥ (५।१५)

jnanena tu tad ajnanam
yesam nasitam atmanah
tesam adityavaj jnanam
prakasayati tat param (16)

ज्ञानेन तु तदज्ञानं येषां नाशितमात्मान: ।
तेषामादित्यवज्ज्ञानं प्रकाशयति तत्परम् ॥ (५।१६)

tadbuddhayas tadatmanas
tannisthas tatparayanah
gacchanty apunaravrttim
jnananirdhutakalmasah (17)

तद्बुद्धयस्तदात्मानस्तन्निष्ठास्तत्परायणा: ।
गच्छन्त्यपुनरावृत्तिं ज्ञाननिर्धूतकल्मषा: ॥ (५।१७)

vidyavinayasampanne
brahmane gavi hastini
suni cai va svapake ca
panditah samadarsinah (18)

विद्याविनयसम्पन्ने ब्राह्मणे गवि हस्तिनि ।
शुनि चैव श्वपाके च पण्डिता: समदर्शिन: ॥ (५।१८)

ihai va tair jitah sargo
yesam samye sthitam manah
nirdosam hi samam brahma
tasmad brahmani te sthitah (19)

इहैव तैर्जितः सर्गो येषां साम्ये स्थितं मनः ।
निर्दोषं हि समं ब्रह्म तस्माद्ब्रह्मणि ते स्थिताः ।। (५ । १९)

na prahrsyet priyam prapya
no dvijet prapya ca priyam
sthirabuddhir asammudho
brahmavid brahmani sthitah (20)

न प्रहृष्येत्प्रियं प्राप्य नोद्विजेत्प्राप्य चाप्रियम् ।
स्थिरबुद्धिरसम्मूढो ब्रह्मविद् ब्रह्मणि स्तितः ।। (५ । २०)

bahyasparsesv asaktatma
vindaty atmani yat sukham
sa brahmayogayuktatma
sukham aksayam asnute (21)

बाह्यस्पर्शाष्विसक्तात्मा विन्दत्यात्मनि यत्सुखम् ।
स ब्रह्मयोगयुक्तात्मा सुखमक्षयमश्नुते ।। (५ । २१)

ye hi samsparsaja bhoga
duhkhayonaya eva te
adyantavantah kaunteya
na tesu ramate budhah (22)

ये हि संस्पर्शजा भोगा दुःखयोनय एव ते ।
आद्यन्तवन्तः कौन्तेय न तेषु रमते बुधः ।। (५ । २२)

saknoti hai va yah sodhum
prak sariravimoksanat
kamakrodhodbhavam vegam
sa yuktah sa sukhi narah (23)

शक्नोतीहैव यः सोढु प्राक्शरीरविमोक्षणात् ।
कामक्रोधोद्भवं वेगं स युक्तः स सुखी नरः ।। (५ । २३)

The embodied (soul) who has controlled his nature, renounces all actions by mind, dwells at ease (peace) in the city of nine gates, neither working nor causing work to be done.

(Nine gates are the two eyes, the two ears, the two nostrills, the mouth and two organs of excretion and generation. Soul at peace acts as witness only. It is free from all bondage).

The sovereign self does not create for the people agency nor does He act. Nor does He connect works with their fruits. Nature works out all this. The all pervading spirit does not take on the sin or the merit of any. Creatures are bewildered (confused) due to their ignorance which is destroyed by wisdom just as darkness is removed by sun. When thoughts, aims, actions are devoted to the soul all sins are washed and no rebirth will be there. This wisdom brings out the excellent performance. Sages will not differentiate between learned and humble brahmin, a cow and an elephant, a dog or an outcaste. Wisdom brings great humility and equality. Wise will see God in all creatures as well as within self. Thus, they will become persons established in God. They will not rejoice on obtaining pleasant nor sorrow on obtaining unpleasant. Such self–controlled and self–realised persons enjoy eternal bliss.

Pleasures born of external contacts with objects of senses are really sources of sorrow. They have a beginning and an end. Wiseman will not delight in them. One who is able to resist the rush of desire and anger in this life will be happy (emancipated). He is yogin.

It is clear that emancipation can be attained while living and are working with the help of Janana yoga and Karma yoga.

3. Self-contentment (Inner Peace)

yo ntahsukho ntararamas
tatha ntarjyotir eva yah
sa yogi brahmanirvanam
brahmabhuto dhigacchati (24)

योऽन्तःसुखोऽन्तरारामस्तथान्तर्ज्योतिरेव यः ।
स योगी ब्रह्मनिर्वाणं ब्रह्मभूतोऽधिगच्छति ॥ (५ । २४)

labhante brahmanirvanam
rsayah ksinakalmasah
chinnadvaidha yatatmanah
sarvabhutahite ratah (25)

लभन्ते ब्रह्मनिर्वाणमृषय: क्षीणकल्मषा: ।
छिन्नद्वैधा यतात्मान: सर्वभूतहिते रता: ॥ (५ । २५)

kamakrodhaviyuktanam
yatinam yatacetasam
abhito brahmanirvanam
vartate vidatatmanam (26)

कामक्रोधवियुक्तानां यतीनां यतचेतसाम् ।
अभितो ब्रह्मनिर्वाणं वर्तते विमितात्मनाम् ॥ (५ । २६)

sparsan krtva bahir bahyams
caksus cai va ntare bhruvoh
pranapanau samau krtva
nasabhyantaracarinau (27)

स्पर्शान्कृत्वा बहिर्बाह्यांश्चक्षुश्चैवान्तरे भ्रुवो: ।
प्राणापानौ समौ कृत्वा नासाभ्यन्तरचारिणौ ॥ (५ । २७)

yatendriyamanobuddhir
munir moksaparayanah
vigatecchbhayakrodho
yah sada mukta eva sah (28)

यतेन्द्रियमनोबुद्धिर्मुनिर्मोक्षपरायण: ।
विगतेच्छाभयक्रोधो य:सदा मुक्त एव स: ॥ (५ । २८)

bhoktaram yajnatapasam
sarvolokamahesvaram
suhrdam sarvabhutanam
jnatva mam santim rcchati (29)

भोक्तारं यज्ञतपसां सर्वलोकमहेश्वरम् ।
सुहृदं सर्वभूतानां ज्ञात्वा मां शान्तिमृच्छति ॥ (५ । २९)

One who finds his happiness within, has joy within and light within, that yogin becomes divine and attains ***Brahma nirvana*** or beautitude of the God. It is a state full of bliss, knowledge, self-possession and detached action for maintenance of the world organisation. Sins are destroyed, doubts and duals are cut, mind is disciplined and good to all creatures is done. Such self-realised souls (Yogins) are delivered from desire and anger. They have subdued their minds and have knowledge of the Self/God.

Shutting out all external objects, fixing the vision between the eyebrows, making even the flow of breath, the sage (yogin) who has controlled the senses, mind and understanding, who is intent on liberation, who has cast away desire, fear and anger, he is freed for ever. Knowing me (God) as the enjoyer of all sacrifices and austerities, the great Lord of all the worlds, the friend of all–beings, he (the yogin) attains peace.

(For a karma yogi, the realisation of Self/God and enjoyment of eternal bliss, emancipation becomes possible on earth while living and working, the invisible God becomes a personal friend, philosopher and guide for him).

SUMMARY

The subtle difference between renunciation of work and their unselfish-performance is explained. Renunciation of work and unselfish-performance bring the same result (bliss, peace and freedom from bondage) for yogins or men of wisdom. But for ordinary mortals/ignorant, work is emphasized. The karma yogi performs duty in the spirit of renunciation (of desires, ego, fruits). He is free from dualities and released from bondage very easily. Renunciation is a mental and spiritual phenomenon. It is not physical. Duty should not be given up in the grab of renunciation. Ignorants do that. True renunciation can be done by yogins or men of wisdom only. It is inwardly only. Soul of karma yogi is purified through detached performance. Such a soul acts as witness only and enjoys eternal bliss and peace. It realises God/Self on this earth. Invisible God becomes a personal God for a karma yogi. He attains great humility and equality. He sees light everywhere and spreads light everywhere.

Control rush of passions and rage, do duty as offering to God and be peaceful and liberated.

THE TRUE YOGA OF MEDITATION (EXECUTIVE HEALTH MANAGEMENT)

Contents

1. Renunciation and the Action are the Same

sribhagavan uvaca
griasritah karmaphalami
karyam karma karoti yah
sa samnyasi ca yogi ca
na miragnir na ca kriyah (1)

श्रीभगवानुवाच
अनाश्रित: कर्मफलं कार्यं कर्म करोति य: ।
स सन्न्यासी च योगी च न निरग्निर्न चाक्रिय: ॥ (६ । १)

Srikrṣna said, He is samyasin, he is the yogin who does the work without seeking fruits and not the one who gives up rituals like lighting the sacred fire and performing rites.

(Samyasin is an inward attitude of detachment to fruits. It has nothing to do with physical renunciation of work).

Samkara has given alternative interpretation to this verse. According to him "A samyasin is not only one who lights the sacred fire and performs rites but also one who does work without seeking fruits," However, this does not seem to be quite fair to the text, in the opinion of Dr. S. Radhakrishnan (see p.187 the *Bhagvadgita*.)

yam sanyasamiti prahur
yogam tam viddhi pandava
na hyasamnyastasamkalpo
yogi bhavati kascana (2)

यं सन्न्यासमिति प्राहुर्योगं तं विद्धि पाण्डव ।
न ह्यसन्न्यस्तसङ्कल्पो योगी भवति कश्चन ॥ (६ । २)

"O Pandava (Arjuna)! No one becomes yogin without renouncing his (selfish) purpose. Renunciation is disciplined activity (yoga).

(Thus, the renunciation and disciplined action are the same. These are synonyms or interchangeable words to describe unselfish work).

2. The Goal

aruruksor muner yogam
karma karanam ucyate
yogarudhasya tasyai va
samah karanam ucyate (3)

आरुरुक्षोर्मुनेर्योगं कर्म कारणमुच्यते ।
योगारूढस्य तस्यैव शमः कारणमुच्यते ॥ (६ । ३)

yada hi ne ndrivarthesu
na karmasv anusajjate
sarvasamkalpasamnyasi
yogarudhas tado cyate (4)

यदा हि नेन्द्रियार्थेषच न कर्मस्वनुषज्जते ।
सर्वसङ्कल्पसन्यासी योगारूढस्तदोच्यते ॥ (६।४)

uddhared atmana tmanam
na tmanam avasadayet
atmai va hy atmano bandhur
atmai va ripur atmanah (5)

उद्धरेदात्मनात्मानं नात्मानमवसादयेत् ।
आत्मैव ह्यात्मनो बन्धुरात्मैव रिपुरात्मन: ॥ (६।५)

bandhur atma tmanas tasya
yena tmai va tmana jitah
anatmanas tu satrutve
varteta tmai va satruvat (6)

बन्धुरात्मात्मनस्तस्य येनात्मौवात्मना जित: ।
अनात्मनस्तु शत्रुत्वे वर्तेतात्मैव शत्रुवत् ॥ (६।६)

jitatmanah prasantasya
paramatma samahitah
sitosnasukhaduhkhesu
tatha manapamananayoh (7)

जितात्मन: प्रशान्तस्य परमात्मा समाहित: ।
शीतोष्णसुखदु:खेषु तथा मानापमानायो: ॥ (६।७)

jnanavijnanatrptatma
kutastho vijitendriyah
yukta ity ucyate yogi
samalostasmakancanah (8)

ज्ञानविज्ञानतृप्तात्मा कूटस्थो विजितेन्द्रिय: ।
युक्त इत्युच्यते योगी समलोष्टश्मकाञ्चन: ॥ (६ ८)

suhrnmitraryudasina–
madhyasthadvesyabandhusu
sadhusu api ca papesu
samabuddhir visisyate (9,

सुहृन्मित्रार्युदासीनमध्यस्थद्वेष्यबन्धुषु ।
साधुष्वपि च पापेषु समबुद्धिर्विशिष्यते ॥ (६।९)

Work (or performance of duty) is said to be the means of the sage to attain yoga when yoga is attained. Serenity is said to be means (to perform duty).

(Through doing our duty with detachment we obtain self-control and through self-control we attain peace. When duty is done with detachment to fruits and with equanimity, we are filled with spontaneous inner vitality and strength leads to excellent performance.)

One is said to have attained yoga when he is detached from the objects of sense, work and its fruits. This is true renouncement. Let a man lift himself by Himself; let him not degrade Himself (by attachments). Self (atman) alone is the friend as well as enemy of the self (person). Self is friend of self for one who has conquered his (lower) self by the higher (self). Self is an enemy of self for one who has not possessed his higher self.

(Lower self means desire/passions, ego, anger, attachment, aversion, lust, greed, jealousy etc. If it is controlled by the higher self. (Spirit), then self becomes pure and full of inner strength, lower self can't be destroyed. It can only be regulated by practice and determination. However, if not controlled by higher self it results into lower performance, conflicts, stress and strain. Self becomes enemy of self in such a case.The control of lower self by higher self has to be done by self. It can't be done by others. Thus, self is the Lord of self and also the goal of the self. The major determinants of excellent performance are psycho–spiritual rather than physical. Everyone is free to rise or fall and, therefore, everyone is the maker of his own destiny.)

When one has conquered his lower self and has attained the calm of self-mastery (self-control), his supreme self abides ever concentrate; he is at peace in cold and heat, in pleasure and pain, in honour and dishonour.

(When self is bound by lower self or modes of nature it is called Ksetrajna and when it is freed from them, it is called atman or supreme 'self.' It becomes free from attachments and duality. It is filled with spontaneous energy to attain mission of serving the humanity with equanimity and concentration).

Such a person is yogi whose soul is satisfied with wisdom and knowledge, who is stable (concentrate) and master of his senses (self-controlled). To him a clod, a stone and a piece of gold are the same. He is equal minded among friends, companions, and foes, among those who are neutral and related, among saints and sinners. He excels (in performance).

3. The Eternal Vigilance

yogi yunjita satatam
atmanam rahasi sthitah
ekaki yatacittatma
nirasir aparigrahah (10)

योगी युञ्जीत सततमात्मानं रहसि स्थित: ।
एकाकी यतचित्तात्मा निराशीरपरिग्रह: ॥ (६ । १०)

sucau dese pratisthapya
sthiram asanam atmanah
na tyucchritam na tinicam
cailajinakusottaram (11)

शुचौ देशे प्रतिष्ठाप्य स्थिरमासनमात्मन: ।
नात्युच्छ्रितं नातिनीचं चैलाजिनकुशोत्तरम् ॥ (६ । ११)

tatran kargram manah krtva
yatacittendriyakriyah
upavisya sane yunjyad
yogam atmavisuddhaye (12)

तत्रैकाग्रं मन: कृत्वा यतचित्तेन्द्रियक्रिय: ।
उपविश्यासने युञ्ज्याद्योगमात्मविशुद्धये ॥ (६ । १२)

samam kayasirogrivam
dharayann acalam sthirah
sampreksya nasikagram svam
disas ca navalokayan (13)

समं कायशिरोग्रीवं धारयन्नचलं स्थिर: ।
सम्प्रेक्ष्य नासिकाग्रं स्वं दिशश्चानवलोकयन् ॥ (६ । १३)

prasantatma vigatabhir
brahmacarivrate sthitah
manah samyamya maccitto
yukta asita matparah (14)

प्रशान्तात्मा विगतभीर्ब्रह्मचारिव्रते स्थित: ।
मन: संयम्य मच्चित्तो युक्त आसीत मत्पर: ॥ (६ । १४)

yunjann evam sada tmanam
yogi niyatamanasah
santim nirvanaparamam
matsamstham adhigacchati (15)

युञ्जन्नेवं सदात्मानं योगी नियतमानस: ।
शान्तिं निर्वाणपरमां मत्संस्थामधिगच्छति ॥ (६ । १५)

na tyasnatas tu yogo sti
na cai kantam anasnatah
na ca tisvapnasilasya
jagrato nan va ca rjuna (16)

नात्यश्नतस्तु योगोऽस्ति न चैकान्तमनश्नत: ।
न चाति स्वप्नशीलस्य जाग्रतो नैव चार्जुन ॥ (६ । १६)

yuktaharaviharasya
yuktacestasya karmasu
yuktasvapnavabodhasya
yogo bhavati duhkhaha (17)

युक्ताहारविहारस्य युक्तचेष्टस्य कर्मसु ।
युक्तस्वप्नावबोधस्य योगो भवति दु:खहा ॥ (६ । १७)

'This yoga can be attained by constant concentration of mind (on supreme self), remaining in solitude and alone, self–controlled free from desires and or longing for possessions.

(The technique of mental discipline given above is on the lines of "Patanjalis yogasutra." This is called "Meditation." This practice must be constant. Self-controlled means he must not be excited, strained and anxious).

For meditation, sit in a clean place on firm seat, neither too high nor too low, covered with sacred grass, a deer skin, a cloth, one over the other. Take seat, make mind single–pointed, control thoughts and sense. Then practice yoga (Dhyan Yoga) for the purification of soul.

(Here, the word yoga denotes meditation or Dhyan Yoga.This a process of *citasuddhi* or purification of soul).

Hold the body, head and neck erect and still. Look fixedly at the tip of your nose, without looking around.

(Posture should be steady and pleasing to aid in concentration. A right posture gives serenity of body. Body must be clean and unstitched loose cotton or silk clothes be used to wear. Very light *sattvik* food be taken).

Sit serene and fearless, firm in the vow of celibacy, subdued in mind, harmonized, your mind turned to Me and intent on Me (God) alone.

(Celibacy for meditation means abstinence from sexual intercourse in thought; word and deed in all conditions, places and times. A householder who regulates sex is also called *brahmachari*. A housholder may also practice meditation. When this is done he must also observe vow to celibacy as stated above or regulated sex is allowed may be a debatable issue. The majority favours the latter view. The third meaning of *brahmacharya* is unity with *brahma* (The spreme being) through purity of thought and action. This is more relevant to contemporary world in practice. It is withdrawn from external objects of senses but concentrated on the supreme self).

The yogin of subdued mind, ever keeping himself harmonized, obtains to peace, the supreme *nirvana* which abides in Me (God).

This yoga of meditation is not meant for him who eats too much or abstains too much from eating. It is not for him, O Arjuna, who sleeps too much or keeps awake too much. For the man who is temperate in food and recreation, who is restrained in his actions, whose sleep and waking are regulated there ensures discipline (Yoga) which destroys all sorrow.

Srikṛsna has emphasized need for avoiding extremes in food, sleep and recreation. Regulated moderate living is essential for an excellent executive. This will keep him physically fit and mentally alert. Through meditation, he will be saved of stress, strain and other diseases like blood pressure, sugar and heart ailments. Excellent performance comes through pure and regulated spirit, mind, living (body) and action.

4. Qualities of a Perfect Yogi

yada viniyatam cittam
atmamy eva vatosthate
nihsprhah sarvakamebhyo
yukta ity ucyate tada (18)

यदा विनियतं चित्तमात्मन्येवावतिष्ठते ।
निःस्पृहः सर्वकामेभ्यो युक्त इत्युच्यते तदा ॥ (६ । १८)

yatha dipo nivatastho
ne ngate so pama smrta

yogino yatacittasya
yunjato yogam atmanah (19)

यथा दीपो निवातस्थो नेङ्गते सोपमा स्मृता ।
योगिनो यतचित्तस्य युञ्जतो योगमात्मनः ॥ (६ । १९)

yatro paramate cittam
niruddham yogasevaya
yatra cai va tmana tmanam
pasyann atmani tusyati (20)

यत्रोपरमते चित्तं निरुद्धं योगसेवया ।
यत्र चैवात्मानं पश्यन्नत्मनि तुष्यति ॥ (६ । २०)

sukham atyantikam yat tad
buddhigrahyam atindriyam
vetti yatra na cai va yam
sthitas calati tattvatah. (21)

सुखमात्यन्तिकं यत्तद्बुद्धिग्राह्यमतीन्द्रियम् ।
वेत्ति यत्र न चैवायं स्थितश्चलति तत्त्वतः ॥ (६ । २१)

yam labhva ca param labham
manyate na dhikam tatah
yasmin sthito na duhkhena
guruna pi vicalyate (22)

यं लब्ध्वा चापरं लाभं मन्यते नाधिकं ततः ।
यस्मिन्स्थितो न दुःखेन गुरुणापि विचाल्यते ॥ (६ । २२)

tam vidyad duhkhasamyoga–
viyogam yogasamjnitam
sa niscayena yoktavyo
yogo nirvinnacetasa (23)

तं विद्याद् दुःखसंयोगवियोगं योगसञ्ज्ञितम् ।
स निश्चयेन योक्तव्यो योगोऽनिर्विण्णचेतसा ॥ (६ । २३)

samkalpaprabhavan kamams
tyaktva sarvan asesatah

manasai ve ndriyagramam
viniyamya samantatah. (24)

सङ्कल्पप्रभवान्कामांस्त्यक्त्वा सर्वनशेषतः ।
मनसैवेन्द्रियग्रामं विनियम्य समन्ततः ॥ (६ । २४)

sanaih–sanair uparamed
buddhya dhrtigrhitaya
atmasamstham manah krtva
na kimcid api cintayet (25)

शनैः शनैरुपरमेद्बुद्ध्या धृतिगृहीतया ।
आत्मसंस्थं मनः कृत्वा न किञ्चिदपि चिन्तयेत् ॥ (६ । २५)

yato–yato niscarati
manas cancalam asthiram
tatas tato niyamyai tad
atmany eva vasam nayet. (26)

यतो यतो निश्चरति मनश्चञ्चलमस्थिरम् ।
ततस्ततो नियम्यैतदात्मन्येव वशं नयेत् ॥ (६ । २६)

prasantamanasam hy enam
yoginam sukham uttamam
upaiti santarajasam
brahmabhutam akalmasam (27)

प्रशान्तमनसं ह्येनं योगिनं सुखमुत्तमम् ।
उपैति शान्तरजसं ब्रह्मभूतमकल्मषम् ॥ (६ । २७)

yunjann evam sada tmanam
yogi vigatakalmasah
sukhena brahmasamsparsam
atyantam sukham asnute (28)

युञ्जन्नेवं सदात्मानं योगी विगतकल्मषः ।
सुखेन ब्रह्मसंस्पर्शमत्यन्तं सुखमश्नुते ॥ (६ । २८)

sarvabhutastham atmanam
sarvabhutani cha tmani

iksate yogayuktama
sarvatra samadarsanah. (29)

सर्वभूतस्थमात्मानं सर्वभूतानि चात्मनि ।
ईक्षते योगयुक्तात्मा सर्वत्र समदर्शन: ॥ (६ । २९)

yo man pasyati sarvatra
sarvam ca mayi pasyati
tasya ham na pranasyami
sa ca me na pranasyati (30)

यो मां पश्यति सर्वत्र सर्वं च मयि पश्यति ।
तस्याहं न प्रणश्यामि स च मे न प्रणश्यति ॥ (६ । ३०)

sarvabhutasthitam yo mam
bhajaty ekatvam asthitah
sarvatha vartamano pi
sa yogi mayi vartate (31)

सर्वभूतस्थितं यो मां भजत्येकत्वमास्थित: ।
सर्वथा वर्तमानोऽपि स योगी मयि वर्तते ॥ (६ । ३१)

atmaupamyena sarvatra
samam pasyati yo rjuna
sukham va yadi va duhkham
sa yogi paramo matah (32)

आत्मौपम्येन सर्वत्र समं पश्यति योऽर्जुन ।
सुखं वा यदि वा दु:खं स योगी परमो मत: ॥ (६ । ३२)

When the disciplined mind is established in the self alone, liberated from all desires then he is called harmonized (in Yoga). He is stable himself like a lamp in a windless place. His thought is at rest, restrained by the practice of concentration. He beholds the self through the self and rejoices in the self. He finds supreme delight (bliss), perceived by the intelligence and beyond the reach of the senses. This makes him firm in truth (God). He thinks there is no greater gain than this. (Self-realisation and enjoyment of eternal bliss). So, established, he is not shaken even by the heaviest sorrow. This disconnection from the union with pain is called 'yoga'. This yoga should be practised with determination, with heart free from dismay, abandoning all desires born of (selfish) will, restraining with the mind all senses on every side. Thus, yogi gradually gains tranquillity by means of reason controlled by steadiness and having fixed the mind on self. He does not think of anything (else). He restrains and brings back the wandering, wavering and unsteady mind to the control of the self alone. Supreme happiness (bliss) comes to such a yogin whose mind is peaceful, passions are at rest, stainless and who has become one with God/ Self. With harmonized (pure) self, free from sins, the yogin easily experiences the infinite bliss of contact with the eternal and sees the self-abiding in all-beings and all–beings in the self. He who sees Me (God) everywhere and sees all in Me (God), I (God) am not lost to him nor he is lost to Me (God). Howsoever he may be active, the yogin remains one with Me (God) and worships Me abiding in all–beings lives in Me.

O Arjuna! He is a perfect yogin who sees with equality everything in the image of his own self, whether in pleasure or pain. It means a yogin considers others pain as his own pain and others good as own good. He fears nothing but embraces all in equality. He is perfectly secular and completely humanist.)

5. Control of Mind is Difficult but not Impossible

arjuna vuaca
yo yam yogas tvaya proktah
samyena madhusudana
etasya ham na pasyami
cancalatvat sthitim sthiram (33)

अर्जुन उवाच
योऽयं योगस्त्वा प्रोक्तः साम्येन मधुसूदन ।
एतस्याहं न पश्चामि चञ्चलत्वात्स्थितिं स्थिराम् ॥ (६ । ३३)

cancalam hi manah krsna
pramathi balavad draham
tasya ham nigraham manye
vayor iva suduskarma (34)

चञ्चलं हि मनः कृष्ण प्रमाथि बलवदृढम् ।
तस्याहं निग्रहं मन्ये वायोरिव सुदुष्करम् ॥ (६ । ३४)

Shribhagavan uvaca
asamsayam mahabaho
mano durnigraham calam
abhyasena tu kaunteya
vairagyena ca grhyate (35)

श्रीभगवानुवाच
असंशयं महाबाहो मनो दुर्निग्रहं चलम्।
अभ्यासेन तु कौन्तेय वैराग्येण च गृह्यते ॥ (६। ३५)

asamyatatmana yogo
dusprapa iti me matih
vasyatmana tu yatata
sakyo vaptum upayatah (36)

असंयतात्मना योगो दुष्प्राप इति मे मतिः।
वश्यात्मना तु यतता शक्योऽवाप्तुमुपायतः ॥ (६। ३६)

arjuna uvaca
ayatih sraddhayo peto
yogac calitamanasah
aprapya yogasamsiddhim
kam gatim krsna gacchati (37)

अर्जुन उवाच
अयतिः श्रद्धयोपेतो योगाच्चलितमानसः।
अप्राप्य योगसंसिद्धिं कां गतिं कृष्ण गच्छति ॥ (६। ३७)

kaccin no bhayavibhrastas
chinnabhram iva nasyati
apratistho mahabaho
vimudho brahmanah pathi (38)

कच्चिन्नोभयविभ्रष्टश्छिन्नाभ्रमिव नश्यति।
अप्रतिष्ठो महाबाहो विमूढो ब्रह्मणः पथि ॥ (६। ३८)

etan me samsayam krsna
chettum arhasy asesatah
tvadanyah samsayasya sya
chetta na hy upapadyate (39)

एतन्मे सांयं कृष्णा छेत्तुमर्हस्यशेषतः।
त्वदन्यः संशयस्यास्य छेत्ता न ह्युपपद्यते ॥ (६। ३९)

shribhagavan uvaca
partha nai ve ha na mutra
vinasas tasya vidyate
na hi kalyanakrt kascid
durgatim tata gacchati (40)

श्रीभगवानुवाच
पार्थ नैवेह नामुत्र विनाशस्तस्य विद्यते ।
न हि कल्याणकृत्कश्चिद् दुर्गतिं तात गच्छति ।। (६ । ४०)

prapya punyakrtam lokan
ysitva sasvatih samah
sucinam srimatam gehe
yuogabhrasto bhijayate (41)

प्राप्य पुण्यकृतां लोकानुषित्वा शाश्वती: समा: ।
शुचीनां श्रीमतां गेहे योगभ्रष्टोऽभिजायते ।। (६ । ४१)

athava yoginam eva
kule bhavati dhimatam
etad dhi durlabhataram
loke janma yad isrsam (42)

अथवा योगिनामेव कुले भवति धीमताम् ।
एतद्धि दुर्लभतरं लोके जन्म यदीदृशम् ।। (६ । ४२)

tra tam buddhisamyogam
labhate paurvadehikam
yatate ca tato bhuyah
samsiddhau kurunandana (43)

तत्र तं बुद्धिसंयोगं लभते पौर्वदेहिकम् ।
यतते च ततो भूय:संसिध्दौ कुरुनन्दन ।। (६ । ४३)

purvabhyasena tenai va
hriyate by avaso pi sah

jijnasur api yogasya
sabdabrahma tivartate (44)

पूर्वाभ्यासेन तेनैव ह्रियते ह्यवशोऽपि सः ।
जिज्ञासुरपि योगस्य शब्दब्रह्मातिवर्तते ॥ (६ । ४४)

prayatnad yatamanas tu
yogi samsuddhakilbisah
anekajanmasamsiddhas
tato yati param gatim. (45)

प्रयत्नाद्यतमानस्तु योगी संशुद्धकिल्बिषः ।
अनेकजन्मसंसिद्धस्ततो याति परां गतिम् ॥ (६ । ४५)

Arjuna raised a very practical point for discussion. He said; "O Madhusudan (Kṛsna), you declare yoga to be evenness of mind but I find that mind is unstable on account of restlessness." Srikṛsna readily agreed with him by saying "O Arjuna! No doubt mind is difficult to control. It is restless. But, however, it can be controlled by constant practise and non–attachment. Yoga is difficult to attain by one who is not self-controlled but the self controlled can attain it by striving through proper means (which have been explained in preceding sections).

Arjuna raised another relevant query,"What happens to the soul which attempts to attain yoga position but fails. Does he not perish like a rent cloud fallen from *Maya* as well as God? O Kṛsna! Only you can completely dispel my doubt." Srikṛsna clarifies his doubt by stating, "O Partha (Arjuna)! He will never come to grief (who starts practise of Yoga). Such a fallen yogi will born again in the home of pure and prosperous persons or in the family of yogins, who are endowed with wisdom. It is difficult to get birth in such families normally. There he (fallen yogi of last birth) will regain his (mental) impressions (of the union with the Divine) which he had developed in his previous birth. With this as starting point he strives again for perfection. Yogi goes beyond vedic rule (of rituals leading to heaven.) He seeks unity with God, the supreme goal (complete emancipation for self and well–being/ harmony of the humanity)

(Thus, perfection in yoga may not be attained in one's lifetime. It may spread over next birth with better environment and good samskaras).

6. Yogi with Devotion

Having explained Buddhi Yoga and Karma Yoga, now Srikṛsna turns focus to devotion (Bhakti yoga). The combination of three yogas makes a perfect yogi or an excellent performer.

tapasvibhya dhika yogi
jnanibhyo' pi mato dhikah
karmibhyas ca dhiko yogi
tasmad yogi bhava Arjuna (46)

तपस्विभ्योऽधिको योगी ज्ञानिभ्योऽपि मतोऽधिकः ।
कर्मिभ्यश्चाधिको योगी तस्माद्योगी भवार्जुन ॥ (६ । ४६)

yoginan api sarvesani
madgatena ntaratnana
sraddhovan bhajte yo mami
sa me yuktatemo matah (47)

योगिनागपि सर्वेषां मद्‌गतेनान्तरात्मना ।
श्रद्धावान्भजते यो मां स मे युक्ततमो मतः ॥ (६ । ४७)

The yogin is greater than the ascetic (tapasvi); he is considered greater than the man of knowledge; greater than the man of rituals (vedic). Therefore, you (Arjuna) become a yogin.

And of all Yogins a devotee (Bhakta) is the best. He worships Me with full faith, with his inner self abiding in Me (God). In my opinion, he is the most attuned (to Me in Yoga). (The greatest yogin is a combination of knowledge, action and devotion. In fact, all the three elements are essentials of the excellent performance or the best productivity).

Chapter 6 entitled the yoga of meditation is over.

SUMMARY

Samyasin is one who does work without seeking fruits or selfish purpose. Renunciation is disciplined activity. The yogi performs duty with serenity. This yogic position has to be obtained by self-efforts. Man is the maker of his destiny. He has to control his lower self-desire, ego,etc., by control of his/herself. Action with uncontrolled lower self leads to stress, strain, conflicts, etc. Self-control of senses, concentration, wisdom and knowledge, equanimity makes a karma yogi– the effective excellent performer. For this, constant practise of meditation is recommended. For effective meditation and performance one must avoid extreme points in work, sleep and consumption.

A perfect yogi or an excellent executive has the following qualities which make him an excellent performer :

1. *Disciplined mind and regulated life*
2. *Free from desires*
3. *Self-controlled and harmonious*
4. *Concentration–no wavering thoughts*
5. *Self-realised– njoyer of eternal bliss*
6. *Firm in truth*
7. *Tranquillity*
8. *Stainless*
9. *Free from sins*
10. *Holistic view of self and universe–secular and humanist.*

It is difficult to control mind but it can be attained through constant practise. If one fails to realise self in one birth then his efforts will not go invain. He will get next birth with good environment and samskaras ,where he will start his journey onward from the last point for self-realization. Perfect yogi or excellent performer is made by devotion (Thus, knowledge and action must be combined with devotion).

GOD AND HIS CREATION

Contents

1. What is God ?

Sri Bhagvana uvaca
mayy asaktamanah partha
yogain yunjan massausrayah
asamsayam samagran mami
yatha jnasyasi tac chrnu. (1)

श्रीभगवानुवाच
मय्यासक्तमना: पार्थ योगं युञ्जन्मदाश्रय: ।
असंशयं समग्रं मांयथा ज्ञास्यसि तच्छृणु ॥ (७ । १)

Srikṛsna said :

"O Partha (Arjuna), how practising yoga with the mind clinging to me with me as your refuge, you shall know me fully without any doubt.

jananam tehami savijnanam
idam vaksyuany asestah
yaj jnatva ne' ha bhuyo nyaj
jnatavyam avasisyate (2)

ज्ञानं तेऽहं सविज्ञानमिदं वक्ष्याम्यशेषतः ।
यज्ज्ञात्वा नेह भूयोऽन्यज्ज्ञातव्यमवशिष्यते ॥ (७।२)

I will declare to you this full wisdom together with knowledge by knowing which there will remain nothing more to be known. (knowledge of self as God is incomplete without knowing his creations rationally. Jananam and Vijnanam both make complete knowledge.).

manusyanam sahasresu
kascid yatati siddhaye
yatatam api siddhanam
kascim man vetti tattvatah (3)

मनुष्याणां सहस्त्रेषु कश्चिद्यतति सिद्धये ।
यततामपि सिद्धानां कश्चिन्मां वेत्ति तत्त्वतः ॥ (७।३)

One amongst thousands strives for perfection and of those who do so successfully scarcely one knows Me truly.

(Most of the people do not feel the need for attaining perfection. Out of those who try very few succeed. Those who succeed, very few practice. Knowledge of God self–realisation leads to full knowledge of God when we actually live by it).

2. Two Natures of The God

bhumir apo nato vayuh
kham mano buddhir eva ca
ahamkara iti yam me
bhinna prakrtir astadha (4)

भूमिरापोऽनलो वायुःखं मनो बुद्धिरेव च ।
अहङ्कार इतीयं मे भिन्ना प्रकृतिरष्टधा ॥ (७।४)

apare yam itas tu anyam
prakrtim viddhi me param

jivabhutam mahabaho
yaye dam dharyate jagat (5)

अपरेयमितस्त्वन्यां प्रकृतिं विद्धि मे पराम् ।
जीवभूतां महाबाहो ययेदं धार्यते जगत् ॥ (७।५)

etadyonini bhutani
sarvani ty upadharaya
aham krtsnasya jagatah
prabhavah pralayas tatha (6)

एतद्योनीनि भूतानि सर्वणीत्युपधारय ।
अहं कृत्स्नस्य जगत: प्रभाव: प्रलयस्तथा ॥ (७।६)

mattah parataram na nyat
kimcid asti dhanamjaya
amyi sarvam idam protam
sutre manigana tva. (7)

मत्त: परतरं नान्यत्किञ्चिदस्ति धनञ्जय ।
मयि सर्वमिदं प्रोतं सूत्रे मणिगणा इव ॥ (७।७)

raso ham apsu kaunteya
prabha smi sasisuryayoh
pranavah sarvavedesu
sabdah khe paurusam nrsu (8)

रसोऽहमप्सु कौन्तेय प्रभास्मि शशिसूर्ययो: ।
प्रणव: सर्ववेदेषु शब्द: खे पौरुषं नृषु ॥ (७।८)

punyo gandhah prthivyam ca
tejas ca smi vibhavasau
jivanam sarvabhutesu
tapas ca smi tapasvisu. (9)

पुण्यो गन्ध: पृथिव्यां च तेजश्चास्मि विभावसौ ।
जीवनं सर्वभूतेषु तपश्चास्मि तपस्विषु ॥ (७।९)

bijam mam sarvabhutanam
viddhi partha sanatanam

buddhir buddhimatam asmi
tejas tejasvinam aham (10)

बीजं मां सर्वभूतानां विद्धि पार्थ सनातनम् ।
बुद्धिर्बुद्धिमतामस्मि तेजस्तेजस्विनामहम् ॥ (७।१०)

balam balavatam ca ham
kamaragavivarjitam
dharmaviruddho bhutesu
samo smi bharatarsabha (11)

बलं बलवतां चाहं कामरागविवर्जितम् ।
धर्माविरुद्धो भूतेषु कामोऽस्मि भरतर्षभ ॥ (७।११)

ye cai va sattvika bhava
rajasas tamasas ca ye
matta eve ti tan viddhi
na tv aham tesu te mayi (12)

ये चैव सात्त्विका भावा राजसास्तामसाश्च ये ।
मत्त एवेति तान्विद्धि न त्वहं तेषु ते मयि ॥ (७।१२)

Earth, water, fire, air, ether, mind, understanding and self–sense (ego) this is eight–fold division of My nature.

(This is one type of nature of the God which is called *shakti* or *maya,* the basis of the objective world).

This is my lower nature. Know my other and higher nature which is called soul which upholds the world, O Arjuna. All–beings have their birth in this. I am the origin as well as dissolution of this world. There is nothing higher than I(God). All that is here is strung on Me as rows of gems on a string. I am the taste in the waters, I am the light in the Moon and the Sun, I am *Om* in all the *vedas* I am the sound in ether and manhood in men. I am the pure fragrance in earth and brightness in fire. I am the life in all existences and the austerity in ascetics. Know Me, O Arjuna, to be the eternal seed of all existences, I am the intelligence of the intelligence; I am the splendour of the splendid . I am the strength of the strong, devoid of desire and passion. In beings, I am the ethical desire.

(All desires are not bad *per–se*. In fact, selfish desires are to be avoided and God's desires or divine will are to be accomplished through detached and determined action).

Whatever states of being there may be, they may be pure or harmonious (*sattvika*), passionate (*rajasik*) and slothful/dark or ignorant (*tamasik*). They are all from Me alone. I am not in them, they are in Me. (Gita propounds that nature is dependent on God. Creatures of God are dependent on Him, but He is not dependent on His creations.

3. Three modes of Nature

tribhir gunamayair bhavair
ebhih sarvam idam jagat
mohitam na bhijanati
mam ebhyah param avyayam (13)

त्रिभिर्गुणमयैर्भावैभिः सर्वमिदं जगत्।
मोहितं नाभिजानाति मामेभ्यः परमव्ययम्॥ (७। १३)

daivi hy esa gunamayi
mama maya duratyaya
mam eva ye prapadyante
mayam etam taranti te (14)

दैवी ह्येषा गुणमयी मम माया दुरत्यया।
मामेव ये प्रपद्यन्ते मायामेतां तरन्ति ते॥ (७। १४)

Deluded by these three–fold modes of nature – *sattva, rajas, tamas,* this whole world does not recognize Me (God). I am above them and imperishable.

(God has expressed regret that His own creation bound by trinity of *gunas* fail to recognise Him who is eternal, pure, enlightened, free, the self of all–beings, devoid of attributes or *gunas*, by knowing whom the seed of the evil of *samsara* (bondage of rebirth) is burnt up. We see shadows but not the light from which shadows emanate.)

This divine *maya* of Mine (God), consisting of trinity of *gunas* is hard to overcome. But those who take refuge in Me alone cross it (they become free of delusion and *agunateeta*).

4 . The Evil Doers

na mami duskrtino mudhah
prapadyante naradhamah
mayaya, pahrta jnana
asuram bhavam asritah (15)

न मां दुष्कृतिनो मूढा: प्रपद्यन्ते नराधमा: ।
माययापहृतज्ञाना आसुरं भावमाश्रिता: ॥ (७। १५)

The evil doers (sinners) are foolish, low in human scale, have minds carried away by illusion and are demonaic by nature. They do not seek refuge in Me (God).

(They can't realise God because their mind and will are insturments of passion and ego. They do not have control over senses.)

5. Different Kinds of Devotion

caturvidha bhajante mam
janah sukrtino rjuna
arto jijnasur arthathi
jnani ca bharatarsabha (16)

चतुर्विधा भजन्ते मां जना: सुकृतिनोऽर्जुन ।
आर्तो जिज्ञासुरर्थार्थी ज्ञानी च भरतर्षभ ॥ (७। १६)

tesam jnani nityayukta
ekabhaktir visisyate
priyo hi jnanino tyartham
aham sa ca mama priyah. (17)

तेषां ज्ञानी नित्ययुक्त एकभक्तिर्विशिष्यते ।
प्रियो हि ज्ञानिनोऽत्यर्थमहं स च मम प्रिय: ॥ (७। १७)

udarah sarva evai te
jnani tv atmai va me matam
asthitah sa hi yuktama
mam eva nuttamam gatim (18)

उदारा: सर्व एवैते ज्ञानी त्वात्मैव मे मतम्।
आस्थित: स हि युक्तात्मा मामेवानुत्तमां गतिम्॥ (७।१८)

bahunam janmanam ante
jnanavan mam prapadyate
vasudevah sarvam iti
sa mahatma sudurlabhah (19)

बहूनां जन्मनामन्ते ज्ञानवान्मां प्रपद्यते।
वासुदेव: सर्वमिति स महात्मा सुसुलेभ:॥ (७।१९)

There are four kinds of virtuous devotees who worship Me–the man in distress (*arta*), the seeker of knowledge (Janani), the seeker of wealth (artharthi) and the man of wisdom (*buddhiman*). Of these the wise one, who is in constant union with the Divine (God), whose devotion is single– minded, is the best. I am supremely dear to him and he is dear to Me.

(There is absence of duality in devotee of wisdom. He is the best. Other three kinds of devotees live in dual seeker and giver).

All the four kinds of devotees are noble but I hold the sage (yogin) verily Myself. Perfectly harmonized, he resorts to Me alone as the highest goal.

(Prayer is always good. First, three kinds of devotees attempt to use God as per their will, whereas the last one kind of devotee (wise) belong to God to be used as per His will. That is the ultimate state of devotion. One may pass through various stages of prayers and then reach the ultimate.)

At the end of many lives (births), the man of widsom resorts to Me knowing that Vasudeva (the Supreme) is all that is. Such a great soul is rare.

(The process of evolution in devotion is a slow and time–consuming process spread over several lives or births. It is not quick over–night activity).

6. Tolerance

kamais tais–tair hrtajnanah
prapadyante nyadevatah.
tam–tam niyamam asthaya
prakrtya niyatah svaya (20)

कामैस्तैस्तैर्हृतज्ञाना: प्रपद्यन्तेऽन्यदेवता:।
तं तं नियममास्थाय प्रकृत्या नियता: स्वया॥ (७।२०)

yo–yo yam–yam tanum bhaktah
sraddhaya rcitum icchati
tasya–tasya calam sraddham
tam eva vidadhamy aham (21)

यो यो यां यां तनुं भक्त: श्रद्धयार्चितुमिच्छति ।
तस्य तस्याचलां श्रद्धां तामेव विदधाम्यहम् ॥ (७। २१)

sa taya sraddhaya yuktas
tasya radhanam ihate
labhate ca tatah kaman
mayai va vihitan hi tan (22)

स तया श्रद्धया युक्तस्तस्याराधनमीहते ।
लभते च तत: कामान्मयैव विहितान्हि तान् ॥ (७। २२)

antavat tu phalam tesam
tad bhavaty alpamedhasam
devan devayajo yanti
madbhakta yanti mam api (23)

अन्तवत्तु फलं तेषां तद्भवत्यल्पमेधसाम् ।
देवान्देवयजो यान्ति मद्भक्ता यान्ति मामपि ॥ (७। २३)

Those whose minds are distorted by desires resort to worship other Gods (Vedic Gods like Indra, Varun, Kuber, Fire, etc.), observe various rites/ rituals, constrained by their own natures. Whatever form any devotee with faith wishes to worship, I make his faith steady. Endowed with that faith, he seeks the propitiation of such a one and from him he obtains his desires, the benefits being decreed by Me alone.

(All forms of Gods are the forms of one Supreme. Every surface derives soil from the depths and every shadow reflects the nature of the substance. All worship elevates if our reverence is serious.)

But fruits so granted are temporary. The worshippers of Gods go to the Gods but My devotee (devotee of the God or the Supreme) comes to Me. Various Gods have relevance at lower levels of evolution of devotion.

(Ultimate *bhakti* and *mukti* are granted by the devotion to the supreme God. Gita teaches tolerance of worship of various Gods. Thus, it emphasises tolerance rather than communal conflicts).

(In organisational context, it may be interpreted like formation of groups, caucuses, coteries, etc., based on selfish interest. People seek benefits through devotion to particular executives at middle and lower levels of management hierarchy. The CEO. tolerates it. Benefits are granted by executives on the basis of delegated authority by the chief. However, these benefits are temporary. The real, sustainable benefits come only when the will of the CEO. as revealed by corporate mission and objectives is carried out with full devotion. National awards like *bharat ratna, padma vibhushan,* etc., are conferred by the President only when some extra-ordinary contribution to the nation is made by an individual. It can't be got by serving executives at lower and middle level. Some temporary gains like promotion, postings, etc., may be gained through such services. Sometimes, undue personal enrichment even at the cost of organizational effectiveness may be got as a personal favour by politicking, leg pulling, serving an individual or a group for selfish purposes. But these are temporary gains and not sustainable. These lead to more organisational conflicts).

7. The Power of Ignorance

avyaktam vyaktim apannam
manyante mam abuddhayah
param bhavam ajananto
mama vyayam anuttamam (24)

अव्यक्तं व्यक्तिमापन्नं मन्यन्ते मामबुद्धयः ।
परं भावमजानन्तो ममाव्ययमनुत्तमम् ॥ (७। २४)

na ham prakasah sarvasya
yogamayasamavrtah
mudho yam na bhijanati
loko mam ajam avyayam (25)

नाहं प्रकाशः सर्वस्य योगमायासमावृतः ।
मूढोऽयं नाभिजानाति लोको मामजमव्ययम् ॥ (७। २५)

veda ham samatitani
vartamanan ca rjuna
bhavisyani ca bhutani
mam tu veda na kascana (26)

वेदाहं समतीतानि वर्तमानानि चार्जुन ।
भविष्याणि च भूतानि मां तु वेद न कश्चन ॥ (७। २६)

icchadvesasamutthena
dvandvamohena bharata
sarvabhutani sammoham
sarge yanti paramtapa (27)

इच्छाद्वेषसमुत्थेन द्वन्द्वमोहेन भारत ।
सर्वभूतानि सम्मोहं सर्गे यान्ति परन्तप ॥ (७। २७)

Men of no understanding (ignorant) think of Me, the unmanifest, as having manifestation, not knowing My higher nature, changeless and Supreme.

(Ignorant people impose several forms on God due to their own limitations. All Gods except the one unmanifest eternal, are forms imposed on Him. God is not one among many Gods. He is the one behind several everchanging forms. In management parlance, there may be several executives at middle and lower level but none is a substitude for the CEO. His authority is Supreme).

Veiled by *yogamaya* (My creative power), I am not revealed to all. This bewildered or confused world does not know Me, the unborn, the unchanging. I know the beings–past, pesent and future but no one knows Me. O Arjuna, all–beings are born to delusion overcome by dualities which arise from wish and hate.

(This is the power of ignorance which creates delusion and confusion, prevents identification of real source of authority in an organisation–the CEO.)

8. The Objective of Knowledge

yesam tv antagatam papam
jananam punyakarmanam
ie dvamdvamohanirmukta
bhajante mam drdhavratah (28)

येषां त्वन्तगतं पापं जनानां पुण्यकर्मणाम् ।
ते द्वन्द्वेमोहनिर्मुक्ता भजन्ते मां दृढव्रता: ॥ (७। २८)

jaramaranamoksaya
mam asritya yatanti ye
te brahma tad viduh krtsnam
adhyatmam karma ca khilam (29)

जरामरणमोक्षाय मामाश्रित्य यतन्ति ये ।
ते ब्रह्म तद्विदु: कृत्स्नमध्यात्मां कर्म चाखिलम् ॥ (७। २९)

sadhibhutadhidaivam mam
sadhiyajnam ca ye viduh
prayanakale pi ca mam
te vidur yuktacetasah (30)

साधिभूताधिदैवं मां साधियज्ञं च ये विदु: ।
प्रयाणकालेऽपि च मां ते विदुर्युक्तचेतस: ॥ (७। ३०)

But those men of virtuous deeds who are free from sin and delusion of dualities worship Me firm in their vows. Those who take refuge in Me and strive for deliverance from old age and death, they know the Brahman (or absolute), entire self and all about action/duty. Those who know Me as the controller of material (empirical) and the divine aspects (spirituality), and all sacrifices they with their minds harmonized have knowledge of Me even at the time of their departure (from the world).

(It is advisable that at the moment of departure or death, we should not confuse mind of a devotee by several schools of thought. He should know Him as universal and supreme, trust Him and worship Him).

Seventh Chapter entitled 'jananavijnana yoga' (the yoga of wisdom and knowledge). is over.

SUMMARY

Complete knowledge covers science of empirical and knowledge of the God (spiritual) both. Very rare people have this complete knowledge. Very few practise it. My s'akti or Maya consists of my natural creations– earth, water, fire,air, ether, mind and ego. This is my lower nature. You can see Me in all creations of nature. But I am independent of nature and its three modes. Deluded by three modes of nature, people fail to realise God. Those who seek refuge in God, can cross over trinity of gunas.

Out of various kinds of devotees wise is the best. He is free from duality. After several births of prayers, one is able to reach the ultimate in devotion.

We should be tolerant to various modes of prayers and worships. Ultimate emancipation comes through devotion to the Supreme God. All other worships bring temporary gains only.

Ignorant people impose several forms on God. Veiled by Yogmaya, the Supreme God is not revealed to all. I (God) am the controller of empirical and spiritual both. In the final moments of departure, it is useless to preach various schools of thought. Devotion to the Supreme is the only option to get emancipation.

(Realise that the CEO is the ultimate source of all authority in an organisation. Be devoted to the duty as per his will as reflected in corporate mission and object statement. This will make you an excellent performer. Don't get attracted by temporary benefits of becoming loyal to certain individuals and groups as part of organizational politics.)

THE COURSE OF COSMIC EVOLUTION

Contents

1. Basic Terminology

arjuna uvaca
kim tad brahma kim adhyatmami
kim karma purusottama
adhibhutam ca kim proktam
adhidaivam kim ucyate (1)

अर्जुन उवाच
किं तद्ब्रह्म किमध्यात्मं किं कर्म पुरुषोत्तम।
अधिभूतं च किं प्रोक्तमधिदैवं किमुच्यते॥ (८।१)

Arjuna asked meaning of basic terms:
What is *brahman* (or the absolute)?
What is self or *adhyatmam*?
What is action or Karma?
What is *adhibhutam*?
What is *adhidaivam*?

adhiyajnah kathami ko tra
dehe smin madhusudan
prayan kale ca katham
jneyo si niyatatmabhih (2)

अधियज्ञ: कथं कोऽत्र देहेऽस्मिन्मधुसूदन ।
प्रयाणकाले च कथं ज्ञेयोऽसि नियतात्मभि: ।। (८ । २)

What is *adhiyajnah*?

How are you to be known at the time of death (departure) by the self–controlled ?

Sribhagvan uvaca
aksarambrahma parmam
svabhavo' dhyatmam ucvate
bhutabhavodbhavakaro
visargah karmasamjnitrah (3)

श्रीभगवानुवाच
अक्षरं ब्रह्म परमं स्वभावोऽध्यात्ममुच्यते ।
भूतभावोद्भवकरो विसर्ग: कर्मसञ्ज्ञित: ।। (८ । ३)

adhibhutam ksaro bhava
purusas' ca' didaivatam
adjouakmp ja, eva'tra
dehe dehabhrtam vara (4)

अधिभूतं क्षरो भाव: पुरुषश्चाधिदैवतम् ।
अधियज्ञोऽहमेवात्र देहे देहभृतां वर ।। (८ । ४)

Srikṛsna defines various terms:

Brahman (or the Absolute) is indestructible, the Supreme (higher than all else).

The essential nature is called self the Brahman assumes the form of jiva. Therefore, donation, offering as mandated by scriptures is called "karma".

All perishable creations are called *adhibhuta*?

Hiranyamaya purusha in called *adhideva* (macro – God).

Vasudeva residing in all bodies (soul) is called *adhiyajna*. (micro – God).

2. THE PROCESS OF TRANSMISSION OF SOUL

antakale ca mam eva
smaran muktva kalevaram
yeh prayati sa madbhavam
yati na sty atra samsayah (5)

अन्तकाले च मामेव स्मरन्मुक्त्वा कलेवरम् ।
य: प्रयाति स मद्भावं याति नास्त्यत्र संशय: ।। (८ । ५)

Whosoever, at the time of death, gives up his body and departs, remembering Me alone, he comes to My status (of being) without any doubt.

(Mind devoted to God at the time of death/departure takes soul to the God irrespective of whether he is a good person or a sinner).

yam–yam vaapi smaranbhavam
tyajaty ante kalevaram
tam tam evai ti kaunteya
sada tadbhavabhavitah (6)

यं यं वापि स्मरन्भावं त्यजत्यन्ते कलेवरम् ।
तं तं तमेवैति कौन्तेय सदा तद्भावभावित: ।। (८ । ६)

He attains to that being of which he thinks at the time of death he thinks at the time of death of what he is being ever absorbed in the thought (during his whole life).

(The soul leaves body and goes to that being of which he thinks at the time of death. This does not happen casually. Normally it depends on our persistent efforts to think throughout our life. Thus, what we think we live. What we live we think at the time of death. What we live and what we think we become after death. Our past thoughts determine our present birth and our present thoughts will determine the next birth. We can determine our future if we wish.)

(Cases of Ajamil, and Pingla Prostitute, elephant getting emancipation even by last moment utterances of the name of God are exceptions and not the general rule. God is merciful to even sinners. But constant practise of remembering God in our life as a matter of habit is recommended for those who need emancipation.

tasmat sarvesu kalesu
mam anusmara yadhya ca

mayy arpitamanobuddhir
mam evai 'sasy as amsayah' (7)

तस्मात्सर्वेषु कालेषु मामनुस्मर युध्य च ।
मय्यर्पितमनोबुद्धिर्मामेवैष्यस्यसंशयम् ॥ (८ । ७)

Therefore, you remember Me all times while fighting (doing your duty). When your mind and understanding are set on Me you will come to Me alone undoubtedly.

(Here a mantra of practical successful life is given by the Lord. You do your normal duties and constantly remember God. This will ensure that after death you merge into Him (God) without any doubt. Thus, renunciation of duty is not advised. Duty and devotion both must go simultaneously. You need not run away to forest to meet God. If this advice is followed in practise, country can convert millions of physically fit sadhu–sanyasis into productive manpower and increase national income and per capita income to a large extent. Worker, *sanyasin* and devotee are not exclusive but can coexist . Do your normal duty with devotion and renunciation of selfish motives, ego,etc. This will ensure excellent performance).

abhyasayogayuktena
chetasa na nyagamina
paramam purusam divyam
yaati partha nucintayan (8)

अभ्यासयोगयुक्तेन चेतसा नान्यगामिना ।
परमं पुरुषं दिव्यं याति पार्थानुचिन्तयन् ॥ (८ । ८)

kavim puranamanusasitaram
mianor aniyamsam anusmared yah
sarvasya dhataram acintyarupam
madityavarnam tamasah parastat (9)

कविं पुराणमनुशासितार मणोरणीयांसमनुस्मरेद्यः ।
सर्वस्य धातारमचिन्त्यरूप मादित्यवर्णं तमसः परस्तात् ॥ (८ । ९)

prayanakate manasa calena
bhaktya yukto yogabalena cai va
bhruvor madhye pranam avesya samyak
sa tam param purusam upaiti divyam (10)

प्रयाणकाले मनसाचलेन
भक्त्या युक्तो योगबलेन चैव।
भ्रुवोर्मध्ये प्राणमावेश्य सम्यक् –
स तं परं पुरुषमुपैति दिव्यम् ॥ (८।१०)

yad akṣaram vedavido vadanti
visanti yad yatayo vitaragah
yad icchanto brahmacaryam caranti
tat te padam samgrahena pravakṣye (11)

यदक्षरं वेदविदो वदन्ति
विशन्ति यद्यतयो वीतरागा:।
यदिच्छन्तो ब्रह्मचर्यं चरन्ति
तत्ते पदं सङ्ग्रहेण प्रवक्ष्ये ॥ (८।११)

sarvadvarani samyamya
mano hrdi nirudhya ca
murdhny adhaya tmanah pranam
asthito yogadhiranam. (12)

सर्वद्वाराणि संयम्य मनो हृदि निरुध्य च।
मूर्ध्न्याधायात्मन: प्राणमास्थितो योगधारणाम् ॥ (८।१२)

aum ity ekakṣaram brahma
vyaharan mam anusmaran
yah prayati tyajan deham
saa yaati paramam gatim (13)

ओमित्येकाक्षरं ब्रह्म व्याहरन्मामनुस्मरन्।
य: प्रयाति त्यजन्देहं स याति परमां गतिम् ॥ (८।१३)

ananyacetah satatam
yo mam smarati nityasah
tasya ham sulabhah partha
nityayukṭasya yoginah (14)

अनन्यचेता: सततं यो मां स्मरति नित्यश:।
तस्याहं सुलभ: पार्थ नित्ययूक्तस्य योगिन: ॥ (८।१४)

mam upetya punarjanma
duhkhalayam asasvatam
na pnuvanti maharmanah
samsiddhim paramam gatah (15)

मामुपेत्य पुनर्जन्म दु:खालयमशाश्वतम् ।
नाप्नुवन्ति महात्मान: संसिद्धिं परमां गता: ॥ (८ । १५)

a brahmabhuvanallokah
punaravartino rjuna
mam upetya tu kaunteya
punarjanma na vidyate (16)

आब्रह्मभुवनाल्लोका: पुनरावर्तिनोऽर्जुन ।
मामुपेत्य तु कौन्तेय पुनर्जन्म न विद्यते ॥ (८ । १६)

sahasrayugaparyantam
ahar yad brahmano viduh
rartim yugasahasrantam
te haratravido janah. (17)

सहस्त्रयुगपर्यन्तमहर्यद्ब्रह्मणो विदु: ।
रात्रिं युगसहस्त्रान्तां तेऽहोरात्रविदो जना: ॥ (८ । १७)

avyaktad vyaktayah sarvah
prabhavanty aharagame
ratryagame praliyante
tatrai va vyaktasamjnake (18)

अव्यक्ताद्व्यक्तय: सर्वा: प्रभवन्त्यहरागमे ।
रात्र्यागमे प्रलीयन्ते तत्रैवाव्यक्तसञ्ज्ञके ॥ (८ । १८)

bhutagramah sa eva yam
bhutva bhutva praliyate
ratryagame vasah partha
prabhavaty aharagame (19)

भूतग्रामः स एवायं भूत्वा भूत्वा प्रलीयते ।
रात्र्यागमेऽवशः पार्थ प्रभवत्यहरागमे ॥ (८ । १९)

paras tasmat tu bhavo nyo
vyakto vyaktat sanatanah
yah sa sarvesu bhutesu
nasyatsu na vinasyati (20)

परस्तस्मात्तु भावोऽन्योऽव्यक्तोऽव्यक्तात्सनातनः ।
यः स सर्वेषु भूतेषु नश्यत्सु न विनश्यति ॥ (८ । २०)

avyakto ksara ity uktas
tam ahuh paramam gatim
yam prapya na nivartante
tad dhama paramam mama (21)

अव्यक्तोऽक्षर इत्युक्तस्तमाहुः परमां गतिम् ।
यं प्राप्य न निवर्तन्ते तद्धाम परमं मम ॥ (८ । २१)

purusah sa parah partha
bhaktya labhyas tv ananyaya
yasya ntahsthani bhutani
yena sarvam idam tatam (22)

पुरुषः स परः पार्थ भक्त्या लभ्यस्त्वनन्यया ।
यस्यान्तःस्थानि भूतानि येन सर्वमिदं ततम् ॥ (८ । २२)

He who meditates on the Supreme (God) with his thought attuned by constant practice and not wandering after anything else, he, O, Arjuna reaches the Person, Supreme and divine.

(Constant and unwavering devotion and concentration on the God is recommended rather than death–bed repentence).

He who meditates on seer (omniscient God) the ancient, the ruler, the most subtle, the supporter of all whose form is beyond conception, who is full of light (he is personal God or Isvara) at the time of his departure (death) should be done with a steady mind, devotion and strength of yoga and setting his *prana* (life force) in the centre of eyebrows.

(This type of death is possible for yogin who has power to choose moment of death or who gets advance indication of moment of death).

The imperishable state (mukti, moksha, freedom from rebirth) is described now by Srikṛsna. This state is accessible only to those who lead a life of self-control and detachment for attaining it. All the nine gates of body are kept restrained, the mind is confined within the heart, *prana* fixed in the head, established in concentration by yoga. While giving up body he utters *aum*. He goes to the highest goal – moksa, mukti or paramdham, freedom from rebirth. I am easily reached by self-disciplined yogins (united with the supreme) who constantly meditate on Me thinking of none else. Having come to Me these great souls do not go to rebirth, the place of sorrow, impermanent, for they have reached the highest perfection/the ultimate destination or goal.

The imperishable state (freedom from rebirth) is granted only to the devotees of Kṛsna/Visnu because all worlds up to the realm of Brahma are subject to rebirth. Those who know that the day of Brahma is of the fixed duration and that night of Brahma is also of equal duration. At the beginning of day of Brahma the universe is manifested or created (born) and at the end of it or at the start of night of Brahma the whole universe merges in the unmanifest. This cycle gets repeated during days and nights of Brahma (The periodic emergence and dissolution of all existences does not affect the Supreme God who has created Brahma). Beyond this unmanifested, there is yet another unmanifested eternal Supreme being (Parabrahman or Narayana) who does not perish when all existences perish. Redeemed great souls merge into Him.That is my Supreme abode (Vaikuntha or Goloka), unmanifested, imperishable, Supreme status where these great souls reach. They do not return from there.

The Supreme Person (God or Parabrahman Narayana) is the person in whom all existences abide and by whom all this is pervaded. He can be gained by unswerving devotion.

(In management parlance, it can be interpreted as the way to reach the top status. Those who give excellent performance through detached involvement reach the highest status in the corporate hierarchy. Once they reach there, they will never return to middle and lower level positions. A happy blending of knowledge yoga, action yoga and devotion yoga makes one fit for attaining the top status).

3. The two ways – Emancipation and Rebirth

yatra kale tv anavrttim
avrttim cai va yoginah
prayata yanti tam kalam
vaksyami bharatarsabha (23)

यत्र काले त्वनावृत्तिमावृत्तिं चैव योगिनः ।
प्रयाता यान्ति तं कालं वक्ष्यामि भरतर्षभ ॥ (८।२३)

agnir jyotir ahah suklah
shanmasa uttarayanam
tatra prayata gacchanti
brahma brahmavido janah (24)

अग्निर्ज्योतिरहः शुक्लः षण्मासा उत्तरायणम् ।
तत्र प्रयाता गच्छन्ति ब्रह्म ब्रह्मविदो जनाः ॥ (८।२४)

dhumo ratris tatha krsnah
shanmasa daksinayanam
tatra chandramasam jyotir
yogi prapya nivartate (25)

धूमो रात्रिन्तथा कृष्णः षण्मासा दक्षिणायनम् ।
तत्र चान्द्रमसं ज्योतिर्योगी प्राप्य निवर्तते ॥ (८।२५)

suklakrsne gati hy ete
jagatah sasvate mate
ekaya yaty anavrttim
anyaya vartate punah (26)

शुक्लकृष्णे गती ह्योते जगतः शाश्वते मते ।
एकया यात्यनावृत्तिमन्ययावर्तते पुनः ॥ (८।२६)

nai te smrti partha janan
yogi muhyati kaschana

tasmat sarvesu kalesu
yogayukto bhava rjuna (27)

नैते स्मृती पार्थ जानन्योगी मुह्यति कश्चन।
तस्मात्सर्वेषु कालेषु योगयुक्तो भवार्जुन॥ (८।२७)

vedesu yajnesu tapahsu cai va
danesu yat punyaphalam pradistam
atyeti tat sarvam idam viditva
yogi param sthanam upaiti ca dyam (28)

वेदेषु यज्ञेषु तपःसु चैव
दानेषु यत्पुण्यफलं प्रदिष्टम्।
अत्येति तत्सर्वमिदं विदित्वा
योगी परं स्थानमुपैति चाद्यम्॥ (८।२८)

O Arjuna, now I tell you the time in which yogins departing never return and also in which departing they return.

Fire, light, day, the shukla paksha (bright half part of the month ending on full moon day), uttarayana (six months from makarasamkranti or Jan. 14) then leaving this body and going forth the men who know the Supreme (absolute) go to Him.

Smoke, night krsnapaksa (dark half part of month ending on amavasya) the six months of Daks'inayanan (begining from July 14) then going forth, the yogin obtains the lunar light and takes rebirth on earth.

These two paths–one of light and another of darkness, are thought to be the world's everlasting paths. By the former one goes not to return, by the latter one goes to return.

(Those who lead a life of knowledge (light) they get emancipation but those who lead a life of ignorance they are reborn).

The Yogin who knows these paths will never be deluded. O Arjuna, therefore, you be firm in yoga. (Do your duty in union of the Supreme)

The yogin who knows all this goes beyond the fruits of good deeds as given in vedas and attains to the Supreme status.

(Sacrifices, austerities and gifts–incentives and motivation are the tools and techniques for ordinary performers. Excellent performance comes from those who are firm in three yogas – buddhi, devotion, and action, and accept duty as will of the God or His work. They will reach the supreme status).

The chapter 8 entitled "aksarabrahmayoga" (The yoga of the imperishable Absoulute) is over.

SUMMARY

Arjuna wanted to know the meanings of basic terms. Lord Srikṛsna defined these terms clearly. Conceptual clarity is essential for effective communication. Brahma is Supreme and indestructible. Essential nature is called 'self'. The Brahma assumes the form of 'jeev' or 'atman'. Therefore, it is called 'adhyatma' . Karma is the creative force. It is also the expenditure on sacrifice, donation, offering as mandated by scriptures. All perishable creations are called adhibhuta. Macro – God is 'adhideva' and micro – God vasudeva who resides in all bodies is called'adhiyajna.

Mind devoted to God at the time of death grants freedom from rebirth. It generally comes through constant practise of meditation. What we did and thought determined our present birth; what we do now and think will determine our next birth/emancipation. Thus, we are the master of our own destiny. Therefore, action with devotion is recommended. Firm devotion and meditation (concentration) lead to excellence of performance. This is the way to attain the supreme status. No return to middle level and lower level of hierarchy will be there after attaining the top position. Parabrahma Narayana is the Supreme, Imperishable/ unmanifest. He can be gained by firm devotion.

Man has two options–(1) Lead life through dark way (ignorance) and continue the cycle of rebirth, (2) Lead life through light way (knowledge, devotion, etc), and attain the Supreme status of no rebirth.

Motivation and incentives are the tools of performance for ordinary souls. Self-realised and self-controlled souls accept duty as Dharma and do it excellently with knowledge, devotion and action (buddhi, bhakti and karma yogas). They will attain the Supreme status. They are fit for top positions in an organisations.

SUPREMACY OF THE LORD

Contents

1. The Sovereign Mystery/Secret

Sribhagavan uvaca
idami tute guhyatamani
pravaksya my anasuyave
jnanam vijnasahitami
yaj jnatva moksyase'subhat (1)

श्रीभगवानुवाच
इदं तु ते गुह्यतमं प्रवक्ष्याम्यनसूयवे।
ज्ञानं विज्ञानसहितं यज्ज्ञात्वा मोक्ष्यसेऽशुभात्॥ (९।१)

rajvidya raja guhyam
pavitram idam uttaman
bratyaska vagamani dharmyam
susukham kartum avyayam (2)

राजविद्या राजगृह्यं पवित्रतिदमुत्तमम्।
प्रत्यक्षावगमं धर्म्यं सुसुखं कर्तुमव्ययम्॥ (९।२)

as' raddadhanah purusha
dharmashy 'sya paramitapa
aprapya mam nivartante
mrtyusamisara–vartmani (3)

अश्रद्दधानाः पुरुषा धर्मस्यास्य परन्तप ।
अप्राप्य मां निवर्तन्ते मृत्युसंसारवर्त्मनि ॥ (९ । ३)

Srikṛsna said:

"O Arjuna, I shall now reveal the profound secret of wisdom combined with scientific knowledge, by knowing which you will be released from evil (depression and inaction). This is sovereign knowledge, sovereign mystery or secret, supreme sanctity, known by direct experience, in accord with the Dharma (duty), very easy to practise and is imperishable. Those who have no faith, will not attain Me and take rebirth in this world (samsara).

2. The Supreme Reality

maya tatam idam sarvam
jagad avyaktamurtina
matsthani sarvabhutani
na cha ham tesu avasthitah (4)

मया ततमिदं सर्वं जगदव्यक्तमूर्तिना ।
मत्स्थानि सर्वभूतानि न चाहं तेष्ववस्थितः ॥ (९ । ४)

na ca matsthani bhutani
pasya me yogam aisvaram
bhutabhrn na ca bhutastho
mama tma bhutabhavanah (5)

न च मत्स्थानि भूतानि पश्य मे योगमैश्वरम् ।
भूतभृन्न च भूतस्थो ममात्मा भूतभावनः ॥ (९ । ५)

ya ha kasasthito ni yam
vayuh sarvatrago mahan
atha sarvani bhutani
matsthani ty upadharaya (6)

यथाकाशस्थितो नित्यं वायु: सर्वत्रगो महान् ।
तथा सर्वाणि भूतानि मत्स्थानीत्युपधारय ॥ (९।६)

sarvabhu ani kaun ya
prakrtim yani mamikam
kalpaksaye punas tam
kalpadau visrjamy aham (7)

सर्वभूतानि कौन्तेय प्रकृतिं यान्ति मामिकाम् ।
कल्पक्षये पुनस्तानि कल्पादौ विसृजाम्यहम् ॥ (९।७)

prakrtim svam avastabhya
visrjami punah
bhutagramam imam krtsnam
avasam prakrter vasat (8)

प्रकृतिं स्वामवष्टभ्य विसृजामि पुन: पुन: ।
भूतग्राममिमं कृत्स्नमवशं प्रकृतेर्वशात् ॥ (९।८)

na ca mam tam karmani
nibadhnanti dhanamjaya
udasinavad asinam
asaktam tesu karmasu (9)

न च मां तानि कर्माणि निबध्नन्ति धनञ्जय ।
उदासीनवदासीनमसक्तं तेषु कर्मसु ॥ (९।९)

maya dhyaksena prakrtih
suyate sacaracaram
hetuna nena kaunteya
jagad viparivartate (10)

मयाध्यक्षेण प्रकृति: सूयते सचाराचरम् ।
हेतुनानेन कौन्तेय जगद्विपरिवर्तते ॥ (९।१०)

avajananti mam mudha
manusim tanum asritam
param bhavam ajananto
mama bhutamahesvaram (11)

अवजानन्ति मां मूढा मानुषीं तनुमाश्रितम् ।
परं भावमजानन्तो मम भूतमहेश्वरम् ॥ (९ । ११)

moghasa moghakarmano
moghajnana vicetasah
Raksasim asurim cai va
prakrtim mohinim srtitah (12)

मोघाशा मोघकर्माणो मोघज्ञाना विचेतसः ।
राक्षसीमासुरीं चैव प्रकृतिं मोहिनीं श्रिताः ॥ (९ । १२)

mahatmanas tu mam partha
daivim prakrtim asritah
bhajanty ananyamanaso
jnatva bhutadim avyayam (13)

महात्मानस्तु मां पार्थ दैवीं प्रकृतिमाश्रिताः ।
भजन्त्यनन्यमनसो ज्ञात्वा भूतादिमव्ययम् ॥ (९ । १३)

satatam kirtayanto mam
yatantas ca drdhavratah
namasyantas ca mam bhaktya
nityayukta upasate (14)

सततं कीर्तयन्तो मां यतन्तश्च दृढव्रताः ।
नमस्यन्तश्च मां भक्त्या नित्ययुक्ता उपासते ॥ (९ । १४)

jnanayajnena ca py anye
yajanto mam upasate
ekatvena prthaktvena
bahudha visvatomukham (15)

ज्ञानयज्ञेन चाप्यन्ये यजन्तो मामुपासते ।
एकात्वेन पृथक्त्वेन बहुधा विश्वतोमुखम् ॥ (९ । १५)

aham kratur aham yajnah
svadha ham aham ausadham
mantro ham aham eva jyam
aham agnir aham hutam. (16)

अहं क्रतुरहं यज्ञ: स्वधाहमहमौषधम् ।
मन्त्रोऽहमहमेवाज्यमहमग्निरहं हुतम् ॥ (९। १६)

pita ham asya jagato
mata dhata pitamahah
vedyam pavirtam aumkara
rk sama yajur eva ca (17)

पिताहमस्य जगतो माता धाता पितामह: ।
वेद्यं पवित्रमोङ्कार ऋक्साम यजुरेव च ॥ (९। १७)

gatir bharta prabhuh saksi
nivasah saranam suhrt
prabhavah pralayah sthanam
nidhanam bijam avyayam (18)

गतिर्भर्ता प्रभु: साक्षी निवास: शरणं सुहृत् ।
प्रभव: प्रलय: स्थानं निधानं बीजमव्ययम् ॥ (९। १८)

tapamy aham aham varsam
nigrhnamy utsrjami ca
amrtam cai va mrtyus ca
sadasacca ham arjuna (19)

तपाम्यहमहं वर्षं निगृह्णाम्युत्सृजामि च ।
अमृतं चैव मृत्युश्च सदासच्चाहमर्जुन ॥ (९। १९)

traividya mam somapah putapapa
yajnair istva svargatim prarthayante
te punyam asadya surendralokam
asnanti divyan divi devabhogan (20)

त्रैविद्या मां सोमपा: पूतपापा–
यज्ञैरिष्ट्वा स्वर्गतिं प्रार्थयन्ते ।
ते पुण्यमासाद्य सुरेन्द्रलोक–
मश्नन्ति दिव्यान्दिवि देवभोगान् ॥ (९। २०)

te tam bhuktva svaralokam visalam
kstne punye martyalokam visanti

evam trayidharmam anuprapanna
gatagat imkamaama labhat'e (21)

ते तं भुक्त्वा स्वर्गलोकं विशालं-
क्षीणे पुण्ये मर्त्यलोकं विशन्ति ।
एवं त्रयीधर्ममनुप्रपन्ना-
गतागतं कामकामा लभन्ते ॥ (९ । २१)

anayas cintayanto mam
ye janah paryupasate
lesam nityabhiyuktanam
yogaksemam vahamy aham (22)

अनन्याश्चिन्तयन्तो मां ये जना: पर्युपासते ।
तेषां नित्याभियुक्तानां योगक्षेमं वहाम्यहम् ॥ (९ । २२)

ye py anyadevatabhakta
yajante sraddhaya nvitah
te pi mam eva kaunteya
yajanty avidhipurvakam (23)

येऽप्यन्यदेवता भक्ता यजन्ते श्रद्धयान्विता: ।
तेऽपि मामेव कौन्तेय तत्कुरुखा मदर्पणम् ॥ (९ । २३)

aham hi sarvayajnanam
bhokta ca prabhur eva ca
na tu mam abhijananti
tattvena tas cyavanti te (24)

अहं हि सर्वयज्ञानां भोक्ता च प्रभुरेव च ।
न तु मामभिजानन्ति तत्त्वेनातश्च्यवन्ति ते ॥ (९ । २४)

yanti devavrata devan
pitrn yanti pitrvratah
bhutani yanti bhutejya
yanti madyajino pi mam (25)

यान्ति देवव्रता देवान्पितॄन्यान्ति पितृव्रता: ।
भूतानि यान्ति भूतेज्या यान्ति मद्याजिनोऽपि माम् ॥ (९ । २५)

This whole universe is pervaded by my unmanifested form. All being abide in Me but I do not abide in them. The beings do not dwell in Me. My spirit which is the source of all–beings sustains them but does not abide in them. (The writ of top management/Leader runs throughout the organisation. All other executives and functionaries derive existence/ authority from the leader or chief but he has his independent status. He is not revealed in all these positions dependent on him. Leader or chief is not expected to obey the desires of his subordinates.)

(Though the mortal world is a loving manifestation of God, it does not fully and finally express Him).

As the mighty air, moving everywhere, ever abides in sky (etheric space), in the same way all existences abide in Me. All–beings pass into nature, which is My own, at the end of the cycle; and at the beginning of the (next) cycle, I send them forth (into existence). All–beings are under the control of nature (prakarati or attitude) and, therefore, I go on repeating this process of birth and death. These actions do not bind Me because I am unattached to these actions. The nature gives birth to all things–moving and unmoving, under my guidance. Thus, the world revolves. The deluded do not know (this secret) that I am the Lord of all existences. Rakasi (fendish) and *asurim* (demonaic) nature people have aspiration, actions and knowledge of no avail (invain). They are devoid of judgement. They are victims of deceitful nature (*mohini prakarati*). As against this, great souls, who abide in divine nature (*daivi prakrati*) know Me as Imperishable source of all–beings, worship Me with a devoted mind. They always glorify Me, they are firm in their vows, they bow down to Me with devotion, they worship Me, ever disciplined.

(Highest perfection is a combination of buddhi yoga, bhakti yoga and action yoga. Divine people respect the leader, whereas fendish and demonic people fail to respect the authority of the Leader and continue to suffer on that account).

Different people (*Dvaita, advaita, visistadvaita*) worship Me in different ways. I am the ritual action, I am the herb, I am the (sacred) hyms, I am the offering, (everything merges in him). I am the father of this world, the mother, the supporter, the grandsire. I am the object of knowledge, the purifier, the AUM, the sama and the yajus as well (rigved, samveda and yajurveda also). I am the goal, the upholder, the Lord, the witness, the abode, the refuge and the friend. I am the origin and the dissolution, the ground, the resting place and the imperishable seed (of the universe).

(As sun), I give heat; I withhold and send forth the rain, I am immortality and also death, I am being as well as non–being (The Supreme Lord is top leader. He is all powerful. He grants our prayer in whatever form we worship Him).

Vedic rituals (yagna, etc), take one to Indraloka (heaven). He will enjoy pleasures of the Gods there, Having enjoyed these pleasures, he takes rebirth in this mortal world, as soon as punyas (merits) are exhausted. Thus, vedas do not make one free from rebirth because rituals are performed with attachment to desires. But those who worship Me, meditating on Me alone, I undertake responsibility of providing what they do not have and security of what they have. (Yogakshema of devotees is guaranteed by the Supreme God).

(Those who are ardent devotees of the Chief/Leader in any organisation, their well-being becomes the responsibility of the Leader).

Even those who are devotees of other Gods, (or worship them with faith,) they also sacrifice to Me alone, though not according to the true law. I am the enjoyer of all sacrifices but these men do not know Me in my true nature and, that is why. they fall (to rebirth). Worshippers of Gods go to the Gods, worshippers of men go to men, sacrificers to the spirits go to the spirits and those who sacrifice to Me come to Me.

(In management parlance, those who obey the orders of middle–level manager/lower–level manager under whom they are formally placed and work for the attainments of corporate goals/ mission, their sacrifice also reaches to the chief of the organisation. But if they develop personal loyalties to individuals, then their sacrifice does not reach the chief. Such devotion at lower level will bring lower temporary rewards. The devotion to the chief will bring rich sustainable rewards).

3. Devotion and its Effects

pattram puspam phalam toyam
yo me bhaktya prayacchati
tad aham bhaktyupahrtam
asnami prayatatmanah (26)

पत्रं पुष्पं फलं तोयं यो मे भक्त्या प्रयच्छति ।
तदहं भक्त्युपहृतमश्नामि प्रयतात्मनः ॥ (९ । २६)

yat karosi yad asnasi
yaj juhosi dadasi yat
yat tapasyasi kaunteya
tat kurusva madarpanam (27)

यत्करोषि यदश्नासि यज्जुहोषि ददासि यत् ।
यत्तपस्यसि कौन्तेय तत्कुरुष्व मदर्पणम् ॥ (९ । २७)

subhasubhaphalair evam
moksyase karmabandhanaih
samnyasayogayuktatma
vimukto mam upaisyasi. (28)

शुभाशुभफलैरेवं मोक्ष्यसे कर्मबन्धनैः ।
सन्न्यसयोगयुक्तात्मा विमुक्तो मामुपैष्यसि ॥ (९। २८)

samo ham sarvabhutesu
na me dvesy sti na priyah
ye bhajanti tu mam bhaktya
mayi te tesu ca py aham (29)

समोऽहं सर्वभूतेषु न मे द्वेष्योऽस्ति न प्रियः ।
ये भजन्ति तु मां भक्त्या मयि ते तेषु चाप्यहम् ॥ (९। २९)

api cet suduracaro
bhajate mam ananyabhak
sadhur eva sa mantavyah
samyag vyavasito hi sah. (30)

अपि चेत्सुदुराचारो भजते मामनन्यभाक् ।
साधुरेव स मन्तव्यः सम्यग्व्यवसितो हि सः ॥ (९। ३०)

ksipram bhavati dharmatma
sasvacchantim nigacchati
kaunteya pratijanihi
na me bhaktah pranasyati (31)

क्षिप्रं भवति धर्मात्मा शश्वच्छान्तिं निगच्छति ।
कौन्तेय प्रतिजानीहि न मे भक्तः प्रणश्यति ॥ (९। ३१)

mam hi partha vyapasritya
ye pi syuh papayonayah
striyo vaisyas tatha sudras
te pi yanti param gatim (32)

मां हि पार्थ व्यपाश्रित्य येऽपि स्युः पापयोनयः ।
स्त्रियो वैश्यास्तथा शूद्रास्तेऽपि यान्ति परां गतिम् ॥ (९। ३२)

kim punar brahmanah punya
bhakta rajarsayas tatha
anityam asukham lokam
imam prapya bhajasva mam. (33)

किं पुनर्ब्राह्मणा: पुण्या भक्ता राजर्षयस्तथा ।
अनित्यमसुखं लोकमिमं प्राप्य भजस्व माम् ॥ (९ । ३३)

manmana bhava madbhakto
madyaji mam namaskuru
mam evai syasi yuktvai vam
atmanam matparayanah (34)

मन्माना भव मद्भक्तो मद्याजी मां नमस्कुरु ।
मामेवैष्यसि युक्त्वैवमात्मानं मत्परायण: ॥ (९ । ३४)

Whosoever offers Me with devotion a leaf, a flower, a fruit, or water, I accept that offering of love, of the pure heart I accept.

(Love and purity of heart pleases the God most. Whatever, you do, you eat, you offer, you give away, you practice, O Arjuna, make it all as an offering to Me.)

(All tasks/actions are sanctified when done with devotion and detachment–as an offering to the God. Then work becomes a worship to the God and workplace becomes a temple. No separate rituals need be performed to please the God).

This type of devotion and detachment will make you free from good and evil results or bonds of your action. With your mind firmly set on renunciation (of selfish objectives), you will become free and attain to Me.

I am the same in all–beings. None is hateful nor dear to Me. But those who worship Me with devotion they are in Me and I am also in them. (Devotion merges separate identities into one or *advaita* is attained by devotion). Everyone is free to elect his way to Him.

Even if a man of the most sinful conduct worships Me with firm devotion, he must be counted as righteous, for he has rightly resolved.

(This is not an easy escape from penalty for sins.This is a reformist way. If a sinner sincerely repents for his past sins and firmly resolves not to repeat these sins in future, he is acceped as 'purified or reformed.' It is very difficult proposition in practice. There is no unforgivable sin for the God).

Such a reformed person will obtain lasting peace. O Arjuna, know it for certain that my devotee will never perish.

(When we are sincerely devoted to God, He protects us. It is his Sovereign Guarantee to his devotees).

Those who take refuge in Me, O Arjuna, they attain the hightest goal (emancipation) irrespective of their caste, race, sex, vocation, etc.

(Thus, Srikṛsna, the teacher of Gita does not approve of social discrimination. He is accessible to all devotees).

My path becomes easier for those Brahmins and royal sages who are self–realised.

(Everyone is welcome to be a devotee of the Supreme God).

Fix your mind on Me; be devoted to Me; worship Me; revere Me; have unification with Me as thy goal, you will come to Me.

(The result of fusion of knowledge, devotion and action is unification with the Supreme God. Joy, peace and excellence will follow).

The ninth chapter entitled,"raja vidya rajguha yoga' (The yoga of sovereign knowledge and sovereign mystery) is over.

Summary

The sovereign knowledge is knowledge and science both. It is imperishable. Only devotees are entitled to it. All–beings abide in God but God does not abide in beings. The mortal world is a living manifestation of God but it is not his full expression. People of devlish/ demonic nature repeatedly suffer the agony of birth, death, rebirth. People of divine nature become devotees of the God. Those who worship Gods, pitras, bhutas, they go to them, whereas those who are devotees of the supreme God go to Him. They are emancipated. Vedic ritual people who perform it with an object will go to heaven. But after enjoyment of heaven, they also come back to this mortal world. My devotees, who meditate on Me alone, get emancipated. Devotion may be in the form of offerings to Me with pure heart and love or it may be in the form of offering of all actions. This will also entitle you to protection by the God. God will accept a reformed sinner also. His devotee will never perish. It is his sovereign guarantee. Those who take refuge in him, they are emancipated. No social discrimination is allowed by God. He is accessible to all devotees. All are welcome to be his devotees.

From management viewpoint, The top leader must be impartial, independent, kind and merciful. He should adopt a reformist approach and be equally accessible to low and high people. Combination of devotion with knowledge and action brings out excellent performance. The leader must be protector of his devotees/good performers without selfish motives and ego. Employee should also comply with policy decision of top manangement instead of seeking short-term gains through loyalty to middle-level or lower-level executive or by forming cliques and coteries. Devotion to top management policy will bring about enduring gains and job security, promotion, rewards, etc.

EXCELLENCE IS REFLECTION OF GOD

Contents

1. Nature of God

Shribhagavan uvaca
bhuya eva mahabaho
srnu me paramaim vacah
yat te'ham priyamanaya
vaksyami hitkamyaya (1)

श्रीभगवानुउवाच
भूय एव महाबाहो शृणु मे परमं वच: ।
यत्तेऽहं प्रीयमाणाय वक्ष्यामि हितकाम्यया ॥ (१०।१)

na me viduh suraganah
prabhavam na maharsayah
aham adir hi devanam
maharsinam ca saruasah (2)

न मे विदुः सुरगणाः प्रभवं न महर्षयः ।
अहमादिर्हि देवानां महार्षीणां च सर्वशः ॥ (१० । २)

yo mam ajam anadim ca
vetti lokamahesvaram
asammudhah sa martyesu
sarvapapaih pramucyate (3)

यो मामजमनादिं च वेत्ति लोकमहेश्वरम् ।
असम्मूढः स मर्त्येषु सर्वपापैः प्रमुच्यते ॥ (१० । ३)

buddhir jnanam asammohah
ksama satyam damah samah
sukham duhkham bhavo bhavo
bhayam ca bhayam eva ca (4)

बुद्धिर्ज्ञानमसम्मोहः क्षमा सत्यं दमः शमः ।
सुखं दुःखं भवोऽभावो भयं चाभयमेव च ॥ (१० । ४)

ahimsa samata tustis
tapo danam yaso yasah
bhavanti bhava bhutanam
matta eva prthagvidhah (5)

अहिंसा समता तुष्टिस्तपो दानं यशोऽयशः ।
भवन्ति भावा भूतानां मत्त एव पृथग्विधाः ॥ (१० । ५)

maharsayah sapta purve
catvaro manavas tatha
madbhava manasa jata
yesam loka imah prajah (6)

महर्षयः सप्त पूर्वे चत्वारो मनवस्तथा ।
मद्भावा मानसा जाता येषां लोक इमाः प्रजाः ॥ (१० । ६)

etam vibhutim yogam ca
mama yo vetti tattvatah
so vikampena yogena
yujyate na tra samsayah (7)

एतां विभूतिं योगं च मम यो वेत्ति तत्त्वतः ।
सोऽविकल्पेन योगेन युज्यते नात्र संशयः ॥ (१० । ७)

Srikṛsna said:

O Arjuna, now listen to My Supreme words which I say for your good because you take delight (in my words). I am the source of the Gods and the great sages. Therefore, they also do not know my origin. I am unborn, without any beginning and the mighty Lord of the worlds. Those who know this among mortals become free from delusion and all sins. Understanding, knowledge, freedom from bewilderment, patience, truth, self-control and calmness; pleasure, existence and non-existence, fear and fearlessness, non-violence, equal-mindedness, contentment, austerity, charity, fame and ill-fame are the different stages of beings which proceed from Me alone. The great seven sages (saptarishis) and the four *manus* are also of my nature and born of My mind. All the creatures in the world have originated from them. He who knows truly My this glory and power are united (with Me) by unfaltering yoga. There is no doubt about it.

(The Supreme God is unborn. All creation of this world-good or bad, are originated from Him. Those who know this are united with God).

2. Knowledge and Devotion

aham sarvasya prabhavo
mattah sarvam pravartate
iti matva bhajante mam
budha bhavasamanvitah (8)

अहं सर्वस्य प्रभवो मत्तः सर्वं प्रवर्तते ।
इति मत्वा भजन्ते मां बुधा भावसमन्विताः ॥ (१० । ८)

maccitta madgataprana
bodhayantah parasparam
kathayantas ca mam nityam
tusyanti ca ramanti ca (9)

मच्चित्ता मद्गतप्राणा बोधयन्तः परस्परम् ।
कथयन्तश्च मां नित्यं तुष्यन्ति च रमन्ति च ॥ (१० । ९)

tesam satatayuktanam
bhajatam pritipurvakam

dadami buddhiyogam tam
yena mam upaynti te (10)

तेषां सततयुक्तनां भजतां प्रीतिपूर्वतम् ।
ददामि बुद्धियोगं तं येन मामुपयान्ति ते ॥ (१० । १०)

tesam eva nukampartham
aham ajnanajam tamah
nasayamy atmavhavastho
jnanadipena bhasvata (11)

तेषामेवानुकम्पार्थमहमज्ञानजं तमः ।
नाशयाम्यात्मभावस्थो ज्ञानदीपेन भास्वता ॥ (१० । ११)

Those who know that I am the origin of all and the whole creation proceeds from Me, they are endowed with conviction and worship Me. Their thoughts (are fixed) in Me, their lives are fully given –up to Me, they converse of Me and enlighten each other, they are contented and rejoicing in Me. I grant the concentration of understanding to such constant devotees and worshippers with love by which they come to Me. (They are emancipated). They remain in My true state. I destroy the darkness born of ignorance by shining the lamp of wisdom in them.

(Devotion also leads to knowledge and emancipation. Lamp of knowledge is lit by the God in the soul of devotees or *bhaktas*).

3. What is God and his Manifestation ?

arjuna uvaca
param brahma param dhama
pavitram paramam bhavan
purusam sasvatam divyam
adidevam ajam vidhum (12)

अर्जुन उवाच
परं ब्रह्म परं धाम पवित्रं परमं भवान् ।
पुरुषं शाश्वतं दिव्यमादिदेवमजं विभुम् ॥ (१० । १२)

ahus tvam rsayah sarve
devarsir naradas tatha
asito devalo vyasah
svayam cai va bravisi me (13)

आहुस्त्वामृषयः सर्वे देवर्षिर्नारदस्तथा ।
असितो देवलो व्यासः स्वयं चैव ब्रवीषि मे ॥ (१० । १३)

sarvam etad rtam manye
yan mam vadasi kesava
na hi te bhagavan vyaktim
vidur deva na danavah (14)

सर्वमेतद् ऋग्तं मन्ये यन्मां वदसि केशव ।
न हि ते भगवन् व्यक्तिं विदुर्देवा न दानवाः ॥ (१० । १४)

svayam eva tmana tmanam
vetha tvam purusottama
bhutabhavana bhutesa
devadeva jagatpate (15)

स्वयमेवात्मनात्मानं वेत्थ त्वं पुराषोत्तम ।
भूतभावना भूतेश देवदेव जगत्पते ॥ (१० । १५)

vaktum arhasy asesena
divya hy atmavibhutayah
yabhir vibhutibhir lokan
imams tvam vyapya tisthasi (16)

वक्तुमर्हस्यशेषेण दिव्या ह्यात्मविभूतयः ।
याभिर्विभूतिभिर्लोकानिमांस्त्वं व्याप्य तिष्ठसि ॥ (१० । १६)

katham vidyam aham yogims
tvam sada paricintayan
kesu kesu ca bhaveshu
cintyo si bhagavn maya (17)

कथं विद्यामहं योगिंस्त्वां सदा परिचिन्तयन् ।
केषु केषु च भावेषु चिन्त्योऽसि भगवन्मया ॥ (१० ।१७)

vistarena tmano yogam
vibhutim ca janardana
bhuyah kathaya trptir hi
srnvato na sti me mrtam (18)

विस्तरेणात्मनो योगं विभूतिं च जनार्दन ।
भूय: कथय तृप्तिर्हि शृण्वतो नास्ति मेऽमृतम् ॥ (१० । १८)

Arjuna said:

"O Kesava (Kṛsna), you are the Supreme Brahman, the Supreme Abobe, the Supreme Purifier, the Eternal, Divine person, the first of the Gods, the unborn, the all–pervading. All the sages say this about you. Divine seers Ṅarada, Asita, Devals, Vyasa and yourself have told this to me. I hold as true all what you say to me; neither the Gods nor the demons know your manifestations.Verily, you yourself know by yourself, O Supreme person; the source of beings, the Lord of creatures, the God of gods, the Lord of the world you should tell me of your divine (excellent) manifestations (forms), without exception. You do abide (in them and beyond). How may I know you by constant meditation. O Lord, in what various aspects you are to be thought by me. O Janardana (Kṛsna), kindly tell me in detail of your power and manifestation, for I am not satisfied by listening your nectar–like speech.

4. EXCELLENCE IS THE REFLECTION OF GOD

sribhagwan uvaca
hanta te kathayisyami
divya hy atmavibhutayah
pradhanyatah kurusrestha
na sty anto vistarasya me (19)

श्रीभगवानुवाच
हन्त ते कथयिष्यामि दिव्या ह्यात्मविभूतय: ।
प्राधान्यत: कुरुश्रेष्ठ नास्त्यन्तो विस्तरस्य मे ॥ (१० । १९)

aham atma gudakesa
sarvabhutasayasthitah
aham adis ca madhyam ca
bhutanam anta eva ca (20)

अहमात्मा गुडाकेश सर्वभूताशयस्थित: ।
अहमादिश्च मध्यं च भूतानामन्त एव च ॥ (१० । २०)

adityanam aham visnur
jyotisam ravir amsuman
maricir marutam asmi
naksatranam aham sasi (21)

आदित्यानामहं विष्णुर्ज्योतिषां रविरंशुमान् ।
मरीचिर्मरुतामस्मि नक्षत्राणामहं शशी ॥ (१० । २१)

vedanam samavedo smi
devanam asmi vsavah
indriyanam manas ca smi
bhutanam asmi cetana (22)

वेदानां सामवेदोऽस्मि देवानामस्मि वासव: ।
इन्द्रियाणां मनश्चास्मि भूतानामस्मि चेतना ॥ (१० ।२२)

rudranam samkaras ca smi
vitteso yaksarakasam
vasunam pavakas ca smi
meruh sikharinam aham (23)

रुद्राणां शङ्करश्चास्मि वित्तेशो यक्षरक्षसाम् ।
वसूनां पावकश्चास्मि मेरु: शिखरिणामहम् ॥ (१० । २३)

purodhasam ca mukhyam mam
viddhi partha brhaspatim
senaninam aham skanadah
sarasam asmi sagarah (24)

पुरोधसां च मुख्यं मां विद्धि पार्थ बृहस्पतिम् ।
सेनानीनामहं स्कन्द: सरसामस्मि सागर: ॥ (१० । २४)

maharsinam bhrgur aham
giram asmy ekam aksaram
yajnanam japayajno smi
sthavaranam himalayah (25)

महर्षीणां भृगुरहं गिरामस्म्येकमत्ररम् ।
यज्ञानां जपयज्ञोऽस्मि स्थावराणां हिमालय: ॥ (१० । २५)

asvatthah sarvavrksanam
devarsinam ca naradah
gandharvanam citraathah
siddhanam kapilo munih (26)

अश्वत्थ: सर्ववृक्षाणां देवर्षीणां च नारद: ।
गन्धर्वाणां चित्ररथ: सिद्धांनां कपिलो मुनि: ॥ (१० । २६)

uccaihsravasam asvanam
viddhi mam amrtodbhavam
airavatam gajendranam
naranam ca naradhipam (27)

उच्चै:श्रवसमश्वानां विद्धि माममृतोद्भवम् ।
ऐरावतं गजेन्द्राणां नराणां च नराधिपम् ॥ (१० । २७)

ayudhanam aham vajram
dhenunam asmi kamadhuk
prajanas ca smi kandrpah
sarpanam asmi vasukih (28)

आयुधानामहं वज्रं धेनूनामस्मि कामधुक् ।
प्रजनश्चास्मि कन्दर्प: सर्पाणामस्मि वासुकि: ॥ (१० । २८)

anantas cha smi naganam
vruno yadsam aham
pitrnam aryama ca smi
yamah samyamatam aham (29)

अनन्तश्चास्मि नागानां वरुणो यादसामहम् ।
पितृणामर्यमा चास्मि यम: संयमतामहम् ॥ (१० । २९)

prahladas ca smi daityanam
kalah kalayatam aham
mrganam ca mrgendro ham
vainateyas ca paksinam (30)

प्रह्लादश्चास्मि दैत्यांनां काल: कलयतामहम् ।
मृगाणां च मृगेन्द्रोऽहं वैनतेयश्च पक्षिणाम् ॥ (१० । ३०)

pavanah pavatam asmi
ramah sastrabhrtam aham
jhasanam makaras ca smi
srotasamasmi jahnavi (31)

पवन: पवतामस्मि राम: शस्त्रभृतामहम् ।
झषाणां मकरश्चास्मि स्रोतसामस्मि जाह्नवी ॥ (१० । ३१)

sarganam adir antas ca
madhyam cai va ham arjuna
adhyatmavidya vidyanam
vadah pravadatam aham (32)

सर्गाणामादिरन्तश्च मध्यं चैवाहमर्जुन।
अध्यात्मविद्या विद्यानां वाद: प्रवदतामहम् ॥ (१० । ३२)

aksaranam akaro smi
dvandvah samasikasya ca
aham eva ksayah kalo
dhata ham visuatomukhah (33)

अक्षराणामकारोऽस्मि द्वन्द्व: सामासिकस्य च।
अहमेवाक्षय: कालो धाताहं विश्वतोमुख: ॥ (१० । ३३)

mrtyuh sarvaharas ca ham
udbhavas ca bhavisyatam
kirtih srir vak ca narinam
smrtir medha dhrith ksama (34)

मृत्यु: सर्वहरश्चाहमुद्भवश्च भविष्यताम्।
कीर्ति: श्रीर्वाच्क नारीणां स्मृतिर्मेधा धृति: क्षमा ॥ (१० । ३४)

brhatsama tatha samnam
gayarti chandasam aham
masanam margasitso ham
rtunam kusumakarah (35)

बृहत्साम तथा साम्नांगायत्री छन्दसामहम्।
मासानां मार्गशिर्षोऽहमृतूना कुसुमाकर: ॥ (१० । ३५)

dyutam chalayatam asmi
tejas tejasvinam aham
jayo smi vyavasayo smi
sattvam sattvavatam aham (36)

द्यूतं छलयतामतस्म तेजस्तेजस्विनामहम्।
जयोऽस्मि व्यवसायोऽस्मि सत्त्वं सत्त्ववतामहम् ॥ (१० । ३६)

vrsninam vasudevo smi
pandavanam dhanamjayah
muninam apy aham vyasah
kavinam usana kavih (37)

वृष्णीनां वासुदेवोऽस्मि पाण्डवानां धनञ्जय: ।
मुनीनामप्यहं व्यास: कवीनामुशना कवि: ॥ (१० । ३७)

dando damayatam asmi
nitir asmi jigisatam
maunam cai va smi guhyanam
jnanam jnanavatam aham (38)

दण्डोदमयतामस्मि नीतिरस्मि जिगीषताम् ।
मौनं चैवास्मि गुह्यानां ज्ञानं ज्ञानवतामहम् ॥ (१० । ३८)

yac ca pi sarvabhutanam
bijam tad aham arjuna
na tad asti vina yat syan
maya bhutam caracaram (39)

यच्चापि सर्वभूतानां बीजं तदहमर्जुन ।
न तदस्ति विना यत्स्यान्माया भूतं चराचरम् ॥ (१० । ३९)

na nto sti mama divyanam
vibhutinam paramtapa
esa tu ddesatah prokto
vibhuter vistaro maya (40)

नान्तोऽस्ति मम दिव्यांना विभूतीनां परन्तप ।
एष तूद्देशत: प्रोक्तो विभूतेर्विस्तरो मया ॥ (१० । ४०)

yad–yad vibhutimat sttvam
srimad urjitam eva va
tat tad eva vagaccha tvam
mama tejomsasambhavam (41)

यद्यद्विभूतिमत्सत्त्वं श्रीमदूर्जितमेव वा ।
तत्तदेवावगच्छ त्वं मम तेजोंऽशसम्भवम् ॥ (१० । ४१)

athava bahunai tena
kim jnatena tava rjuna
vistabhya ham idam krtsnam
ekamsena sthito jagat (42)

अथवा बहुनैतैन किं ज्ञातेन तवार्जुन ।
विष्टभ्याहमिदं कृत्स्नमेकांशेन स्थितो जगत् ॥ (१० । ४२)

Srikrsna said:

"O Arjuna, I declare to you only prominent divine forms (manifestations) of Mine, because there is no end to My extent (the details). I am self-seated in the hearts of all creatures. I am the beginning, the middle and the very end of beings. What is excellent in any category of creation is My reflection.(Excellence is my reflection-sat-cit-anand form).

Category	The Best/ excellent is my form
1. Adtiyas (12)	Vishnu
2. Lights	Sun
3. Maruts (59)	Marici
4. Stars	Moon
5. Vedas	Samveda
6. Gods(vedic Gods)	Indra
7. Senses	Mind
8. Being	Conciousness
9. Rudras	Samkara (siva)
10. Yakshas and Rakhsas	Kubera
11. Vasus	Agni (fire)
12. Mountain peaks	Meru (sumeru)
13. Household priests	Brahaspati
14. War Generals	Skanda (Kartikeya)
15. Lakes	Ocean
16. Sages	Bhrugu
17. Utterances	Aum
18. Offerings	Meditation
19– Unmovable things	Himalaya
20. Trees	Asvattha (Pipal tree)
21. Divine seers	Narada
22. Gandharvas	Chitraratha

23. Perfected ones	Kapila sage
24. Horses	Ucchaisrava
25. Elephant	Airavata
26. Men	Monarch/ king/ leader
27. Weapons	Thunder bolt (vajra)
28. Cows	Kamdhenu
29. Progenitors	God of love (Kamdeva)
30. Sarpents	Vasuki
31. Nagas	Ananta
32. Dwellers in water	Varuna
33. Departed ancestors (pitras)	Aryama
34. Administrators (Exceutors of Law and order)	Yama
35. Titans	Prahlada
36. Calculators	Time
37. Beasts	Lion
38. Birds	Garuda
39. Purifiers	Air
40. Warriors	Rama
41. Fdfishes	Alligator
42. Rivers	Gangas
43. Creations	Beginning, Middle and end.
44. Sciences	Science of Self /atman janam
45. Debates/controversies	Dialectic
46. Letters	A
47. Compounds	Dual

I am imperishable Time. I am the creator whose face is turned on all sides. I am death. I am the origin of the things that are yet to be. I am fame, prosperity, speech, memory, intelligence, firmness and patience. (All divine qualities leading to excellence in performance are My Manifestations).

Of Hymns I am Brihatsaman, of metres I am Gayatri of months, I am Margashrsa and of seasons I am spring. Of the deceitful, I am gambling; of the splendid I am the splendour; I am victory, I am effort and I am the goodness of the good. Of Vrsnis, I am Vasudeva; of sages I am Vyạsa; of Pandavas I am Arjuna, of Poets I am Usana; of those who chastise I am the rod/*danda*; those who seek victory I am the wise Policy/ ethics; of secrets, I am the silence and of knowers of wisdom, I am the wisdom.

O Arjuna, I am the seed of all existences. There is nothing moving or fixed which can exist without Me. My divine manifestations have no end. What I have told you is only illustrative of My infinite glory. Whatsoever being there is, endowed with glory, grace and vigour, it represents fragment of my splendour. (Excellence is reflection of God). There is no need for detailed knowledge (of My manifestation). I support this entire universe pervading it with a single fraction of Myself.

(This cosmos is partial revelation of the Infinite, is illumined by one ray of His shining light. The Supreme dwells beyond all this cosmos, beyond time and space. He reflects through excellence which is an outcome of divine qualities and devoted detached action).

Now chapter 10 entited " vibhutiyoga" is over.

SUMMARY

The Supreme God is unborn, without origin, middle and end. Devotion leads to knowledge or "self-realisation." What is excellent in this world is the manifestation of fragment of His splendour.

Divine qualities and detached and devoted action leads to excellent performance. Excellence is one form of God (sat–chit–anand). List of excellent manifestations given in this chapter is not exhaustive but illustrative only.

(Experience presence of God through excellent performance).

THREE FORMS OF GOD

Contents

1. The macro or universal form of God

madanugrahaya paramam
guhyam adhyatmasamjnitam
yat tvayo ktam vacas tena
moho yam vigato mama (1)

मदनुग्रहाय परमं गुह्यमध्यात्मसञ्ज्ञितम् ।
यत्त्वयोक्तं वचस्तेन मोहोऽयं विगतो मम ॥ (११ । १)

bhavapyayau hi bhutanam
srutau vistaraso maya
tvattah kamalapattraksa
mahatmyam api ca uyayam (2)

भवाप्ययौ हि भूतानां श्रुतौ विस्तरशो मया ।
त्वत्तः कमलपत्राक्ष माहात्म्यमपि चाव्ययम् ॥ (११ । २)

evam etad yatha ttha tvam
atmanam paramesvara
drastum icchami te rupam
aisvaram purusotiama (3)

एवमेतद्यथात्थ त्वमात्मानं परमेश्वर ।
द्रष्टुमिच्छामि ते रुपमैश्वरं पुरुषोत्तम ॥ (११ । ३)

manyase yadi tac chakyam
maya drastum iti prabho
yogesvara tato me tvam
darsaya tmanam avyayam (4)

मन्यसे यदि तच्छक्यं मया द्रष्टुमिति प्रभो ।
योगेश्वर ततो मे त्वं दर्शयात्मानमव्ययम् ॥ (११। ४)

Arjuna said:

My illusion/bewilderment is over after listening your discourse regarding the supreme mystery and the self, the birth and passing away of things and also your Imperishable Majesty, O lotus eyed (Kṛsna). As you have declared yourself to be (the Supreme Lord) and it is true but I desire to see your divine (universal macro) form, O Supreme Person. If you think that it can be seen by me, then reveal to me your Imperishable self, O Yogesvara (Kṛsna).

2. The Revelation of the Lord

shribhagwan uvaca
pasya me partha rupani
sataso tha sahasrasah

nanavidhani divyani
nanavarnakṛtini ca (5)

श्रीभगवानुवाच
पश्य मे पार्थ रूपाणि शतशोऽथ सहस्रशः ।
नानाविधानि दिव्यानि नानावर्णाकृतीनि च ॥ (११ । ५)

pasya dityan vasun rudran
asvinau marutas tatha
bahuny.adrstapurvani
pasya scaryani bharata (6)

पश्यादित्यान्वसून्रुद्रानश्विनौ मरुतस्तथा ।
बहून्यदृष्टपूर्वाणि पश्याश्चर्याणि भारत ॥ (११ । ६)

ihai kastham jagat kṛtsnam
pasya dya sacaracaram
mama dehe gudakesa
yac ca nyad drstum icchasi (7)

इहैकस्थं जगत्कृत्स्नं पश्यद्य सचराचरम् ।
मम देहे गुडाकेश यच्चान्यद्द्रष्टुमिच्छसि ॥ (११ । ७)

na tu mam sakyase drastum
anenai va svacakṣusa
divyam dadami te cakṣuh
pasya me yogm aisvaram (8)

न तु मां शक्यसे द्रष्टुमनेनैव स्वचक्षुषा ।
दिव्यं ददामि ते चक्षुः पश्य मे योगमैश्वरम् ॥ (११ । ८)

Srikṛsna said :

"Behold, O Partha (Arjuna), My forms are of Hundred and thousand fold, various in kind, divine, of various colours and shapes. Behold the Adityas (Suns), the Vasus, the Rudras, the two Asvins and also the Maruts. Behold O Bharata (Arjuna), many wonders never seen earlier. Here today, behold the whole universe, moving and unmoving and whatever else you wish to see, O Gudakesa (Arjuna), all unified in My body.

Gudakesa: One who has controlled sleep. A unique power of Arjuna described by this name.

But, however, you can't see (My macroform) with (ordinary human) eyes of yours; I will bestow on you the supernatural eyes. Behold My divine power.

3. DESCRIPTION OF MACRO FORM BY SAMJAYA

evam uktva tato rajan
mahayogesvaro harih
darsayam asa parthaya
paramam rupam aisvaram (9)

एवमुक्त्वा ततो राजन्महायोगेश्वरो हरिः ।
दर्शयामास पार्थय परमं रूपमैश्वरम् ॥ (११।९)

anekavakrtanayanam
anekadbhutadarsanam
anekadivyadharanam
divyanekodyatayudham (10)

अनेकवक्त्रनयनमनेकाद्भुतदर्शनम् ।
अनेकदिव्याभरणं दिव्यानेकोद्यतायुधम् ॥ (११।१०)

divyamalyambaradharam
divyagandhanulepanam
sarvascaryamayam devam
anantam visvatomukham (11)

दिव्यमाल्याम्बरधरं दिव्यगन्धानुलेपनम् ।
सर्वाश्चर्यमयं देवमनन्तं विश्वतोमुखम् ॥ (११।११)

divi suryasahasrasya
bhaved yugapad utthita
yadi bhah sadrsi sa syad
bhasas tasya mahatmanah (12)

दिवि सूर्यसहस्त्रस्य भवेद्युगपदुत्थिता ।
यदि भाः सदृशी सा स्माद्भासस्तस्य महात्मनः ॥ (११।१२)

tatrai kastham yagat krtsnam
pravibhaktam anekadha

apasyad devadevasya
sarire pandavastada (13)

तत्रैकस्थं जगत्कृत्स्नं प्रविभक्तमनेकधा ।
अपश्यद्देवदेवस्य शरीरे पाण्डवस्तदा ॥ (११ । १३)

Samjaya said :

"O king (Dhritarastra), having this spoken Yogesvara (Kṛsna) then revealed to Partha (Arjuna) his Supreme and Divine form having many mouths and eyes, of many visions of marvel, of many divine ornaments, of many divine uplifted weapons.

(Such a description of macro form or univesal form of the God is found in Pursasukta (Rigvedas X,90) – *sahasrasirsa purusah, sahasraksah saharsrapat*, meaning thereby the God has thousands heads, eyes and feet, thereby describing a top leader/CEO who acts through thousand employees.)

Wearing divine garlands and ornaments with divine perfumes and creams made-up of all wonders, resplendent, boundles with face turned everywhere. The splendour of the universal form of God may resemble the light of a thousand Suns, blazed in the sky at once (an imagination of nuclear explosion). Arjuna seen the whole universe with manifold divisions gathered together in one body of the Supreme God.

(The vision is a revelation of the potential divinity of all empirical life).

tatah sa vismayavisto
hrsta–roma dhananjayah
pranamya shirasa devam
krtanjalir abhasata (14)

ततः स विस्मयाविष्टो हृष्ट रोमा धनञ्जयः ।
प्रणम्य शिरसा देवं कृताञ्जलिरभाषत ॥ (११ । १४)

Arjuna uvaca
pashyaami devaamstav dev dehe
sarvaams tatha bhuta visesa sanghan
brahmanam isam kamalaasana–stham
rsims ca sarvan uragams ca divyaan (15)

अर्जुन उवाच
पश्यामि देवांस्तव देव देहे
सर्वांस्तथा भूतविशेषसङ्घान् ।

ब्रह्माणमीशं कमलासनस्थ–
ऋषींश्च सर्वानुरगांश्च दिव्यान् ॥ (११ । १५)

aneka–bahudara–vaktra–netram
pashyami tvam sarvato–anantroopam
naantam na madhyam na punas tvaadim
pashaami vishveshvara vishva–roopa (16)

अनेकबाहूदरवक्त्रनेत्रं–
पश्यामि त्वां सर्वतोऽनन्तरुपम् ।
नान्तं न मध्यं न पुनस्तवादिं–
पश्यातम विश्वेश्वर विश्वरूप ॥ (११ । १६)

kireetinamgadinam chakrinamca
tejo–raashim sarvato deeptimantam
pashyamitvamdunireekhshyamsamantad
diptanalarka–dutimaprameyam (17)

किरीटीनं गदिनं चक्रिणं च
तेजोराशिं सर्वतो दीप्तिमन्तम् ।
पश्यमि त्वां दुर्निरीक्ष्यं समन्ता –
द्दीप्तानलार्कद्युतिमप्रमेयम् ॥ (११ । १७)

tvamakhsharamparamamveditavyam
tvamasya vishvasya param nidhanam
tvamavyayahaashvatdharamagoptaa
sanatanastvama purusho mato me (18)

त्वमक्षरं परमं वेदितव्यं–
त्वमस्य विश्वस्य परं निधानम्
त्वमव्यय: शाश्वतधर्मगोप्ता
सनातनस्त्वं पुरुषो मतो मे ॥ (११ । १८)

anadi–madhyantam ananta–viryam
ananta–bahum sasi–surya–netram
pashyaamitvamdiptahutasa vaktram
sva–tejasa vishvam idam tapantam (19)

अनादिमध्यान्तमनन्तवीर्य–
मनन्तबेहुं शशिसूर्यनेत्रम ।
पश्यामि त्वां दीप्तहुताशवक्त्रं–
स्वतेजसा विश्वमिदं तपन्तम् ॥ (११ । १९)

dyaavaaprithvyoridaman tramhi
vyaaptam tvayaiken dishashcha sarvaah
drishtvaadbhutam roopamugram tavedam
lokatryam pravyathitam mahaatmana (20)

द्यावापृथिव्योरिदमन्तरं हि
व्याप्तं त्वयअकेन दिशश्चसर्वाः ।
दृष्ट्वाद्भुतं रूपमुग्रं तवेदं–
लोकत्रय प्रव्यथितं महात्मन् ॥ (११ । २०)

ami hi tvaam sursanghaa vishanti
kechidbheetaah praanjalyo grinanti
svasteetyuktvaa maharshisiddhasanghaah
stuvanti tvam stutibhih pushkalaabhih (21)

अमी हि त्वां सुरसङ्घा विशन्ति
केचिद्भीताःपाञ्जलयो गृणन्ति ।
स्वस्ती त्वां स्तुतिभिः पुष्कलाभिः ॥ (११ । २१)

rudraadityaa vasavo ye cha saadhyaa
vishve–ashvinau marutashchoshmapashch
gandharvayakhshaasursidhsangaa
veekhshante tvaam vismataashchaiva sarve (22)

रुद्रादित्या वसवो ये च साध्या–
विश्वेऽश्विनौ मरुतश्चोष्मपाश्च ।
गन्धर्वयक्षासुरसिद्धसङ्घा
वीक्षन्ते त्वां विस्मिताश्चैव सर्वे ॥ (११ । २२)

roopam mahatte bahuvaktranetram
mahaabaaho bahubaahoorupaadam
bahoodaram bahudanshtraakaraalam
drishtvaa lokaah pravyathitaasthaaham (23)

रूपं महत्ते बहुवक्त्रनेत्रं–
महाबाहो बहुबाहूरुपादम् ।
बहूदरं बहुदंष्ट्राकरालं–
दृष्ट्वा लोकाः प्रव्यथितास्तथाहम् ॥ (११। २३)

nabhahsprisham deeptamanekvarnam
vyat–taananam deeptivishaalnetram
drishtvaa hi tvaam pravyathitantaraatmaa
dhritim na vindaami shamam cha vishno (24)

नभःस्पृशं दीप्तमनेकवर्णं–
व्यात्ताननं दीप्तविशालनेत्रम् ।
दृष्ट्वा हि त्वां प्रव्यथितान्तरात्मा
धृतिं न विन्दामि शमं च विष्णो ॥ (११ । २४)

dranshtaakaraalaani cha te mukhaani
drishtaiva kaalaanalasannibhaani
disho na jane na labhe cha sharma
praseed devesh jagannivaasa (25)

दंष्ट्राकरालानि च ते मुखानि
दृष्ट्वैव कालानलसन्निभानि ।
दिशो न जाने न लभे च शर्म
प्रसीद देवेश जगन्निवास ॥ (११ । २५)

ami cha tvam dhritraashtrasya putraah
sarve sahaaivaavnipaalsangaih
bheeshmo dronah sootaputrastathaasau
sahaasmadeeyairapi yodhmukhyaih (26)

अमी च त्वां धृतराष्ट्रस्य पुत्राः
सर्वे सहैवावीनिपालसङ्घैः ।
भीष्मो द्रोणः सूतपुत्रस्तथासौ
सहास्मदीयैरपि योधमुख्यैः ॥ (११ । २६)

vaktraaani te tvarmaalaa vishanti
dranshtaakaraalaani bhayaanakaani
kechidvilagnaa dashaantareshu
sandrishyante choornitairuttmangai (27)

वक्त्राणि तेत्वरमाणा विशन्ति
दंष्ट्राकरालानि भयानकानि ।
केचिद्विलग्ना दशनान्तरेषु
सन्दृश्यन्ते चूर्णितैरुत्तमाङ्गैः ॥ (११ । २७)

yathaa nadeenaam bahvo–ambuvegaah
samudraamevaabhimukhaa dravanti
tathaa tavaami naralokaveeraa
vishanti vaktraanyabhivijvalanti (28)

यथा नदीनां बहवोऽम्बुवेगाः
समुद्रमेवाभिमुखा द्रवन्ति ।
तथा तवामी नरलोकवीरा–
विशन्ति वक्त्राण्यभिविज्वलन्ति ॥ (११ । २८)

yathaa pradeeptam jvalnam patangaa
vishanti naashaaye samridhvegaah
tathaiva naashaaye vishanti lokaa–
stvaapi vaktraani samridhvegaah (29)

यथा प्रदीप्तं ज्वलनं पतङ्गा–
विशन्ति नाशाय समृद्धवेगाः ।
तथैव नाशाय विशन्ति लोका–
स्तवापि वक्त्राणि समृद्धवेगाः ॥ (११ । २९)

lelihyase grasamaanah samantaa
l–lokaaansmagaraanvadnairjvaladbhih
tejobhiraapurya jagatsamagram
bhaasastvogaraah pratpanti vishno (30)

लेलिह्यसे ग्रसमान:समन्ता–
ल्लोकान्समग्रान्वदनैर्ज्वलद्भिः ।
तेजोभिरापूर्य जगत्समग्रं–
भासस्तवोग्राः प्रतपन्ति विष्णो ॥ (११ । ३०)

aakhyaahi me ko bhavaanugraroopo
namo–astu te devavaar praseeda
vigyaatumich–chchaami bhavantamaadyam
na hi prajaanaami tava pravrittam (31)

आख्याहि मे को भवानुग्ररूपो-
नमोऽस्तु ते देववर प्रसीद।
विज्ञातुमिच्छामि भवन्तमाद्यं-
नहि प्रजानामि तव प्रवृत्तिम्॥ (११।३१)

Then Arjuna stuck with amazement his hair standing on end, bowed down his head to the Supreme Lord, with folded hands started praying.

"In your body, O Lord I see all the Gods and the varied hosts of beings as well. Brahma, the Lord seated on the lotus throne and all the sages and heavenly *nagas.* I behold your infinite form on all sides with numerous arms, bellies, faces and eyes. But, O Lord of the universe, O universal Lord, I do not see your end, middle or your beginning. I behold you with your crown, mace and discus glowing everywhere as a mass of light, dazzling on all sides with the radiance of the flaming fire and sun, incomparable. You are imperishable the supreme to be realised. You are the ultimate resting place of the universe; you are the undying guardian of the eternal law/ (Sanatan Dharma).you are the primal person, I think.

I behold you as one without beginning, middle or end, of infinite power of numerous arms, with moon and sun as your eyes, with your face as a flaming fire whose radiance burns up this universe. The space between heaven and earth is with all directions covered by you alone. O Lord, three worlds tremble on seeing this wonderful and terrible form of yours. Hosts of Gods enter you and some in fear extol you, with folded hands. Bands of great seers and perfected ones cry hail and adore you by chanting hymns of abounding praise. The Rudras, the Adityas, the Vasus, the Sadhyas, the Visvedevas, two Asvins, the Maruts, the *Manes* and the host of Gandharvas, Yakshas, Asuras and Siddhas all gaze at you and are quite amazed. On seeing your universal form/macro form with many mouths, eyes, arms, thighs, feet, bellies and many tusks, the worlds tremble so do I. My in most soul trembles in fear. I find neither steadiness nor peace. I lose sense of the directions. Be gracious, O Lord of Gods, refuge of the worlds.

"All sons of Dhritarastra with hosts of Kings and also Bhishma, Drona, Karna along with chief warriors on our side too are rushing into your fearful mouths set with terrible tusks. Some caught with teeth are seen with their heads crushed to powder. As the many rushing torrents of rivers race towards the ocean. So, do the heroes of the human world rush into your flaming mouths. As moths rush fast into a blazing fire to perish so do these heroes rush into your mouth swiftly to their own destruction. (People blinded by ignorance/destiny rush to their destruction, God simply witness them because they suffer on account of their own deeds. The same applies to top Management. People are punished on account of their misdeeds. The divine/ chief executes the law impartially.)

"Devouring all the worlds on every side with Your flaming mouths, You lick them up . Your fiery rays fill this whole universe and scorch it with their fierce radiance, O Vishnu! tell me, who are you with such a terrible form. My salutations to you. Be merciful. I want to know who are you, the primal one, for I do not know your working.

5. God as the Judge – Mahakal

kalo smi lokaksayakri pravrddho
lokan samahartum iha pravrttah
rte pi ivam na bhavisyanti sarve
ye vasthitah pratyanikesu yodhah (32)

कालोऽस्मि लोकक्षयकृत्प्रवृद्धो–
लोकान् समाहर्तुमिह प्रवृत्त: ।
ऋतेऽपि त्वां न भविष्यन्ति सर्वे
येऽवस्थिता: प्रत्यनीकेषु योधा: ॥ (११ । ३२)

tasmat tvam uttistha yaso labhasva
jitva sartun bhunksva rajyam samrddham
mayai vai ve nihatah purvam eva
nimittamatram bhava savyashacin (33)

तस्मात्त्वमुत्तिष्ठ यशो लभस्व
जित्वा शत्रून् भुङ्क्ष्व राज्यं समृद्धम् ।
मयैवैते निहता: पूर्वमेव
निमित्तमात्रं भव सव्यसाचिन् ॥ (११ । ३३)

dronam ca Bhishmam ca jayadratham ca
karnam tatha nyan api yodhaviran
maya hatams tvam jahi ma vyathistha
yudhyasva jetasi rane sapatnan (34)

द्रोणं च भीष्मं च जयद्रथ च
कर्णं तथान्यानपि योधवीरान् ।
मया हतांस्त्वं जहि मा व्यथिष्ठा–
युध्यस्व जेतासि रणे सपत्नान् ॥ (११ । ३४)

etac chrutva vacanam kesavasya
krtanjalir vepamanah kiriti
namaskrtva bhuya eva ha krsnam
sagadgadam bhitabhitah pranamaya (35)

इक्त चरूत्व वाक्यानां केशवस्त्र
कृतांजली विपमानाह कीर्ती
नमस्कृत्वा भूय एवाह कृष्णं–
सगद्गदं भीतभीत: प्रणम्य ॥ (११ । ३५)

Srikrsna said:

"I am Time, world destroying, grown mature, engaged here in subduing the world. Even if you do not fight, all the warriors standing arrayed on the rival side shall cease to be. Therefore, you arise, fight and gain glory and prosperous kingdom.

(Supreme being responsible for creation as well as destruction. Time is great. Human is an instrument only. He is the controller of Time– *Mahakal*).

"You slay Drona, Bhishma, Jaydratha, Karna and other great warriors as well, who are already doomed by Me. Be not afraid. Fight. You will win."

(It appears that Arjuna could not fully grasp Karma yoga of detached and devoted action detailed out by Srikrsna. That is why Lord Krsna has declared the prediction of the outcome of the war. Yet Arjuna will not get motivated. Srikrsna might have put Arjuna to test whether he has any attachment to the fruits of action in spite of his discourse of three yogas.)

Samjaya said:

Having heard these utterances of Keshava (Krsna) Arjuna with folded hands and trembling, saluted again and prostrating himself with great fear, spoke in a faltering voice to Krsna.

6. Praise by Arjuna

sthane hrsikesa tava prakirtya
jagat prahrsyaty anurajyate ca
rakshamsi bhitani diso dravanti
sarve namasyanti ca siddhasamighah (36)

स्थाने हृषीकेश तव प्रकीर्त्या
जगत्प्रहृष्यत्यनुरज्यते च ।

रक्षांसि भीतानि दिशो द्रवन्ति
सर्वे नमस्यन्ति च सिद्धसङ्घा: ॥ (११ । ३६)

kasmac ca te na nameran mahatman
gariyase brahmano py adikartre
ananta devesa jagannivasa
tvam aksaram sad asat tatparam yat (37)

कस्माच्च ते न नमेरन्महात्मन्
गरीयसे ब्रह्मणोऽप्यादिकर्त्रे ।
अनन्त देवेश जगन्निवास
त्वमक्षरं सदसत्तत्परं यत् ॥ (११ । ३७)

tvam adidevah purusah puranas
tvam asya visvasya param nidhanam
vetta si vedyam ca param ca dhama
tvaya tatam visvam anantarupa (38)

त्वमादिदेव: पुरुष: पुराण–
स्त्वमस्य विश्स्य परं च निधानाम् ।
वेत्तासि वेद्यं च परं च धाम
त्वया ततं विश्वमनन्तरूप ॥ (११ । ३८)

vayur yamo gnir varunah sasankah
prajapatis tvam prapitamahas ca
namo namas te stu sahasrakrtvah
punas ca bhuyo pi namo namas te (39)

वायुर्यमोऽग्निर्वरुण: शशाङ्क:
प्रजापतिस्त्वं प्रपितामहश्च ।
नमो नमस्तेऽस्तु सहस्त्रकृत्व:
पुनश्च भूयोऽपि नमो नमस्ते ॥ (११ । ३९)

namah purastad atha prsthatas te
namo stu te sarvata eva sarva
anantaviryamitavikramas tvam
sarvam samapnosi tato si sarvah (40)

नम: पुरस्तादथ पृष्ठतस्ते
नमोऽस्तु ते सर्वत एव सर्व ।

अनन्तवीर्यामितविक्रमस्त्वं–
सर्वं समाप्नोषि ततोऽसि सर्वः ॥ (११।४०)

sakhe ti matva prasabham yad uktam
he krsna he yadava he sakhe ti
ajanata mahimanam tave dam
maya pramadat pranayena va pi (41)

सखेति मत्वा प्रसभं यदुक्तं–
हे कृष्ण हे यादव हे सखेति ।
अजानता महिमानं तवेदं–
मया प्रमादात्प्रणयेन वापि ॥ (११।४१)

yac ca vahasartham asatkrto si
viharasayyasanabhojanesu
eko thava py acyuta tatsamaksam
tat ksamaye tvam aham aprameyam (42)

यच्चवहासार्थमसत्कृतोऽसि
विहारशय्यासनभोजनेषु ।
एकोऽथवाप्यच्युत तत्समक्षं–
तत्क्षामये त्वामहमप्रमेयम् ॥ (११।४२)

pitasi lokasya caracarasya
tvam asya pujyas ca gurur gariyan
na tvatsamo sty abhyadhikah kuto nyo
lokatraye py apratimaprabhava (43)

पितासि लोकस्य चराचरस्य
त्वमस्य पूज्यश्च गुरुर्गरीयान् ।
न त्वत्समोऽस्त्यभ्यधिकः कुतोऽन्यो–
लोकत्रयेऽप्यप्रतिमप्रभाव ॥ (११।४३)

tasmat pranamya pranidhaya kayam
prasadaye tvam aham isam idyam
pite va putrasya sakhe va sakhyuh
priyah priyaya rhasi deva sodhum (44)

तस्मात्प्रणम्य प्रणिधाय कायं-
प्रसादये त्वामहमीशमीड्यम् ।
पितेव पुत्रस्य सखेव सख्युः
प्रियः प्रियायार्हसि देव सोढुम् ॥ (११ । ४४)

Arjuna said:

O Hrisikes a (Kṛsna), the world rightly rejoice and delight in glorifying You. The Raksasas are fleeing in terror in all directions and all hosts of sages are bowing down before You. They should do so because You are greater than Brahma, the originator, creator. O infinite being, Lord of the gods, refuge of the universe, you are imperishable, the being and non–being and what is beyond that. You are the knower and object of knowledge and the supreme goal. This world is pervaded by You. You are Infinite. You are vayu (air), yama (death), agni (fire), varuna (water), sasanka (moon), Prajapati (Brahma), the grandsire (of all). I praise You thousand times, again and again from all sides. You are boundless in power and immeasurable in might You penetrate all and, therefore, You are all."

Arjuna recalls his faults out of ignorance and begs to be excused. "I might have spoken to You in rashness, thinking You as my companion and not aware of your greatness. I might have called You O Kṛsna, O Yadava, O Comrade, out of my negligence or fondness.Disrespect might have been shown to You in jest, while at play or on the bed, or seated or at meals, either alone or in the presence of others. I pray, forgive me, O Immeasurable.

(Whenever unintentionally disrespect is done to a big leader, honest request to be forgiven must be made. Due respect to authority must be maintained.)

Now Arjuna uses Family concept of Management. He says, "You are the father of this world. You are the object of worship and its venerable teacher. None is equal to You, in these three worlds. Therefore, I bow down and prostrate my body before You. O adorable Lord! I seek your grace. O God, You should bear with me as a father to his son, as a friend to his friend, as a husband to his wife."

(Family concept of Management is based on personal relationships. Mistakes are excused and better performance is given due to family well–being as a motivating force. The chief in the role of a father, friend and husband will condone mistakes of subordinates as if they were sons, friends and wives in their own family. Mutual respect and sacrifice are needed for the effective working of family concept of management).

(The pusti marga Vaisnava cult of worship as propounded by Srimad Vallabhacharya is based on family concept of worship).

7. The Four Armed Lord (Middle Level Management)

adrstapurvam hrsito smi drstva
bhayena ca pravyathitam mano me
tad eva me darsaya deva rupam
prasida devesa jagannivasa (45)

अदृष्टपूर्वं हृषितोऽस्मि दृष्ट्वा
भयेन च प्रव्यथितं मनो मे ।
तदेव मे दर्शय देवरूपं–
प्रसीद देवेश जगन्निवास ॥ (११ । ४५)

kiritnam gadinam cakrahastam
icchami tvam drastum aham tathai va
tenai va rupena caturbhujena
sahasrabaho bhava visvamurte (46)

किरीटिनं गदिनं चक्रहस्त–
मिच्छामि त्वां द्रष्टुमहं तथैव ।
तेनैव रूपेण चतुर्भुजेन
सहस्त्रबाहो भव विश्वमूर्ते ॥ (११ । ४६)

O Lord of the universe, I have seen (your universal or macro form) which was never seen before. I rejoice but my heart is shaken with fear. Show me your previous form (of personal God)."

I want to see your "Chaturbhuj swaarupa"– crown, mace, and disc in your hands.

(Four armed form of God is middle management executive form. Two arms are invisible–power and authority. It is less terrifying and less invisible, more close.)

8. The Micro or Human form

(Operating Management)

Two armed human form of Krsna as a companion, friend, charioteer, adviser is free from fear for Arjuna. It is operating management form. It works and motivates others to work in this empirical world. Spiritualism is translated into empirical world of duties/actions through this micro or human form. It grants emancipation through detached action/work. Kṛsna returns to this form and gives assurance to Arjuna.

9. Divine Assurance

shribhagavan uvaca
maya prasannena tava rjuna dam
rupam param darsitam atmayogat
teomayam visvam anantam adyam
yan me tvadanyena na drstapurvam (47)

श्रीभगवानुवाच
मया प्रसन्नेन तवार्जुनेदं–
रूपं परं दर्शितमात्मयोगात् ।
तेजोमयं विश्वमनन्तमाद्यं–
यन्मे त्वदन्येन न दृष्टपूर्वम् ॥ (११ । ४७)

na vedayajnadhayayanair na danair
na ca kriyabhir na tapobhir ugraih
evamrupah sakya aham nrloke
drastum tvadanyena kurupravira (48)

न वेदयज्ञाध्ययनैर्न दानै–
र्न च क्रियाभिर्न तपोभिरुग्रैः ।
एवंरूपः शक्य अहं नृलोके
द्रष्टुं त्वदन्येन कुरुप्रवीर ॥ (११ । ४८)

ma te vyatha ma ca vimudhabhavo
drstva rupam ghoram idrn mame dam
vyapetabhih pritamanah punas tvam
tad eva me rupam idam prapasya (49)

मा ते व्यथा मा च विमूढभावो–
दृष्ट्वा रूपं घोरमीदृङ्ममेदम् ।
व्यपेतभीः प्रीतमनाः पुनस्त्वं–
तदेव मे रूपमिदं प्रपश्य ॥ (११ । ४९)

ityarjunam vasudevasya tatho ktva
svakam rupam darsayam asa bhuyah
asvasayam asa ca bhitam enam
bhutva punah saumyavapur mahatma (50)

इतिर्युजुनाम वसुदेवस्म नभो कव्या-
सकाम रुपम दर्शयाम् अक्षाभुवट:
आश्वासयामास च भीतमेनं–
भूत्वा पुन: सौम्यवपुर्महात्मा ॥ (११।५०)

Arjun uvaca
drstve dam manusam rupam
tava saumyam janardana
idanim asmi samutttah
sacetah prakrtim gatah (51)

अर्जुन उवाच
दृष्ट्वदं मानुषं रूपं तव सौम्यं जनार्दन ।
इदानीमस्मि संवृत्त: सचेता: प्रकृतिं गत: ॥ (११।५१)

sribhagwan uvaca
sudurdarsam idam rupam
drstavan asi yan mama
deva apy asya rupasya
nityam darsanakaniksinah (52)

श्रीभगवानुवाच
सुदुर्दर्शमिदं रूपं दृष्टवानसि यन्मम ।
देवा अप्यस्य रूपस्य नित्यं दर्शनकाङ्क्षिण: ॥ (११ ५२)

na ham vedair na tapasad
na danena na ce jyaya
sakya evamvidho drastum
drstavan asi mam yatha (53)

नाहं वेदैर्न तपसा न दानेन न चेज्यया ।
शक्य एवंविधो द्रष्टुं दृष्टवानसि मां यथा ॥ (११।५३)

bhaktya tu ananyaya sakya
aham evamvidho rjuna
jnatum drastum ca tattvena
pravestum ca paramtapa (54)

भक्त्या त्वनन्यया शक्य अहमेवंविधोऽर्जुन ।
ज्ञातुं द्रष्टुं च तत्त्वेन प्रवेष्टुं च परन्तप ॥ (११।५४)

matkarmakrn matparamo
madbhaktah sangavarjitah
nirvairah sarvabhutesu
yah sa mam eti pandava (55)

मत्कर्मकृन्मत्परमो मद्भक्तः सङ्गवर्जितः ।
निवैरः सर्वभूतेषु यः स मामेति पाण्डव ॥ (११।५५)

Srikṛsna said:

"O Arjuna, you could see My Universal form by My grace, through My divine power which none could see before. None can see it by vedic sacrifices, offerings. Don't be afraid, don't be bewildered on seeing my terrific form. Be glad again by again seeing My former form.(human form)"

Samjaya said:

"Having this spoken to Arjuna, Vasudeva (Kṛsna) revealed to him again his (Human form). In this form of grace he comforted the terrified Arjuna.

Arjuna said:

Beholding again your gracious human form, O Janardana (Kṛsna), I have collected my Mind and restored to My normal nature."

Srikṛsna said:

"This form of Mine is not easy to be seen. You have seen it. Even the Gods are ever eager to see this form. You can't see me in this form by vedic sacrifices. (repetition of verse XI ,48). O Arjuna, I can be thus known, truly seen and entered into by firm devotion to Me."

What is this firm devotion is explained in the last verse 55. Thus, he who does work for Me, he who looks upon Me as his goal, he who worships Me, free from attachment, he who is free from enmity to all creatures, he goes to Me.

(This is the essence of devotion (Bhakti), the substance of the teaching of Gita. We must do our duty directing our spirit to the God with detachment from selfishness and enmity towards anyone. We are bound to attain to the Supreme Lord by our devoted and detached work).

Thus, the chapter 11, entitled *Viswarupa darsanyoga* (The vision of the cosmic/universal/macro form) is over.

SUMMARY

Arjuna requested Kṛsna to show him His Imperishable self. bestowed supernatural vision (eyes) through which Arjuna could have darshan of cosmic or macro form of the God. It had thousands of heads, hands, eyes and legs, boundless, full of decoration, fire and light, sages prayed, demons ran away and several warriors were burning as moths in fire. Krsna predicted favourable result of the war in order to test whether Arjuna was truly detached of the fruits. Arjuna realising great powers of Kṛsna as Lord of the universe, begged to be excused for any disrespect shown out of ignorance. He applied family concept of Management also. Then he prayed for restoration of chaturbhuj swaroopa (middle-level management form of authority) which is more kind and less frightening. Finally he requests to Kṛsna to restore his human form (micro form) of a friend, adviser, charioteer. It was operating form of Management where work was performed as an example. Krsna obliged him and comforted him. ***Finally the essence of Gita message (devotion) was stated– Do your duty as work of God, consider God as your goal, worship Him, be free from attachment and enmity. You will attain to the God by such performance of duty.***

DEVOTION OR BHAKTI YOGA

Contents

1. Choice between *Sagun* and *Nirgun*

Arjuna uvaca
evam satataynkta ye
bhaktas tvam paryupasate
ye chapyaskharamuyattam
tesam ke yogabittamah (1)

अर्जुन उवाच
एवं सततयुक्ता ये भक्तास्त्वां पर्युपासते।
ये चाप्यक्षरमव्यक्तं तेषां के योगवित्तमा:॥ (१२।१)

Arjuna said:

Those devotees who worship you (Kṛsna as personal God or Is'vara) and those who worship the Imperishable and the unmanifested, which of these two have the greater knowledge of yoga.

(Out of sagun devotees and nirgun devotees, which are better?)

Sribhagavan uvaca
mayy avesya manoye mam
nityayukta upasate
sraddhaya parayo'petas
te the yuktatma mamtah (2)

श्रीभगवानुवाच
मय्यावेश्य मनो ये मां नित्ययुक्ता उपासते ।
श्रद्धया परयोपेतास्ते मे युक्ततमा मता: ॥ (१२ । २)

Srikṛsna said:

Those who fixed their minds on Me, worship Me, ever earnest and possessed of supreme faith, I consider them most perfect in yoga.

(I consider sagunopasaka the best devotee).

ye tv akṣaram anirdes'yam
aryaktam paryupasate
sarvatragam acintyam ca
kutastham acalam dhruvam (3)

ये त्वक्षरमनिर्देश्यमव्यक्तं पर्युपासते ।
सर्वत्रगमचिन्त्यं च कूटस्थमचलं ध्रुवम् ॥ (१२ । ३)

samniyamye' ndriyagramam
sarvatra samabuddhyah
te prapnuvanti mam eva
sarvabhutahite ratah (4)

सन्नियम्येन्द्रियग्रामं सर्वत्र समबुद्धय: ।
ते प्राप्नुवन्ति मामेव सर्वभूतहिते रता: ॥ (१२ । ४)

kle'so dhikataras tesam
avyaktas or ktacetasam
avyakta hi gatir duhkham
dehavadbhir avapyate (5)

क्लेशोऽधिकतरस्तेषामव्यक्तासक्तचेतसाम् ।
अव्यक्ता हि गतिर्दु:खं देहवद्भिरवाप्यते ॥ (१२ । ५)

Those who worship Imperishable, unmanifest, undefinable, the omnipresent, the unthinkable, the unchanging, the constant by restraining all the senses, being even–minded in all conditions, rejoicing in the welfare of all creatures, they come to Me.

(Nirgunopasakas also come to Me (or are emancipated) like other devotees. Service to humanity is essential part of Nirgun disciplinenar seva Narayan seva-service of human is service of God).

But devotion to unmanifest (Nirgun upasna) is more difficult because the embodied beings cannot easily give–up body sense. This makes it difficult to reach the goal of the unmanifest.

2. Various Alternatives

ye tu sarvani karmani
mayi samnyasya matparah
ananyenai va yogena
mam dhyayanta upasate (6)

ये तु सर्वाणि कर्माणि मयि सन्न्यस्य मत्पराः।
अनन्येनैव योगेन मां ध्यायन्त उपासते॥ (१२।६)

tesam aham samuddharta
mrtyusamsarasagarat
bhavami nacirat partha
mayy avesitacetasam (7)

तेषामहं समुद्धर्ता मृत्युसंसारसागरात्।
भवामि नचिरात्पार्थ मय्यावेशितचेतसाम्॥ (१२।७)

mayy eva mana adhasva
mayi buddhim nivesaya
nivasisyasi mayy eva
ata urdhvam na samsayah (8)

मय्येव मन आधत्स्व मयि बुद्धिं निवेशय।
निवसिष्यसि मय्येव अत ऊर्ध्वं न संशयः॥ (१२।८)

atha cittam samadhatum
na saknosi mayi sthiram
abhyasayogena tato
mam iccha ptum dhanamjaya (9)

अथ चित्तं समाधातुं न शक्नोषि मयि स्थिरम्।
अभ्यासयोगेन ततो मामिच्छासुं धनंञ्जय॥ (१२।९)

abhyase py asamartho st
matkarmaparamo bhava
madartham api karmani
kurvan siddhim avapsyasi (10)

अभ्योसेऽप्यसमर्थोऽसि मत्कर्मपरमो भव।
मदर्थमपि कर्माणि कुर्वन्सिद्धिमवाप्स्यासि॥ (१२।१०)

athai tad apy asakto si
kartum madyogam asritah
sarvakarmaphalatyagam
tatah kuru yatatmavan (11)

अथैतदप्यशक्तोऽसि कर्तुं मद्योगमाश्रित:।
सर्वकर्मफलत्यागं तत: कुरू यतात्मवान्॥ (१२।११)

streyo hi jnanam abhyasaj
jnanad dhyanam visisyate
dhyanat karmaphalatyagas
tyagac chantir anantaram (12)

श्रयो हि ज्ञानमभ्यासाज्ज्ञानाद्ध्यानं विशिष्यते।
ध्यानात्कर्मफलत्यागस्त्यागाच्छान्तिरनन्तरम्॥ (१२।१२)

I straightaway deliver from the ocean of death–bound existence (I grant emancipation) to those who lay all their actions on Me, intent on Me, worship and meditate on Me with firm devotion and thoughts set on Me. You fix your mind on Me exclusively. Let your understanding dwell in Me. In Me alone you will live thereafter. There is no doubt about it.

If you find it difficult to fix your thought steadily on Me, then seek to reach Me by the practice of concentration (on Me).

If you find difficulty in concentration on Me, then make my service as your Supreme goal. Perform all actions for Me. You will attain perfection.

If you are not able to do even this, then take refuge in Me and renounce the fruits of all your actions with the self–subdued.

Knowledge is better than the practice (of concentration); better than knowledge is meditation; better than meditation is the renunciation of fruits of action because peace follows immediately after renunciation of fruits of action.

(Devotion is better than knowledge and detached action is better than devotion. Peace is very foundation of spiritual life which is gained easily by detachment to fruits).

3. Qualities of A True Devotee

advesta sarvabhutanam
maitrah karuna eva ca
nirmamo nirahamkarah
samaduhkhasukhah ksami (13)

अद्वेष्टा सर्वभूतानां मैत्रः करुण एव च।
निर्ममो निरहङ्कारः समदुःखसुखः क्षमी॥ (१२।१३)

samtustah satatam yogi
yatatma drdhaniscayah
mayy arpitamanobuddhir
yo madbhaktah sa me priyah (14)

सन्तुष्टः सततं योगी यतात्मा दृढनिश्चयः।
मय्यर्पितमनोबुद्धिर्यो मद्भक्तः स मे प्रियः॥ (१२।१४)

yasman no dvijate loko
lokan no dvijate ca yah
harsamarsabhayodvegair
mukto yah sa ca me priyah (15)

यस्मान्नोद्विजते लोको लोकान्नोद्विजते च यः।
हर्षाम र्षभयोद्वेगैर्मुक्तो यः स च मे प्रियः॥ (१२।१५)

anapeksah sucir daksa
udasino gatavyathah
sarvarambhaparityagi
yo madbhaktah sa me priyah (16)

अनपेक्षः शुचिर्दक्ष उदासीनो गतव्यथः।
सर्वारम्भपरित्यागी यो मद्भक्तः स मे प्रियः॥ (१२।१६)

yo na hrsyati na dvesti
na socati na kanksati
subhasubhaparityagi
bhaktiman yah sa me priyah (17)

यो न हृष्यति न द्वेष्टि न शोचति न काङ्क्षति ।
शुभाशुभपरित्यागी भक्तिमान्य: स मे प्रिय: ॥ (१२ । १७)

samah satrau ca mitre ca
tatha manapamanayoh
sitosnasukhaduhkhesu
samah sangavivarjitah (18)

सम: शत्रो च मित्रे च तथा मानापमानयो: ।
शीतोष्णसुखदु:खेषु सम: सङ्गविवर्जित: ॥ (१२ । १८)

tulyanindastutir mauni
samtusto yena kenacit
aniketah sthiramatir
bhaktiman me priyo narah (19)

तुल्यनिन्दास्तुतिर्मौनी सन्तुष्टो येन केनचित् ।
अनिकेत: स्थिरमतिर्भक्तिमान्मे प्रियो नर: ॥ (१२ । १९)

ye tu dharmyamrtam dam
yathoktam paryupasate
sraddhadhana mat parama
bhaktas te tiva me priyah (20)

ये तु धर्म्यामृतमिदं यथोक्तं पर्युपासते ।
श्रद्दधाना मत्परमा भक्तास्तेऽतीव मे प्रिया: ॥ (१२ । २०)

1. He has no ill–will towards any being.
2. He is friendly and compassionate.
3. He is free from ego and self–sense (ahmkara)
4. He is even–minded in all duals.
5. He has patience.
6. He is ever–content.
7. He is self–controlled.
8. He has firm determination.
9. He is free from fear and agitation.
10. He does not become source of grief to anyone and is also not grieved by any body.
11. He has no expectation.
12. He is pure and skilful in action.
13. He is unconcerned and untroubled.
14. He has given–up initiative but accepts duty as Dharma and does it excellently.

15. He neither hates nor rejoices.
16. He has renounced good and evil.
17. He behaves alike to foe and friend.
18. He is not affected by good and bad repute.
19. He is free from all duals and attachments.
20. He holds equal blame and praise.
21. He is silent(restrained in speech).
22. He is content with whatever comes to him.
23. He has no fixed abode.
24. He is firm in mind

A person with the above– stated qualities is a true devotee and is dear to the God.

(A comparison of verses 13–20 chapter 12 with verses 55–72 chapter 2–qualities of a Buddhi yogi will reveal that qualities of a devotee and a buddhi yogi are very much similar. Devotion leads to buddhi as per verse 2 chapter 10).

But those who with faith, holding Me as Supreme aim, follow this immortal wisdom, such devotees are very dear to Me.

Thus, chapter 12 entitled,"*bhakti yoga* (The yoga of devotion) is over.

SUMMARY

Devotion to personal God/Is'vara(sagunopasana) is easy as compared to devotion to the unmanifest (Nirgunopasana) because the latter requires giving up attachment to body which is not easy.

One can attain to God in three alternative ways–

(1) Concentrate on Him (God)

(2) Service to God–All actions are in service of God.

(3) Renounce fruits of your actions and take refuge in Him (God).

Detachment gives instant peace. Therefore, it is the best form of devotion. In fact, it is also the knowledge (buddhi yoga). It brings out excellent performance. It makes you very dear to the God. Cultivate qualites of a good devotee in order to be an excellent performer. These are the same as those of a buddhi yogi.

Chapter12 'Bhakti Yoga' gives three important keys to excellent performance with emotional stability:–

(1) Concentration on Work/Task/Mission.

(2) Consider duty as service to God (or CEO). This is the foundation of 'Servant concept of Leadership.' This gives commitment.

(3) Detached Action–Main source of inspiration. This is anti-thesis of Western concept of motivation and incentives.

FIELD AND ITS KNOWER

Contents

Arjuna requests Kṛsna to give him knowledge of field and its knower, object of knowledge, etc. Answer given by to these queries is the subject–matter of chapter 13.

1. Human body as field and God as its knower

sribhagavan uvaca
idam sariram kaunteya
kṣetram ity abhidhiyate
etad yo vetti tam prahuh
kṣetrajna ititadvidah (1)

श्रीभगवानुवाच
इदं शरीरं कौन्तेय क्षेत्रमित्यभिधीयते ।
एतद्यो वेत्ति तं प्राहुः क्षेत्रज्ञ इति तद्विदः ॥ (१३।१)

O Arjuna, this body (human physical body) is called the 'field' who knows this body is called 'knower'

ksetrajnam ca pi mam viddhi

sarvaksetresu bharata
ksetraksetrajnayor jnanam
yat taj jnanam matam mama. (2)

क्षेत्रज्ञं चापि मां विद्धि सर्वक्षेत्रेषु भारत।
क्षेत्रक्षेत्रज्ञयोर्ज्ञानं यत्तज्ज्ञानं मतं मम॥ (१३।२)

O, Bharata (Arjuna), know Me as knower of the field in all fields. knowledge of the field (Body) and its knower (God) is true knowledge.

tat ksetram yacca yadrk ca
yadvikari yatas ca yat
sa ca yo yatprabhavas' ca
tat samasena me s'rnu (3)

तत्क्षेत्रं यच्च यादृक्च यद्विकारि यतश्च यत्।
स च यो यत्प्रभावश्च तत्समासेन मे शृणु॥ (१३।३)

Hear from Me briefly now what the field is, of what nature, what its modifications are, when it is, what he (the knower of the field) is and what are his powers.

2. The Constituents of the Field

rsibhir bahudha gitam
candobhir vividhaih prathak
brahmasutrapadais' cai' va
hetumadbhir viniscitaih (4)

ऋषिभिर्बहुधा गीतं छन्दोभिर्विविधैः पृथक्।
ब्रह्मसूत्रपदैश्चैव हेतुमद्भिर्विनिश्चितैः॥ (१३।४)

This has been sung by sages in many ways and distinctly, in various hymns/*chandas* (of vedas, upanisads) and also in well–reasoned and conclusive expressions of Brahmasutra.

(Thus, Gita teacher Krsna restates the knowledge sung by sages, contained in vedas, upanisads and Brahmasutra).

mahabhutany ahamkaro
buddhir avyaktam eva ca
indriyani das'ai' kam ca
panca ce ndriyagocarah (5)

महाभूतान्यहङ्कारो बुद्धिरव्यक्तमेव च।
इन्द्रियाणि दशैकं च पञ्च चेन्द्रियगोचराः॥ (१३।५)

Five major or gross elements–earth, water, fire, air, ether self–sense (ahmkar), understanding as also the unmanifested, the ten senses–five of action and five of knowledge–mind and the five objects of senses are the constituents of the field (body).

iccha dvesah sukham duhkham
samghatas' cetana dhrtih
etat ksetram samasena
savidaram udahrtam (6)

इच्छा द्वेषः सुखं दुःखं सङ्घातश्चेतना धृतिः।
एतत्क्षेत्रं समासेन सविकारमुदाहृतम्॥ (१३।६)

Desire and hatred, pleasure and pain, the aggregate (the organism), intelligence and steadfastness is the field along with its modifications. (These are controllble variables. Therefore, these are called modifications. Suffering is the process through which we struggle to realise our true nature/form).

3. Knowledge (Janana)

amanitvam adambhitvam
ahimsa ksantir arjavam
acaryopasanam saucam
sthairyam atmavinigrah (7)

अमानित्वमदम्भित्वमहिंसा क्षान्तिरार्जवम्।
आचार्योपासनं शौचं स्थैर्यमात्मविनिग्रहः॥ (१३।७)

indriyarthesu vairagyam
anahamkara eva ca
janmamrtyujaravyadhi
duhkhadosanudars'anam (8)

इन्दियार्थेषु वैराग्यमनहङ्कार एव च।
जन्ममृत्युजराव्याधिदुःखदोषानुदर्शनम्॥ (१३।८)

asaktir anabhisvangah
putradaragrhadisu
nityam ca samacittat'vam
istanistopapattisu (9)

असक्तिरनाभिष्वङ्गः पुत्रदारगृहादिषु।
पित्यं च समचित्तत्वमिष्टोपपत्तिषु॥ (१३।९)

mayi ca nanyayogena
bhaktir avyabhicarini
viviktades'asevitvam
aratir janasamsadi (10)

मयि चानन्ययोगेन भक्तिरव्यभिचारिणी।
विविक्तदेशसेवित्वमरतिर्जनसंसदि॥ (१३।१०)

adhyatmaj nananityatvam
tattvajnanarthadars'anam
etaj jnanam iti proktam
ajnanam yed ato' nyatha (11)

अध्यात्मज्ञाननित्यत्वं तत्त्वज्ञानार्थदर्शनम्।
एतज्ज्ञानमिति प्रोक्तमज्ञानं यदतोऽन्यथा॥ (१३।११)

yaj jaatva mrtam as'nute
anadimat param brahma
na sat tan na sad ucyate (12)

ज्ञेयं यत्तत्प्रवक्ष्यामि यज्ज्ञात्वामृतमश्नुते।
अनादिमत्परं ब्रह्म न सत्तन्नासदुच्यते॥ (१३।१२)

Humility, integrity, non–violence, patience, uprightness, service of the teacher, purity (of body and mind), steadfastness, self-control, indifference to the objects of sense, self-effacement and perception of the evil of birth, old-age, sickness, pain and death, non-attachment, absence of clinging to son, wife, home and the like, constant equal mindedness to all desirable and undesirable happenings, firm devotion to Me with whole–hearted discipline, resort to solitary places, dislike of crowd of people, constancy in the knowledge of the spirit, insight into the end of knowledge of turth, this is declared to be (true) knowledge. All that is different from it is non-knowledge.

(Moral qualities practised are called knowledge).

I will now describe that which is to be known and by knowing which life eternal is gained. It is Supreme Brahma (*param brahma*) who has no beginning and who is said to be neither existent nor non–existent.

4. The knower of the field (God)

sarvatahpani padam tat
sarvatoksisiromukham
sarvatahs'rutimal loke
sarvam avrtya tisthati (13)

सर्वत:पाणिपादं तत्सर्वतोऽक्षिशिरोमुखम्।
सर्वत: श्रुतिमंल्लोके सर्वम् अर्वत्या तुष्ठति
एतज्ज्ञानमिति प्रोक्तमज्ञानं यदतोऽन्यथा॥ (१३।१३)

sarvendriyagunabhsam
sarvandriyavivarjitam
asaktam sarvabhrc caiva
nirgunam gunabhoktr ca (14)

सर्वेन्द्रियगुणाभासं सर्वेन्द्रियविवर्जितम्।
असक्तं सर्वभृच्चैव निर्गुणं गुणभोक्तृ च॥ (१३।१४)

bahir antas' ca bhutanam
acaram caram eva ca
suksmatvat tad avijneyam
durastham ca' ntike ca tat (15)

बहिरन्तश्च भूतानामचरं चरमेव च।
सूक्ष्मत्वात्तदविज्ञेयं दूरस्थं चान्तिके च तत्॥ (१३।१५)

avibhaktam ca bhutesu
vibhaktam iva ca sthitam
bhutabhartar ca taj jneyam
grasisnu prabhavisnu ca (16)

अविमक्तं च भूतेषु विभक्तमिव च स्थितम्।
भूतभर्तृ च तज्ज्ञेयं ग्रसिष्णु प्रभविष्णु च॥ (१३। १६)

jyotisam api taj jyotis
tamasah param ucyate
jnanam jneyam jnanagamyam
hrdi sarvasya dhisthitam (17)

ज्योतिषामपि तज्ज्योतिस्तमसः परमुच्यते।
ज्ञानं ज्ञेयं ज्ञानगम्यं हृदि सर्वस्य विष्टितम्॥ (१३। १७)

With his hands and feet everywhere, with eyes, heads and faces on all sides, with ears on all sides, He (God) dwells in the world, enveloping all. He appears to have the qualities of all senses and yet is without (any of) the senses, unattached yet supporting all, free from the *gunas* and yet enjoying them, He is without and within all–beings. He is unmoving as also moving. He is too subtle to be known. He is very far away and yet very near. He is indivisible and yet divided among beings. He is supporting creatures, destroying them and creating them afresh. He is the light of lights, said to be beyond darkness. He is knowledge, the object of knowledge and the goal of knowledge-He is seated in the hearts of all.

(God is of two types–one bound by three modes of nature, residing in the hearts of all–beings is called 'Soul' (*atmaram*) of '*ksetrajna.*' In this form, He is very near to all. When '*ksetrajna*' becomes free from three modes of nature, it is called '*param brahma*'. He is very far off and invisible, although soul is his part and both are imperishable).

Many of these verses explaining God are found in various *upanisads*.

(Put in management parlance, Leader dwells in the whole organisation. He is supporting all and yet is independent. His delegated authority runs throughout the organisational structure (all tiers of management) yet all authority and power rests in him. He performs the act of constructive destruction (innovational). He is the supreme power, light, knowledge and authority)

5. The Fruits of Knowledge

iti ksetram tatha jnanam
jneyam co'ktam samasatah
madbhakta etad vijnaya
madbhavayo' papadyate (18)

इति क्षेत्रं तथा ज्ञानं ज्ञेयं चोक्तं समासतः ।
मद्भक्त एतद्विज्ञाय मद्भवायोपपद्यते ॥ (१३ । १८)

By understanding knowledge of *ks'etra*, knowledge and the object of knowledge, My devotee will become worthy of Me.

(He will attain Me. Be liberated/emancipated by this knowledge).

6. Nature and Spirit

prakrtim purusam cai va
viddhy anadi ubhav api
vikarmas ca gunams cai va
viddhi prakrtisambhavan (19)

प्रकृतिं पुरुषं चैव विद्ध्यनादी उभावपि ।
विकारांश्च गुणांश्चैव विद्धि प्रकृतिसम्भवान् ॥ (१३ । १९)

karya karana kartrtve
hetuh prakrtir ucyate
purusah sukhaduhkhanam
bhoktrve hetur ucyate (20)

कार्यकरणकर्तुत्वे हेतुः प्रकृतिरुच्यते ।
पुरुषः सुखदुःखानां भोक्तृत्वे हेतुरुच्यते ॥ (१३ । २०)

purusah prakrtistho hi
bhunkte prakrtijan gunan
karanam gunasango sya
sadasadyonijanmasu (21)

पुरुषः प्रकृतिस्थो हि भुङ्क्ते प्रकृतिजान्गुणान् ।
कारणं गुसङ्गोऽस्य सदासद्योनिजान्मसु ॥ (१३ । २१)

upadrasta numanta ca
bharta bhokta mahesvarah
paramatme ti ca py ukto
dehe smin purusah parah. (22)

उपद्रष्टानुमन्ता च भर्ता भोक्ता महेश्वरः।
परमात्मेति चाप्युक्तो देहेऽस्मिन्पुरुषः परः॥ (१३। २२)

ya evam vetti purusam
prakrtim ca gunaih saha
sarvatha vartamano pi
na sa bhuyo bhijayate (23)

य एवं वेत्ति पुरुषं प्रकृतिं च गुणैः सह।
सर्वथा वर्तमानोऽपि न स भूयोऽभिजायते॥ (१३। २३)

You must know that *prakrati* (nature) and *purusa* (soul) are both beginningless. The forms and modes are born of *prakrati*.

(*Prakrati* and *purusa* are the inferior and superior forms of the Same Supreme God).

Nature is said to be the cause of effect, instrument and agent and the soul is said to be the cause, in regard to the experience of pleasure and pain.

(The body and senses are produced by nature and experience of pleasure and pain is by soul subject to certain limitations. The pure and blissful nature of soul is stained by joy and sorrow due to its identification with the objects of nature or senses.)

The soul in nature enjoys the modes of nature. Attachment to the modes of nature is the cause of its birth in various wombs. The soul acts as witness, the permitter, the supporter the experiencer, the great Lord and the Supreme Self. (Knower of the field and the Supreme Lord are the same – *atma so parmatma* soul is the Supreme God as per Gita.)

He who knows soul and nature together with the modes, he will not be reborn even if acting in every way.

7. Different ways to Salvation

dhyanena tmani pasyanti
kecid atmanam atmana
anye samkhyena yogena
karmayogena ca pare (24)

ध्यानेनात्मनि पश्यन्ति केचिदात्मानमात्मना।
अन्ये साङ्ख्येन योगेन कर्मयोगेन चापरे॥ (१३। २४)

anye tv evam ajanantah
strutva nyebhya upasate
te pi ca titaranty eva
mrtyum srutiparayanah (25)

अन्ये त्वेवमजानन्त: श्रुत्वान्येभ्य उपासते।
तेऽपि चातितरन्त्येव मृत्युं श्रुतिपरायणा: ॥ (१३।२५)

yavat samjayate kimcit
sattvam sthavarajangamam
ksetraksetrajnasamyogat
tad viddhi braratarsabha (26)

यावत्सञ्जायते किञ्चित्सत्त्वं स्थावरजङ्गमम्।
क्षेत्रक्षेत्रज्ञसंयोगात्तद्विद्धि भरतर्षभ ॥ (१३।२६)

samam sarvesu bhutesu
tisthantam paramesvaram
vinasyatsu avinasyantam
yah pasyati sa pasyati (27)

समं सर्वेषु भूतेषु तिष्ठन्तं परमेश्वरम्।
विनश्यत्स्वविनश्यन्तं य: पश्यति स पश्यनि ॥ (१३।२७)

samam pasyan hi sarvatra
samavasthitam isvaram
na hinasty atmana tmanam
tato yati param gatim (28)

समं पश्यन्हि सर्वत्र समवस्थितमीश्वरम्।
न हिनस्त्यात्मनात्मानं ततो याति परां जतिम् ॥ (१३।२८)

prakrtyai va ca karmani
kriyamanani sarvasah
yah pasyati tatha tmanam
akartaram sa pasyati (29)

प्रकृत्यैव च कर्माणि क्रियमाणानि सर्वश:।
य: पश्चति तथात्मानमकर्तारं स पश्यति ॥ (१३।२९)

yada bhutaprthagbhavam
ekastham anupasyati
tata eva ca vistaram
brahma sampadyate tada (30)

यदा भूतपृथग्भावमेकस्थमनुपश्यति ।
तत एव च विस्तारं प्रह्म सम्पद्यते तदा ॥ (१३ । ३०)

anaditvan nirgunatvat
paramatma yam avyayah
sarirastho pi kaunteya
na karoti na lipyate (31)

अनादित्वान्निर्गुणत्वात्परमात्मायमव्ययः ।
शरीरस्थोऽपि कौन्तेय न करोति न लिप्यते ॥ (१३ । ३१)

yatha sarvagatam sauksmyad
akasam no palipyate
sarvatra vasthito dehe
tatha tma no palipyate (32)

यथा सर्वगतं सौक्ष्म्यादाकाशं नोपलिप्यते ।
सर्वत्रावस्थितो देहे तथात्मा नोपलिप्यते ॥ (१३ । ३२)

yatha prakasayaty ekah
kritsnam lokam imam ravih
ksetram ksetri tatha kritsnani
prakasayati bharata (33)

यथा प्रकाशयत्येकः कृत्स्नं लोकमिमं रविः ।
क्षेत्रं क्षेत्री तथा कृत्स्नं प्रकाशयति भारत ॥ (१३ । ३३)

ksetraksetrajnayor evam
antaram jnanacaksusa
bhutaprakrtimoksam ca
ye vidur yanti te param (34)

क्षेत्रक्षेत्रज्ञयोरेवमन्तरं ज्ञानचक्षुषा ।
भूतप्रकृतिमोक्षं च ये विदुर्यान्ति ते परम् ॥ (१३ । ३४)

By meditation some perceive the self in the self by the self.

By path of knowledge (Buddhi Yoga).

By path of action (Karma Yoga)

By worshipping God as they have heard from authority/Guru.

O Arjuna, all moving and unmoving beings are sprung through the union of the field and the knower of the field. (when self is known as separated from body, self–realisation takes place.)

He who sees the Supreme God abiding equally in all–beings will never perish. (God lives and endures even when the universe ceases to exit). He sees the God present equally everywhere and this does not injure his true self by the self. Then he attains the Supreme (God).

When he sees the manifold state of beings is centred in the one (God) and from just that it spreads out, he attains the Supreme God *(parbrahma)*.

Because this Supreme Self is imperishable without beginning, without qualities so O Arjuna, though it resides in the body, it neither acts nor is tainted like ether which is all pervading and untainted.

O Arjuna, as the one sun illuminates this whole world, so does the Lord of field (soul) illuminate this entire field. Those who perceive this by their eye of widsom the distinction between the field (body) and the knower of the field (soul/God), and the deliverance of beings from nature, they attain the Supreme, (God/emancipation).

Thus, chapter 13 entitled, '*Ksetra ksetrajnavibhag yoga.*' (the yoga of the distinction between the field and the knower of the field) is over.

Summary

Human body made of five major elements (earth, air, water, fire, ether) and self-sense (ahmkar), *mind, ten sensuary organs (five action and five knowledge organs with five sense objects) is called field* or ksetra. *Desire, hatred, pleasure and pain, the aggregate (organism), intelligence and steadfastness are modifications to this field or controllable variables.*

Moral qualities practised are called knowledge. It is described in vedas upanisads. *The God is the knower of this field. He resides in the heart of all creations called "soul", bound by nature, it takes rebirth in various wombs. It is called* 'Ksetragya' *(knower of the field). When it is freed from three modes of nature it is liberated and is called* Purusottama. *God is the top leader/CEO of the organisation–supreme light, power, knowledge and authority.*

Body and senses are produced by nature but experience of pleasure and pain is by soul bound by nature. Self-realisation will take place when body and soul are seen separate from each other. Soul is not the doer. It is only witness. Actual doer is nature. Those who know this they attain God/emancipation.

(Body and senses be controlled to make soul pure and obtain excellent performance.)

THREE MODES OF NATURE

Contents

1. The Supreme Wisdom

Sribhagavan uvaca
param bhayah pravaksyami
jnananam jnanam uttamam
yaj jnatva munayah sarve
param sidhim its gatah (1)

श्रीभगवानुवाच
परं भूय: प्रवक्ष्यामि ज्ञानानां ज्ञानमुत्तमम् ।
यज्ज्ञात्वा मुनय: सर्वे; परां सिद्धिमितो गता: ॥ (१४ । १)

Srikṛsna said:

"Now I shall tell you that supreme wisdom, the best wisdọm, by knowing which all sages have attained to the best perfection (excellence).

idam Jnanam upasritya
mama sadharmyam agatah
sarge pi no prajayante
pralaye na vyathanti ca (2)

इदं ज्ञानमुपाश्रित्य मम साधर्म्यमागताः ।
सर्गेऽपि नोपजायन्ते प्रलये न व्यथन्ति च ॥ (१४ । २)

This super wisdom makes one like Me, (of qualities similar to Me) they are not born of the time of creation; nor are they disturbed at the time of dissolution.

mama yonir mahad brahma
tasmin garbham dadhamy aham
samibhavah sarvabhutanam
tato bhavati bharata (3)

मम योनिर्महद्ब्रह्म तस्मिन्गर्भं दधाम्यहम् ।
सम्भवः सर्वभूतानां ततो भवति भारत ॥ (१४ ।३)

O Bharata (Arjuna), the great Brahma (*prakrati*) is my womb, in that I cast the seed from which all–beings are born.

sarvayonisu kaunteya
murtayah sambhavanti yah
tasam brahma mahjad yonir
aham bijapuadah pita (4)

सर्वयोनिषु कौन्तेय मूर्तयः सम्भवन्ति याः ।
तासां ब्रह्म महद्योनिरहं बीजप्रदः पिता ॥ (१४ । ४)

O Arjuna, whatever forms of beings are produced in any wombs,the great Brahma (nature) is their womb and I am the father who casts the seed.

(All–beings of this universe are created by the God and nature as father and mother. Nature alone can't create unless soul is provided by the God. All–beings have the same parentage. Therefore, all must be treated with equality. If this is realised and practised, most of the problems of society and organisations will get resolved and man with such equality of mind will attain to the status of God).

2. Three Modes of Nature (Gunas)

sattvam rajas tama iti
gunah prakrtisambhavah
nibadhnanti mahabaho
dehe dehinam avyayam (5)

सत्त्वं रजस्तम इति गुणाः प्रकृतिसम्भवाः ।
निबध्नन्ति महाबाहो देहे देहिनमव्ययम् ॥ (१४।५)

tatra sattvam nirmaatvat
prakasakam anamayam
sukhasangena badhnati
jnanasangena ca nagha (6)

तत्र सत्त्वं निर्मलत्वात्प्रकाशकमनामयम् ।
सुखसङ्गेन बध्नाति ज्ञानसङ्गेन चानघ ॥ (१४।६)

rajo ragatmakam viddhi
trsnasangasamudbhavam
tan nibadhnati kaunteya
karmasangena dehinam (7)

रजो रागात्मकं विद्धि तृष्णासङ्गसमुद्भवम् ।
तन्निबध्नाति कौन्तेय कर्मसङ्गेनदेहिनम् ॥ (१४।७)

tamas tv ajnanajam viddhi
mohanam sarvadehinam
pramadalasyanidrabhis
tan nibadhnati bharata (8)

तमस्त्वज्ञानजं विद्धि मोहनं सर्वदेहिनेम् ।
प्रमादालस्यनिद्राभिस्तन्निबध्नाति भारत ॥ (१४।८)

sattvam sukhe sanjayati
rajah karmani bharata
jnanam avrtya tu tamah
pramade sanjayaty uta (9)

सत्त्वं सुखे सञ्जयति रजः कर्माणि भारत ।
ज्ञानमावृत्य तु तमः प्रमादे सञ्जयत्युत ॥ (१४।९)

rajas tamas ca bhibhuya
sattvam bhavati bharata
rajah sattvam tamas cai va
tamah sttvam rajas tatha (10)

रजस्तमश्चाभिभूय सत्त्वं भवति भारत।
रजः सत्त्वं तमश्चैव तमः सत्त्वं रजस्तथा॥ (१४।१०)

sarvadvaresu dehe smin
prakasa upajayate.
inanam yada tada vidyad
vivrddham sattvam ity uta (11)

सर्वद्वारेषु देहेऽस्मिन्प्रकाश उपजाते।
ज्ञानं यदा तदा विद्याद्विवृद्धं सत्त्वमित्युत॥ (१४।११)

lobhah pravrttir arambhah
karmanam asamah sprha
rajasy etani jayante
vivrddhe bharatarsabha (12)

लोभः प्रवृत्तिरारम्भः कर्मणामशमः स्पृहा।
रजस्येतानि जायन्ते विवृद्धे भरतर्षभ॥ (१४।१२)

aprakaso pravrttis ca
pramado moha eva ca
tamasy etani jayante
vivrddhe kurunandana (13)

अप्रकाशोऽप्रवृत्तिश्च प्रमादो मोह एव च।
तमस्येतानि जायन्ते विवृद्धे कुरुनन्दन॥ (१४।१३)

yada sattve poravraddhe tu
pralayam yaati dehabhrt
tado ttamavidam lokan
amalan pratipadyate (14)

यदा सत्त्वे प्रवृद्धे तु प्रलयं याति देहभृत्।
तदोत्तमविदां लोकानमलान्प्रतिपद्यते॥ (१४।१४)

rajasi pralayam gatva
karmasangisu jayate
tatha pralinas tamasi
mudhayonisu jayate (15)

रजसि प्रलयं गत्वा कर्मसङ्गिषु जायते ।
तथा प्रलीनस्तमसि मूढयोनिषु जायते ॥ (१४ । १५)

karmanah sukrtasya huh
sattvikam nirmalam phallam
rajasa tu phalam duhkham
ajnanam tamasah phalam (16)

कर्मण: सुकृतस्याहु: सात्त्विकं निर्मलं फलम् ।
रजसस्तु फलं दु:खमज्ञानं तमस: फलम् ॥ (१४ । १६)

sattvat samjayate jnanam
rajaso lobha eva ca
pramadamohau tamaso
bhavato jnanam eva ca (17)

सत्त्वात्सञ्जायते ज्ञानं रजसो लोभ एव च ।
प्रमादमोहौ तमसो भवतोऽज्ञानमेव च ॥ (१४ । १७)

urdhavam gacchanti sattvastha
madhye tisthanti rajasah
jaghanyagunavrtistha
adho gacchanti tamasah (18)

ऊर्ध्वं गच्छन्ति सत्त्वस्था मध्ये तिष्ठन्ति राजसा: ।
जघन्यगुणवृत्तिस्था अधो गच्छन्ति तामसा: ॥ (१४ । १८)

na nyam gunebhyah kartaram
yadạ drasta nupasyati
gunebhyas ca param vetti
madbhavam so shigacchati (19)

नान्यं गुणेभ्य: कर्तारं यदा द्रष्टानुपश्यति ।
गुणेभ्यश्च परं वेत्ति मद्भावं सोऽधिगच्छति ॥ (१४ । १९)

gunan etan atitya trin
dehi dehasamudbhavan
janmamrtyujaraduhkhair
vimukto mrtam asrute (20)

गुणानेतानतीत्य त्रीन्देही देहसमुद्भवान् ।
जन्ममृत्युजरादुःखैर्विमुक्तोऽमृतमश्नुते ॥ (१४।२०)

The three modes (*gunas*) are purity or goodness (*sattva*), passion or action (*rajas*), dullness or idleness (*tamas*). These are born of nature/attitude and bind down soul in body, O Arjuna.

(The immortal, imperishable soul binds in the body and is caught in the cycle of birth and death due to power of modes of nature or gunas).

(*Sattva* is radiance. It is identified with Vishnu, the maintainer of the universe. *Rajas* is outward activity. It is identified with Brahma, the creator. *Tamas* is darkness, idleness, inaction decay and demise. It is identified with Siva. They are responsible for maintenance, creation and destruction/ dissolution of the universe. God wants redemption through God like souls (person of super wisdom). We can get rid of bondage of rebirth if we rise above three modes of nature.We become *Trigunatita*.

Sattva causes illumination and health. It binds (soul) by attachment to happiness and intellectual knowledge. (ego–sense remains. Pure consciousness does not come even with *sattva guna*).

O Arjuna, *Rajas* is the nature of attraction, springing from carving and attachment it binds fast the embodied soul by attachment to action.

(I am doer sense develops in *Rajas* which is the root cause of conflicts, stress and strain.)

O Arjuna, *Tamas* or dullness is born of ignorance and deludes all embodied beings. It binds soul by (developing the qualities of) negligence, indolence, sleep. *Sattva* attaches to happiness, *Rajas* to action and *Tamas* to negligence. *Sattva* prevails overpowering *Rajas* and *Tamas*. *Rajas* prevails overpowering *Sattva* and *Tamas*. *Tamas* prevails overpowering *Sattva* and *Rajas*.

(Thus, all human beings have three modes of nature in varying degrees as long-term, short-term, very short–term and random variables. Attitude may be long-term as well as situational or contingent attribute. *Satvic* temperament people are free, calm and selfless. They may have ego of peace and knowledge. They want appreciation of their qualities. *Rajsika* temperament people are active but full of ego sense of I am doer. They are selfish by nature. They want monetary and non–monetary rewards. They indulge in conflict and organisational politics. *Tamasik* temperament people are negligent, confused and ignorant. They need supervision and control to work even at the minimum level. They enjoy inaction, dullness, sleep. Better management of human resources can be done if managers can correctly classify their subordinates on the basis of three modes of nature and devise appropriate strategies to make them perform well.)

When the light of knowledge spreads in all the (nine) gates of the body, then know that *Sattva* is dominating. While greed, activity, actions, unrest, desires spring up, O Arjuna, then know that *Rajas* is dominating. When darkness of ignorance, inactivity, negligence, a mere delusion arise, O Arjuna, then know that *Tamas* is on rise.

(It means three modes of nature may vary in degree at different times/ situations. A good manager should be able to identify which *guna* is dominating and then devise appropriate tactics to take work from a subordinate).

(Destiny after death depends on dominance of a mode of nature at the moment of death.)

Death in *Sattva* takes soul to heaven. Death in *Rajas* takes one to instant rebirth in this mortal world. Death in *Tamas* will take soul to hell and/or rebirth in lower wombs–insects, immovable, etc. The fruit of *Rajas* is pain (stress, strain, conflict, illness, etc.) and the fruit of *Tamas* is ignorance (negligence/ punishment). Purity gives knowledge, passion gives greed and negligence and errors arise from ignorance and dullness.

Those who are firmly good and pure they rise upwards. They reach to the higher status/positions on the basis of their excellent performance. Those who are selfish performers, remain at middle--level position. Those who are negligent, commit mistakes, they sink downwards (demoted, discharged).

When it is realised that the three modes of nature are the only agents and who is beyond three modes, he attains to My–being. When the embodied soul rises above these three modes that springs from the body it is emancipated.

3. Qualities of Trigunatita

kair lingais trin gunan etan
atito bhavati prabho
kimacarah katham cai tams
trin gunan ativartate (21)

कैर्लिङ्गैस्त्रीन्गुणानेतानतीतो भवति प्रभो।
किमाचार: कथं चैतांस्त्रीन्गुणानतिवर्तते॥ (१४।२१)

shribhagavan uvaca
prakasam ca pravrttim ca
moham eva ca pandava
na dvesti sampravrttani
na nivrttani kanksati (22)

श्रीभगवानुवाच
प्रकाशं च प्रवृत्तिं च मोहमेव च पाण्डव।
न द्वेष्टि सम्प्रवृत्तानि न निवृत्तानि काङ्क्षति॥ (१४। २२)

udasinavad asino
gunair yo na vicalyate
guna vartanta ity eva
yo vatisthati ne ngate (23)

उदासीनवदासीनो गुणैर्यो न विचाल्यते।
गुणा वर्तन्त इत्येव योऽवतिष्ठति नेङ्गते॥ (१४। २३)

samaduhkhasukhah svasthah
samalostasmakancanah
tulyapriyapriyo dhiras
tulyanindatmasamstutih (24)

समदु:खसुख: स्वस्थ: समलोष्टाश्मकाञ्चन:।
तुल्यप्रियाप्रियो धीरस्तुल्यनिन्दात्मसंस्तुति:॥ (१४। २४)

manapamanayos tulyas
tulyo mitraripaksayoh
sarvarambhaparityagi
gunatitah sa ucyate (25)

मानापमानयोस्तुल्यस्तुल्यो मित्रारिपक्षयो:।
सर्वारम्भपरित्यागी गुणातीत: स उच्यते॥ (१४। २५)

mami ca yo vyabhicarena
bhaktiyogena sevate
sa gunan samatityai tan
brahmabhuyya kalpate (26)

मां च योऽव्यभिचारेण भक्तियोगेन सेवते।
स गुणान्समतीत्यैतान्ब्रह्मभूयाय कल्पते॥ (१४। २६)

brahmano hi pratistha ham
amrtasya vyayasya ca
sasvatasya ca dharmasya
sukhasyai kantikasya ca (27)

ब्रह्मणो हि प्रतिष्ठाहममृतस्याव्ययस्य च।
शाश्वतस्य च धर्मस्य सुखस्यैकान्तिकस्य च॥ (१४। २७)

Arjuna said:

O Lord (Krsna), by what marks/qualities a person beyond three modes of nature (*trigunatita*) is characterised? What is his way of life? How does he attain that position?

Sribhagavana said:

O Arjuna, he who does not abhor illumination, activity and delusion when they arise, nor desire them when they cease, he sits like one unconcerned, unperturbed by the modes (of nature), who stands apart, without wavering, knowing that it is only the modes that act. He regards pain and pleasure alike. He dwells in his self. He considers clod, stone and a piece of gold as of equal value. He remains even amongst the pleasant and unpleasant things. He is of firm mind. He regards praise and blame, honour and dishonour, friends and foes as the same. He does not initiate action. Such a person is called *trigunatita.*

"He who serves Me with firm devotion of love, rises above the three modes. He too is fit for becoming *Brahma* (liberated); for I am the abode of *Brahma* the Immortal and the Imperishable of eternal law and absolute bliss."

(If we compare qualities of Trigunatita with those of a devotee (XII, 13 f.f) and of *Buddhiyogi* or *Sthitaprajna* (II 55 f.f) we find them almost the same. From this, it is evident that the goal of liberation and excellence can be achieved through any one of these three ways. All of them are '*Jivanmuktas*". Getting any one leads to emergence of remaining two states.)

Since a thorn is pull out by another thorn, we should renounce world not by leaving it but by renouncing selfish goals and attachments. By *Sattva* we can overpower Rajas and Tamas and then we can renounce selfish goals, ego and any other attachment and go beyond *Sattva* attachment also. One should see mutations of nature but should not get entangled in them).

Thus, the chapter 14 entitled *Gunatryavibhag yoga* (the yoga of the differentiation of three modes of nature, the supreme wisdom) is over.

SUMMARY

Supreme wisdom gives excellence/perfection. It makes persons like God in qualities. They become free from birth and death. First, one should realise that all–beings are creations of God as father and nature as mother. The three modes of nature bind soul with body. These are– Sattva (pure) Rajas (action) and Tamas (ignorance, inaction, darkness). Some mode dominates other two modes.

Sattva gives illumination, happiness, promotion to top status. Rajas gives passion, action, selfishness, conflicts, strain and stress and promotion to middle–level status. Tamas gives idleness, ignorance, errors, punishment, demotion/discharge, etc. God wants redemption to be attained through persons of super wisdom. Liberating can be obtained by going beyond three modes of nature (trigunatita). For that Sattva aptitude is precondition.

Manager should identify and classify people on the basis of three modes of nature and devise human resource utilization strategies and tactics accordingly. Tamas attitude people work out of fear, Rajas attitude people work for monetary and non–monetary incentives (selfish motives) and Sattva attitude people work for a mission and recognition. Trigunatita is a liberated soul that works for self-realisation and takes duty as Dharma service of people. He is tree from self-sense.

Death in Sattva takes soul to heaven, in Rajas to rebirth in this world as human being and in Tamas to hell or rebirth in lower wombs. Death of trigunatitas leads them to empanicpation, merging soul in God.

Qualities of trigunatita are similar to those of a devotee and a stith prajna. Liberation and excellence can be attained by any one of the three ways. Attainment of any one state will lead to emergence of other two states. Observe mutations of nature but don't get entangled in them. This is super wisdom for attaining excellence in Management.

THE YOGA OF SUPREME PERSON

(THE MOST SECRET DOCTRINE)

Contents

1. The Cosmic Tree

sribhagwan uvaca
urdhvamulam adhahsakham
asvattham prahur avyayam
chandamsi yasya parnani
yas tam veda sa vedavit (1)

श्रीभगवानुवाच
ऊर्ध्वमूलमध:शाखमश्वत्थं प्राहुरव्ययम् ।
छन्दांसि यस्य पर्णानि यस्तं वेद स वेदवित् ॥ (१५ । १)

adhas co rdhavam prastas tasya sakha
gunapravrddha visayapravalah
adhas ca mulany anusamtatani
karmanubandhini manusyaloke (2)

अधश्चोर्ध्वं प्रसृतास्तस्य शाखा
गुणप्रवृद्धा विषयप्रवालाः ।
अधश्च मूलान्यनुसन्ततानि
कर्मानुबन्धीनि मनुष्यलोके ॥ (१५ । २)

na rupam asye ha tatho palabhyate
na' nto na ca dir na ca sampratistha
asvattham enam suvirudhamulam
asangasastrena drdhena chittva (3)

न रूपमस्येह तथोपलभ्यते
नान्तो न चादिर्न च सम्प्रतिष्ठा ।
अश्वत्थमेनं सुविरूढमूल–
मसङ्गशस्त्रेण दृढेन छित्त्वा ॥ (१५ । ३)

tatah padam tat parimargitavyam
yasmin gata na nivartanti bhuyah
tam eva ca dyam purusam prapadye
uatah pravriittih prastra purani (4)

ततः पदं तत्परिमार्गितव्यं–
यस्मिन्गता न निवर्तन्ति भूयः ।
तमेव चाद्यं पुरुषं प्रपद्ये
यतः प्रवृत्तिः प्रसृता पुराणी ॥ (१५ । ४)

nirmanamoha jitasangadosa
adhyatmanitya vinivrttakamah
dvandvair vimuktah sukhaduhkhasamjnair
gacchanty amudhah padam avyayam tat (5)

निर्मानमोहा जितसङ्गदोषा–
अध्यात्मनित्या विनिवृत्तकामाः ।
द्वन्द्वैर्विमुक्ताः सुखदुःखसञ्ज्ञै–
र्गच्छन्त्यमूढाः पदमव्ययं तत् ॥ (१५ । ५)

(This world is like an *asvastha* (*peepal*) tree which has its roots above and branches below. Its leaves are *Vedas* and who knows this is the knower of *Vedas*.

(As the world originates in God, it is said to have its roots "above" and as it extends into this world, its branches are said to go downwards. This world is a living organism united with the God. The world is sustained through *vedic* rituals. Therefore, *vedic* hymns are called its leaves which keep this imperishable tree green and growing.

Its branches extend below and above, nourished by three modes of nature, with sense objects for its twigs and below in this mortal world stretch forth the roots resulting in actions.

(Downward spreading roots are desires or *vasanas* which the soul carries as result of past deeds–*Samskara*)

The real form of cosmic tree is not perceived here, nor its end nor beginning nor its foundation (because it has origin above and branches below). Liberation/emanicipation can be sought by cutting off this firm rooted *asvastham* (*peepal*) tree by the strong sword of non–attachment. Say, "I seek refuge only in that primal person from whom this ancient current of the world (life) has originated".

People freed from pride and delusion, who have won the evil of attachment, whose all desires are stilled, who are always devoted to the supreme spirit, who are liberated from the dualities like pleasure and pain and who are not deluded go to that eternal state (of emancipation from rebirth, peace and supreme bliss).

2. The God as Life of the Universe

na tad bhasayate suryo
na sasanko na pavakah
yad gatva na nivartante
tad dhama paramam mama (6)

न तद्भासयते सूर्यो न शशाङ्को न पावक: ।
यद्गत्वा न निवर्तन्ते तद्धाम परमं मम ॥ (१५ । ६)

mamai va mso jivaloke
jivabhutah sanatanah
manahsasthanindriyani
prakrtisthani karsati (7)

ममैवांशो जीवलोके जीवभूत: सनातन: ।
मन:षष्ठानीन्द्रियाणि प्रकृतिस्थानि कर्षति ॥ (१५ । ७)

sariram yad avapnoti
yac ca py utkramati svarah
grhitvai tani samyati
vayur gandhar iva sayat (8)

शरीरं यदवाप्नोति यच्चाप्युत्क्रामतीश्वरः ।
गृहीत्वैतानि संयाति वायुर्गन्धानिवाशयात ॥ (१५ । ८)

srotram caksuh sparsanam ca
rasanam ghranam eva ca
adhisthaya manas ca yam
visayan upasevate (9)

श्रोत्रं चक्षुः स्पर्शनं च रसनं घ्राणमेव च।
अधिष्ठाय मनश्चायं विषयानुपसेवते ॥ (१५ । ९)

utkramantam sthitam va pi
bhunjanam va gunanvitam
vimudha nanupasyanti
pasyanti jnanacaksusah (10)

उत्क्रामन्तं स्थितं वापि भुञ्जानं वा गुणान्वितम् ।
विमुढा नानुपश्यन्ति पश्यन्ति ज्ञानचक्षुषः ॥ (१५ । १०)

yatanto yoginas cai nam
pasyanty atmany avasthitam
yatanto py akrtatmano
nainam pasyanty acetasah (11)

यतन्तो योगिनश्चैनं पश्यन्त्यात्मन्यवस्थितम् ।
यतन्तोऽप्यकृतात्मानो नैनं पश्यन्त्यचेतसः ॥ (१५ । ११)

yad adityagatam tejo
jagad bhasayate khilam
yac candramasi yac ca gnau
tat tejo viddhi mamakam (12)

यदादित्यगतं तेजो जगद्भासयतेऽखिलम् ।
यच्चन्द्रामसि यच्चाग्नौ तत्तेजो विद्धि मामकम् ॥ (१५ । १२)

gamavisya ca bhutani
dharayamy aham ojasa
pusnami cau sadhih saruah
somo bhutva rasatmakah (13)

गामाविश्य च भूतानि धारयाम्यहमोजसा ।
पुष्णामि चौषधी: सर्वा: सोमो भूत्वा रसात्मक: ॥ (१५ । १३)

aham vaisvanaro bhutva
praninam deham asritah
pranapanasamayuktah
pacamy annam caturvidham (14)

अहं वैश्वानरो भूत्वा प्राणिनां देहमाश्रित: ।
प्राणापानसमायुक्त: पचाम्यन्नं चतुर्विधम् ॥ (१५ । १४)

sarvasya ca ham hrdi samnivisto
mattah smritir jnanam apohanam ca
vedais ca sarvair aham eva vedyo
vedantakrd vedvid eva ca ham (15)

सर्वस्य चाहं हृदि सन्निविष्टो–
मत्त: स्मृतिर्ज्ञानमपोहनं च ।
वेदैश्च सर्वैरहमेव वेद्यो–
वेदान्तकृद्वेदविदेव चाहम् ॥ (१५ । १५)

The sun does not illumine that, nor the moon, nor the fire (it is self–illumined). It is my Supreme abode from which those who reach will never return.

(This verse is found in Katha up; V.15 mundaka up II 2–10).

A fragment (or fraction) of Mine self has become soul of living beings in this world. It draws to itself the senses of which mind is the sixth, that rest in nature.

(Human soul is a fragment of the Imperishable God. Therefore, it is also imperishable. But it is bound by sensuary organs and modes of nature. However, it serves as a bridge between this earth and other worlds. If freed from limitations/bondage of senses and modes of nature, it attains emancipation, bound by *sattva*, it attains heaven, bound by *rajas*, it attains rebirth in this world and bound by *tamas* it goes to hell or lower wombs. Self is a part of the Supreme just like space in an earthen jar or a house as part of the universal space. Ramanujacharya considers soul as ams'a of God. It assumes form of Jiva in some mode of nature. It expresses one aspect of multiple forms of divine consciousness. If we choose, it can attain the Supreme again by rising above senses and modes of nature).

When soul takes up a body and when it leaves it, He takes these (senses and mind) and goes even as the wind carries smell from earth. He enjoys the object of senses through eyes, the touch sense, the taste sense, the smell sense, (nose) as also the mind. When he departs, stays or experiences in contact with modes of nature, the deluded can't see (the soul). Only those who have eyes of wisdom can see (the soul).The sages striving perceive Him as established in the self but the unwise whose souls are not disciplined though striving, do not find Him (soul).

The splendour of the Sun that illuminates the whole world and the splendour that of Moon and Fire, known as Mine. My vital energy supports all–beings on earth. I nourish all herbs (plants) through becoming fire of life (*vaiswaner*) in the bodies of living creatures, mingling with the upward and downward breath (*udan, apan vayu*).

I am lodged in the hearts of all (*soul*). Memory and knowledge as well as their loss arise from Me. I am known by all the *vedas*, I am the author of *vedanta* and I am too the knower of *vedas*.

3. THE SUPREME PERSON

dvav imau purusau loke
ksaras ca' ksara eva ca
ksarah sarvani bhutani
kutastho' ksara ucyate (16)

द्वाविमौ पुरुषौ लोको क्षरंश्चाक्षर एव च।
क्षर: सर्वाणि भूतानि कूटस्थोऽक्षर उच्यते ॥ (१५।१६)

uttamah purusas tv anyah
paramatme ty udahrtah
yo lokairayam avisya
bibharaty avyaya isvarah (17)

उत्तम: पुरुषस्त्वन्य: परमात्मेत्युदाहृत:।
यो लोकत्रयमाविश्य बिभर्त्यव्यय ईश्वर: ॥ (१५।१७)

yasmat ksaram atiti ham
aksarad api co ttamah

ato smi loke vede ca
prathitah purusottamah (18)

यस्मात्क्षरमतीतोऽहमक्षरादपि चोत्तमः।
अतोऽस्मि लोके वेदे च प्रथितः पुरुषोत्तमः॥ (१५।१८)

yo mam evam asammudho
janati purusottamam
sa sarvavid bhajati mam
sarvadhavena bharata (19)

यो मामेवमसम्मूढो जानाति पुरुषोत्तमम्।
स सर्वविद्भजति मां सर्वभावेन भारत॥ (१५।१९)

iti guhyatamam sastram
idam uktam maya nagha
etad buddhva buddhiman syat
krtakrtyas ca bharata (20)

इति गुह्यतमं शास्त्रमिदमुक्तं मयानघ।
एतद्बुद्ध्वा बुद्धिमान्स्यात्कृतकृत्यश्च भारत॥(१५।२०)

There are two persons in this world. All existences are perishable, whereas (soul) is unchanging and imperishable. But other than these two there is Supreme person (*Purushottama*) who is undying and enters the three worlds and sustains them.

(This moving mortal world is the creation of the Supreme Lord. He maintains it. He is the Supreme person or Purushottama).

As I surpass the perishable and a higher even then the imperishable (soul), I am celebrated as the Supreme person in the world and in the *vedas*. Who undeluded knows Me as the Supreme person is the knower of all and worships Me with all his being, O Arjuna.

I have taught you this most secret doctrine. By knowing this, you will become wise and fulfil (discharge) all your duties, O Bharata (Arjuna).

This chapter 15, entitled "*Purushottam yoga*" (The yoga of the Supreme person) is over.

SUMMARY

The cosmic tree is a reverse asvasthah (peepal) *tree whose branches extend below and above, nourished by modes of nature and attachment to senses. It has origin in God. Therefore, emancipation or realisation of God is possible by its firm rooted branches by the strong sword of non–attachment. Self-realised (devotee, buddhi yogi, karma yogi) can have this liberation. The Supreme abode of God is self-illumined. One who obtains to it will never return to this world. Soul is the small frcgment of the God. It is bound to the body by modes of nature and attachments. If these bonds are crossed, soul will merge into the God and be liberated (from rebirth).*

*Soul entering body as well as leaving it carries nature and attachment just like air carries smell of earth with it. Soul can be seen by liberated sages only. God creates and manintains the world. It is Supreme person (*purusttama*), much above the perishable body and imperishable soul. It is fire of digestion in human body. Memory, knowledge and their loss are due to Him. This is the most secret doctrine.*

If you achieve some success, it is due to the grace of the Supreme Lord.

In management parlance, top management is Purushottam, middle management is Soul and operating management is Physical Body. All the three parts should be in harmony holistically in order to attain organisational effectiveness.

ABOUT DIVINE AND DEMONAIC PERSONS

Contents

1. Qualities of a Divine Person

sribhagwan uvaca
abhayam sattvasamshuddhir
jnanayogavyavasthitih
danam damas ca yajnas ca
svadhyayas tapa arjavam (1)

श्रीभगवानुवाच
अभयं सत्त्वसंशुद्धिर्ज्ञानयोगव्यवस्थितिः ।
दानं दमश्च यज्ञश्च स्वाध्यायस्तप आर्जवम् ॥ (१६।१)

ahimsa satyam akrodhas
tyagah santir apaisunam

daya bhutesv aloluptvam
mardavam hrir acapalam (2)

अहिंसा सत्यमक्रोधस्त्यागः शान्तिरपैशुनम् ।
दया भूतेष्वलोलुप्त्वं मार्दवं ह्रीरचापलम् ॥ (१६ । २)

tejah ksama dhrtih saucam
adroho na timanita
bhavanti sampadam daivim
abhijatasya bharata (3)

तेजः क्षमा धृतिः शौचम अद्रोहो नातिमानिता ।
भवन्ति सम्पदं दैवीमभिजातस्य भारत ॥ (१६ ।३)

Srikrsna said:

(The qualities of a born divine person are as follows:)

1. Fearlessness
2. Purity of mind
3. Wise apportionment of knowledge and concentration
4. Charity
5. Self–control and sacrifice
6. Study of scriptures
7. Austerity and uprightness
8. Non–violence
9. Truth
10. Freedom from anger
11. Renunciation of selfishness, attachments
12. Tranquillity
13. Aversion to fault finding
14. Compassion of living beings
15. Freedom from covetousness
16. Gentleness
17. Modesty
18. Steadiness or Firmness (In mind and decisions)
19. Vigour

20. Forgiveness (in deserving cases)
21. Fortitude
22. Purity
23. Freedom from malice and excessive pride

2. Qualities of a Demonaic Person

dambho darpo "bhimanas" ca
krodhah parusyam eva ca
ajnanam ca bhijatasya
partha sampadam asurim (4).

दम्भो दर्पोऽभिमानश्च क्रोध: पारुष्यमेव च।
अज्ञानं चाभिजातस्य पार्थ सम्पदमासुरीम्॥ (१६।४)

(Demonaic person has the following major Qualities/ Vices by birth:–)

1. Ostentation
2. Arrogance
3. Excessive pride
4. Anger
5. Harshness
6. Ignorance

(The *Mahabharata* says that pure divine or pure demonaic persons are not possible to have in real life. Nothing is wholly good or nothing is wholly evil. This has an important message for managers. They should analyse the personality of each individual and put him under divine or demonaic category on the basis of dominance of the attributes of either category. Then positive (divine) attributes be fully utilised and negative (demonaic) attributes be controlled. For some specific tasks, even demonaic quality persons are most suitable. Identify appropriate qualities and select right persons for the right task. There will be no need for management if 100% divinity is there and management would not be able to survive if 100% demonaic personalities persist.)

(There has been an eternal conflict between divine and demonaic cultures. Both type of persons are children of the same God. *Vedas*, epics depict this conflict of two value systems (ethics vs. unethics) which is of perennial nature. This is cosmic, universal, organisational and individual also. The Supreme God has to take *'Avtar'* for restoration of ethical order when demonaic persons crush it. Much depends upon qualities of leaders – Divine or demonaic).

3. Consequences of being Divine or Demonaic

daivi sampad vimoksaya
ni banshaya surimata
ma sucah sampadam daivim
abhijato si pandava (5)

दैवी सम्पद्विमोक्षाय निबन्धायासुरी मता ।
मा शुच: सम्पदं दैवीमभिजातोऽसि पाण्डव ।। (१६ । ५)

The divine endowments are for liberation and the demonaic are for bondage. O Arjuna, you are born with divine endowments.

Therefore, you need not worry. (You will be liberated)

(Krsna assures Arjuna that he is born with divine endowments. His attachment and delusion are situational and are bound to vanish when memory/knowledge is regained by him through this discourse and dialogue. Then he would be able to understand his duty due to the force of born divine qualities in him. In management, there may be cases when a divine person may become confused about his duty. The leader should adopt the communication strategy of Srikrsna to bring back such persons on correct path).

4. Philosophy and Approach to the Life of a Demonaic Person

dvau bhutasargau loke smin
daiva asura eva ca
daivo vistarasah prokta
asuram partha me srnu (6)

द्वौ भूतसर्गौ लोकेऽस्मिन्दैव आसुर एवं च ।
दैवो विस्तरश: प्रोक्त आसुरं पार्थ मे शृणु ।। (१६ । ६)

pravrttim ca nivrttim ca
jana na vidur asurah
na saucam na pi ca caro
na satyam tesu vidyate (7)

प्रवृत्तिं च निवृत्तिं च जना न विदुरासुराः ।
न शौचं नापि चाचारो न सत्यं तेषु विद्यते ॥ (१६।७)

asatyam apratistham te
jagad ahur anisvaram
aparasparasambhutam
kim anyat kamahaitukam (8)

असत्यमप्रतिष्ठं ते जगदाहुरनीश्वरम् ।
अपरस्परसम्भूतं किमन्यत्कामहैतुकमख ॥ (१६।८)

etam drstim avastabhya
nastatmano lpabuddhayah
prabhavanty ugrakarmanah
ksayaya jagato hitah (9)

एतां द्रृष्टिमवष्टभ्य नष्टात्मानोऽल्पबुद्धयः ।
प्रभवन्त्युग्रकर्माणः एतावदिति निश्चिताः ॥ (१६।९)

kamam asritya duspuram
dambhamanamadanvitah
mohad grhitva sadgrahan
pravarante sucivratah (10)

कामाश्रित्य दुष्पूरं दम्भमानमदान्विताः ।
मोहादृगृहीत्वासदृग्राहान्प्रवर्तन्तेऽशुचिव्रताः ॥ (१६।१०)

cintam aparimeyam ca
pralayantam upasritah
kamopabhogaparama
etavad iti niscitah (11)

चिन्तामपरिमेयां च प्रलयान्तामुपाश्रिताः ।
कामोपभोगपरमा एकावदिति निश्चिताः ॥ (१६।११)

asapasasatair baddhah
kamakrodhaparayanah
ihante kamabhogartham
anyayena rthasamcayan (12)

आशापाशशतैर्बद्धा: कामक्रोधपरायणा: ।
ईहन्ते कामभोगार्थमन्यायेनार्थसञ्चयान् ॥ (१६ । १२)

idam adya maya labdham
imam prapsye manoratham
idam asti dam api me
bhavisyati punar dhanam (13)

इदमद्य मया लब्धमिमं प्राप्स्ये मनोरथम् ।
इदमस्तीदमपि मे भविष्यति पुनर्धनम् ॥ (१६ । १३)

asau maya hatah satrur
hanisye ca paran api
isvaro ham aham bhogi
siddho ham balavan sukhi (14)

असौ मया हत: शत्रुर्हनिष्ये चापरानपि ।
ईश्वरोऽहमहं भोगी सिद्धोऽहं बलवान्सुखी ॥ (१६ ।१४)

adhyo bhijanavan asmi
k nyo sti sadrso maya
yaksye dasyami modisya
ity ajnanavimohitah (15)

आढ्योऽभिजनवानस्मि कोऽन्योऽस्तिसदृशो मया ।
यक्ष्ये दास्यामि मोदिष्य इत्यज्ञानविमोहिता: ॥ (१६ । १५)

anekacittavibhranta
mohajatasamavrtah
prasaktah kamabhgesu
patanti narake sucau (16)

अनेकचित्तविभ्रान्ता मोहजालसमावृता: ।
प्रसक्ता: कामभोगेषु पतन्ति नरकेऽशुचौ ॥ (१६ । १६)

atmasambhavitah stabdha
dhanamanamadanvitah
yajante namayajnais te
dambhenavidhipuruakam (17)

आत्मासंम्भाविता: स्तब्धा धनमानमदान्विता: ।
यजन्ते नामयज्ञैस्ते दम्भेनविधीपूर्वकम् ॥ (१६ । १७)

ahamkarma balam darpam
kamam krodham ca samsritah
mam atmaparadehesu
pradvisanto bhyasuyakah (18)

अहङ्कारं बलं दर्पं कामं क्रोधं च संश्रिता: ।
मामात्मपरदेहेषु प्रद्विषन्तोऽभ्यसूयका: ॥ (१६ । १८)

tan aham dvisatah krutan
samsaresu naradhaman
ksipamy ajasram asubhan
asurisv eva yonisu (19)

तानहं द्विषत: क्रूरान्संसारेषु नराधमान् ।
क्षिपाम्यजस्त्रमशुभानासुरीष्वेव योनिषु ॥ (१६ । १९)

asurim yonim apanna
mudha janmani– janmani
mam aprapyai va kaunteya
tato yanty adhamam gatim (20)

आसुरीं योनिमापन्ना मूढा जन्मनि जन्मनि ।
मामत्मपरदेहेषु प्रद्विषन्तोऽभ्यसूयका: ॥ (१६ । २०)

There are two types of living creatures in the world–the divine and the demonaic. The divine have been described at length. O Arjuna, now you listen from Me about the demonaic.

They do not know about the way of action and the way of renunciation. They have no purity, good conduct and truth in them. They say the world is unreal, without a basis, without a Lord (God). It is caused by desire (sexual passions). Holding such views (propagating such philosophies), they cause destruction of this world by their cruel deeds of souls of fable understanding. They give up themselves to insatiable desires. They are full of hypocrisy, excessive pride and arrogance, holding wrong view through delusion they act with malafide resolves. They are obsessed with numerous cares which will end only with (their) death. They consider satisfaction of desires as the only goal of life.

(Demonaic persons have a materialistic approach to life–Charvak philosophy explains it very vividly:–

yavad jivet sukham jivet,
rnani krtva ghrtam pibet
bhasmibhutasya dehasya
punar agamanam kutah

(Live comfortably till you are alive, borrow money to drink ghee because this body will be turned into ashes and there will be no coming back to enjoy this life.)

(This is eat, drink and be merry even through borrowing funds culture. This is 'Leverged Consumption' cult which is being promoted now in India. It will lead to more desire, greed, lust, envy, ego, attachment, stress, strain and conflicts and crimes.)

They are slaves of hundreds of ties of desires, lust anger. They amass hoards of wealth by unfair means for satisfaction of these desires.

They always think, "This I have gained today, this I shall attain, this is mine and this wealth also shall be mine (In future). This enemy is slain by me and I shall kill others also. I am the Lord, I am the enjoyer, I am successful, mighty and happy. I am rich and well–born. None is comparable to me. I shall sacrifice, I shall give I shall rejoice. Thus, they are deluded by ignorance (self–ego, attachments, etc.). They fall into a foul hell (of conflicts, war, non–violence, victory, defeat, dissatisfaction) due to bewilderment arising out of many thoughts, entangled in the meshes of delusion and addicted to the satisfaction of desires.

They perform sacrifices for the name sake with ostentation and without any regard to rules. They show their obstinancy, pride, arrogance of wealth through sacrifices. Such malicous people disrespect Me (God) dwelling in the bodies of their own and others (God witnesses their malific acts also). I hurl them constantly into the wombs of demons. They fail to attain Me in spite of repeated births in demonaic wombs. They go down to the lowest state.

5. The Tiriple Gates of Hell

trividham narakasye dam
dvaram nasanam atmanah
kamah krodhas tatha lobhas
kasmad etat trayam tyajet (21)

त्रिविधं नरकस्येदं द्वारं नाशनमात्मनः ।
कामः क्रोधस्तथा लोभस्तस्मादेतत्त्रयं त्यजेत् ॥ (१६ । २१)

etair utmuktah kaunteya
tamodvarais tribhir narah
acaraty atmanah sreyas
tato yati param gatim (22)

एतैर्विमुक्त: कौन्तैय तमोद्वारैस्त्रिभिर्नर: ।
आचरत्यात्मन: श्रेयस्ततो याति परां गतिम् ॥ (१६ । २२)

Lust, anger, and greed are the three gates of hell. They lead to the ruin of soul. Therefore, avoid them carefully. The man who is released from these three gates to hell (darkness), O Arjuna, will do what is good for the soul and then reach the supreme state (of liberation).

6. Scriptures as Guide to Duty

yah sastravidhim utsrjya
vartate kamakaratah
na sa siddhim ava pnoti
na sukham na param gatim (23)

य: शास्त्रविधिमुत्सृज्य वर्तते कामकारत: ।
न स सिद्धिमवाप्नोति न सुखं न परां गतिम् ॥ (१६ ।२३)

tasmac shastram pramanam te
karyakaryavyavasthitau
jnatva sastravidhanoktam
karma kartum iha rhasi (24)

तस्माच्छास्त्रं प्रमाणं ते कार्याकार्यव्यवस्थितौ ।
ज्ञात्वा शास्त्रविधानोक्तं कर्म कर्तुमिहार्हसि ॥ (१६ । २४)

One who acts as per his desires rejecting the law of scriptures, he does not attain either perfection or happiness or the ultimate goal of liberation. Therefore, let the scriptures be your authority for determining your duty what should be done and what should not be done. Know what is mandated by the scriptures and then you should perform your duty in this world.

(The drive of desire, passion, ego, be replaced by mandates of scriptures. This can serve as a good guide to managers in determining duties and performance norms).

Thus, chapter 16 entitled "*Daivasura sampadvibhaga yoga*" (the yoga of the distinction between the divine and demonaic endowments) is over.

SUMMARY

Divine persons are noble persons and detached performers. They attain self–realisation and freedom from rebirth. Devil or demonaic persons are bad persons. They are materialistic and attached performers. They create a hell of violence, enmity, conflicts, etc. They are subjected to rebirth in lower demonaic wombs. They cause destruction of the world and fail to attain peace and liberation. Managers should identify a person with born qualities. Demonaic qualities be controlled and divine qualities be used effectively. Person be choosen according to his qualities and qualities required for a particular job (assignment).

What is duty should be decided by scriptures (rule book) rather than desires or passions.

APPLICATION OF THREE MODES OF NATURE

Contents

1. Three kinds of
   - (1) Faith
   - (2) Food
   - (3) Sacrifice
   - (4) Penance
   - (5) Gift
2. The mystical utterance of AUM TAT SAT

1. THREE KINDS OF FAITH

Arjuna uvaca
ye saastravidhim utsrjya
ajante sraddhaya nvitah
tesam nistha tu ka krsna
sattvam aho rajas tamah (1)

अर्जुन उवाच
ये शास्त्रविधिमुत्सृज्य यजन्ते श्रद्धयान्विता: ।
तेषां निष्ठा तु का कृष्ण सत्त्वमाहो रजस्तम: ॥ (१७। १)

Arjuna said:

Those who offer sacrifices with faith but violate the mandates of scriptures, what is their position, O Kṛsna? Is it sattva, rajas or tamas?

Sri bhagavan uvaca
tividha bhavati sraddha
dehinami sa svabhavaja
sattviki rajasi cai va
tamasi ce ti tam srnu (2)

त्रिविधा भवति श्रध्दा देहिनां सा स्वभावजा।
सात्त्विकी राजसी चैव तामसी चेति तां श्रृणु॥ (१७।२)

Srikṛsna said :

The faith of embodied is of three kinds born of their nature–sattviki, rajasi, and tamasik. Hear now about it.

sat vanurupa sarvasya
sraddha bhavati bharata
sraddhamayo yam puruso
yo yachhadhya sa eva sah (3)

सत्त्वानुरूपा सर्वस्य श्रद्धा भवति भारत।
श्रद्धामयोऽयं पुरुषो यो यच्छ्रद्धः स एव सः॥ (१७।३)

O Bharata (Arjuna), the faith of every individual is as per his own nature. Man is of the nature of his faith. What is his faith variety, he is that.

Sattva: nature, svabhava

Sraddha: faith–striving after self–realisation (not belief)

According to Bhagvata, the fruit of worship follows the faith of the worshipper VIII.17.)

(Evidence of faith is the heart of the believer).

yjante sattvika devan
yksaraksamisi rajasah
petan bhutaganams ca nye
yjante tamsa janah (4)

यजन्ते सात्त्विका देवान्यक्षरक्षांसि राजसाः।
प्रेतान्भूतगणांश्चान्ये यजन्ते तामसा जनाः॥ (१७।४)

Pure men worship God, passionate worship demi Gods and demons and ignorant worship spirits and ghosts.

asastravihitam ghoram
tapyante ye tapo janah
dambhahamkarasamyuktha
kamaragabalanvitah (5)

अशास्त्रविहितं घोरं तप्यन्ते ये तपो जनाः ।
दम्भाहङ्कारसंयुक्ताः कामारागबलान्विताः ॥ (१७।५)

karsayantah sarirastham
bhutagramam acetasah
mam cai va ntahsarirastham
tan viddhy asuraniscayar (6)

कर्शयन्तः शरीरस्थं भूतग्राममचेतसः ।
मां चैवान्तःशरीरस्थं तान्विद्ध्यासुरनिश्चयान् ॥ (१७।६)

Those men, vain and conceited and forced by lust and passion, who perform violent austerities not approved by scriptures are fools. They supress the elements in body and Me (soul) dwelling in the body. Know these as demonaic in their resolves.

(Methods of self–torture are condemned here as demonaic. Such violators of scriptures are called fools by the teacher of Gita, Srikrsna).

2. Three kinds of food

aharas tv api sarvasya
trividho bhavati priyah
yajnas tapas tatha danam
tesam bhedam imam srnu (7)

आहारस्त्वपि सर्वस्य त्रिविधो भवति प्रियः ।
यज्ञस्तपस्तथा दानं तेषां भेदमिमं शृणु ॥ (१७।७)

ayuhsattvabalarogya
sukhapritivivardhanah
rasyah snigdhah sthira hrdya
aharah sattvikapriyah (8)

आयु:सत्त्वबलारोग्य–
सुखप्रीतिविवर्धना: ।
रस्या: स्निग्धा: स्थिरा हृद्या–
आहारा: सात्त्विकप्रिया: ॥ (१७।८)

katvamlalavanatyusna
tiksnaruksavidahinah
ahara rajasasye sta
duhkhasokamayapradah (9)

कट्वम्ललवणात्युष्णतीक्ष्णरूक्षविदाहिन: ।
आहारा राजसस्येष्टा दु:खशोकामयप्रदा: ॥ (१७।९)

yatayamam gatarasam
puti paryusitam ca yat
ucchistam api ca medhyam
bhojanam tamasapriyam (10)

यातयामं गतरसं पूति पर्युषितं च यत् ।
उच्छिष्टपि चामेध्यं भोजनं तामसप्रियम् ॥ (१७।१०)

Even the food dear to all is of three kinds. So are the sacrifices, austerities and gifts. You listen these distinctions now.

The foods which promote life, vitality, strength, health, joy and cheerfulness, which are sweet, soft nourishing and agreeable are dear to *sattvik* (pure) people.

The foods that are bitter, sour, saltish, very hot, pungent, harsh and burning, producing pain, grief and disease are liked by the passionate '*Rajasik*' people.

The foods that are spoiled, tasteless, putrid, stale, refuse and unclean are liked by the 'dull' (*Tamasik*) people.

As the body is built by food the quality of food is important. Best is *sattvik* food, medium is *rajasik* food and the worst is *tamasik* food. Ban *tamsik*, avoid *rajasik* and prefer *sattvik* food. The type of food we take affects our power of self-control also.

3. Three Kinds of Sacrifice

aphalakanksibhir yajno
vidhidrsto to ijyate
yastavyam eve ti manah
samadhaya sa sattvikah (11)

अफलाकाङ्क्षिभिर्यज्ञो विधिदृष्टो य इज्यते ।
यष्टव्यमेवेति मन: समाधाय स सात्त्विक: ॥ (१७। ११)

abhisamdhaya tu phalam
dambhartham api cai va yat
ijyate bharatasrestha
tam yajnam viddhi rajasam (12)

अभिसन्धाय तु फलं दम्भर्थमपि चैव यत् ।
इज्यते भरतश्रेष्ठ तं यज्ञं विद्धि राजसम् ॥ (१७। १२)

vidhihinam asrstannam
mantrahinam adaksinam
sraddhavirahitam yajnam
tamasam paricaksate (13)

विधिहीनमसृष्टान्नं मन्त्रहीन मदक्षिणम् ।
श्रद्धाविरहितं यज्ञं तामसं परिचक्षते ॥ (१७। १३)

The sattvik (pure) sacrifice is one which is offered as per scriptures, with no expectation of reward and with a firm belief that it is my duty to offer sacrifice.

Yajna: Sacrifice of wealth and action to the service of God (Gita uses the word yajna in a sense different and wider than vedic yajna/ hawan, etc. It uses *yajna* as detached action or enterprise.)

The sacrifice becomes *Rajasik* (Passionate) when reward is expected or it is done for the sake of display (for name and fame).

The sacrifice becomes *Tamasik* (dull, dark) if it is not done in accordance with scriptures, no food is distributed, no hymns are chanted and no daksina (fee) is paid and no faith is there.

The best enterprise is *sattvik* where it is undertaken as duty without selfish motives. Gains are distributed amongst various stakeholders in a fair and just manner. It will lead to sustainable growth, peace and harmony. *Rajasik* enterprise will have ups and downs, conflict, etc. *Tamasik* enterprise is full of exploitation and injustice. It is doomed to fail.

4. Three kinds of Penance

devadvijaguruprajna
pujanam saucam arjavam
brahmacaryam ahimsa ca
sariram tapa ucyate (14)

देवद्विजगुरुप्राज्ञपूजनं शौचमार्जवम् ।
ब्रह्मचर्यमहिंसा च शारीरं तप उच्यते ॥ (१७।१३)

anudvegakarma vakyam
satyam priyahitam ca yat
svadhyayabhyasanam cai va
vanmayam tapa ucyate (15)

अनुद्वेगकरं वाक्यं सत्यं प्रियहितं च यत् ।
स्वाध्यायाभ्यसनं चैव वाङ्मयं तप उच्यते ॥ (१७।१५)

manahprasadah saumyatvam
maunam atmavinigrahah
bhavasamsuddhir ity etat
tapo manasam ucyate (16)

मनःप्रसादः सौम्यत्वं मौनमात्मविनिग्रहः ।
भावसंशुद्धिरित्येतत् तपो मानसमुच्यते ॥ (१७।१६)

sraddhaya paraya taptam
tapas tat trividham naraih
aphalakanksibhir yuktih
sattvikam paricaksate (17)

श्रद्धया परया तप्तं तपस्तत्त्रिविधं नरैः ।
अफलाकाङ्क्षिभिर्युक्तैः सात्त्विकं परिचक्षते ॥ (१७।१७)

satkarmaanapujartham
tapo dambhena cai va yat
kriyate tad iha proktam
rajasam calam adhruvam (18)

सत्कारमानपूजार्थंतपो दम्भेन चैव यत् ।
क्रियते तदिह प्रोक्तं राजसं चलमध्रुवम् ॥ (१७।१८)

mudhagrahena tmano yat
pidaya kriyate tapah
parasyo tsadanartham va
tat tamasam udahrtam (19)

मूढग्राहेणात्मनो यत्पीडया क्रियते तपः ।
परस्योत्सादनार्थं वा तत्तामसमुदाहृतम् ॥ (१७।१९)

The penance of body is worship of gods, dvijas, teachers and wise and pure, upright and peaceful people. The penance of speech is the utterance of non–offending words, truthful, pleasant and beneficial, regular recitation of vedic hymns.

(The speaker as well as listener can't be found *easily of what is* disagreeable but beneficial speech, The *Mahabharata,* Santiparva, 63,(7)

The penance of mind is serenity of mind, gentleness, silence, self–control, the purity of mind.

If the penance of body, speech and mind is practised with utmost faith by men of balanced mind, without expecting any reward, it is called 'sattvik' penance. If it is done to earn respect, honour, reverence or for the sake of show, it is called "rajasik" penance. When it is done with a foolish obstinancy by means of self–torture or for harming others, it is called "tamasik" penance.

Satvik penance of body, speech and mind of people will make climate and culture of an organisation as ideal. Average climate and culture organisation is made by *Rajsik* penance. Worst type of climate and culture of organisation will emerge from *Tamasik* penance.

5. Three kinds of Gifts/ donation

datavyam iti yad danam
diyate nupakarine
dese kale ca patre ca
tad danam sattvikam smrutam (20)

दातव्यमिति यद्दानं दीयतेऽनुपकारिणे ।
देशे काले च पात्रे च तद्दानं सात्त्विकं स्मृतम् ॥ (१७। २०)

yat tu pratyupakarartham
phalam uddisya va punah
diyate ca puriklistam
tad dama, rakasa smrutam (21)

यत्तु प्रत्युपकारार्थं फलमुद्दिश्य वा पुनः ।
दीयते च परिक्लिष्टं तद्दानं राजसं स्मृतम् ॥ (१७। २१)

adesakale yad danam
apatrebhyas ca diyate
asatrta, avakmatam
tat tamasam udahrutam (22)

देशे काले यद्दानमपात्रेभ्यश्च दीनते ।
असत्कृतमवज्ञातं तत्तामसमुदाहृतम् ॥ (१७। २२)

The gift or donation or *daan* which is made to one from whom no return is expected, with a feeling of duty, given in proper place, time and to deserving person, it is callled "Sattvik Gift". But a gift made with the hope of a return or future gain, when it hurts to give is called, "Rajasik Gift" A gift made at a wrong place or time or to an undeserving person, without proper ceremony or with contempt, it is called "Tamasik Gift".

Good Manager/leaders should give *sattvik daan*. *Rajasik daan* is a bribe or deal which is unethical. *Tamasik daan* is wastage of wealth. It may take the form of extortion.

6. The Mystical utterance: Aum tat sat

aum tat sad iti nirdeso
brahanas trividhah smrtah
brahmanas tena edas ca
yajnas ca vihitah pura (23)

ॐ तत्सदिति निर्देशो ब्रह्मणस्त्रिविधः स्मृतः ।
ब्राह्मणास्तेन वेदाश्च यज्ञाश्च विहिताः पुरा ॥ (१७। २३)

tasmad aum ity udahrtya
yajnadanatapahkriyah
pravartante vidhanoktah
satam brahmavadinam (24)

तस्मादोमित्युदाहृत्य यज्ञदानतप:क्रिया: ।
प्रवर्तन्ते विधानोक्ता: सततं ब्रह्मवादिनाम् ॥ (१७। २४)

tad ity anabhisamdhaya
phalam yajnatapahkriyah
danakriyas ca vividhah
kriyante moksakanskibhih (25)

तदित्यनभिसन्धाय फलं यज्ञतप:क्रिया: ।
दानक्रियाश्च विविधा: क्रियन्ते मोक्षकाङ्क्षिभि : ॥ (१७। २५)

sadhave sadhubhave ca
sad ity etat prayujyate
prasaste karmani tatha
sacchabdah partha yujyate (26)

सद्भावे साधुभावे च सदित्येतत्प्रयुज्यते ।
प्रशस्ते कर्माणि तथा सच्छब्द: पार्थ युज्यते ॥ (१७। २६)

yajne tapasi dane ca
sthitih sad iti co cyate
karma cai va tadarthiyam
sad ity eva bhidhiyate (27)

यज्ञे तपसि दाने च स्थिति: सदिति चोच्यते ।
कर्म चैव तदर्थीयं सदित्येवाभिधीयते ॥ (१७। २७)

asraddhaya hutam dattam
tapas taptam krtam ca yat
asad ity ucyate partha
na ca tat pretya no iha (28)

अश्रद्धया हुतं दत्तं तपस्तप्तं कृतं च यत् ।
असदित्युच्यते पार्थ न च तत्प्रेत्य नो इह ॥ (१७। २८)

"Aum tat sat" is considered to be the threefold symbol of *Brahman* (the Supreme God.). By this were ordained of old the *Brahmins*, the *Vedas* and the sacrifices.

(''AUM'' expresses the supremacy of God. TAT expresses univesality of God and "SAT" expresses the truth or reality of God).

Therefore, all acts of sacrifices, gift and penance enjcined in scriptures are always undertaken by the expounders of *Brahma* with the utterance of ''AUM''. These acts are performed with the utterance of 'TAT' by those who seek salvation without aiming at any reward. The word 'SAT' is used for reality and purity. So the word 'Sat' is used for praiseworthy action/deed. Steadfastness in sacrifice, penance and gift or *daan* is also called 'sat'. Any action for such purpose is also called 'SAT'. Any offering or gift made or penance performed or rite observed without faith is called "A–sat" (untrue). O Arjuna, it is of no avail here or in other world.

(Purity of faith, purity of food, purity of sacrifice, purity of penance and gifts (*daan*) with chanting of "AUM TAT SAT" is recommended for excellence of performance and perfection of life attaining liberation).

This chapter 17, Entitled "*Sraddhatrya vibhag yoga*" (The yoga of threefold division of faith) is over.

Summary

The faith is born of nature. It may be pure, passionate or dark/dull as per own nature of man. What is his faith, variety, he is that. Worship is also as per faith. It is demonaic to self–torture through violent acts not approved by scriptures. One must avoid such acts.

Prefer pure quality of food because your body is made of food. The type of food will affect your power of self-control also. Therefore, avoid rajasik and tamaysik food. Sacrifice of wealth and deeds be "pure", not for reward and not for ego satisfaction. The penance of body, speech and mind must also be "pure", with no return, as duty and given to deserving person, at right place, right time and in the manner approved by scriptures.

"AUM" be uttered in the beginning of all sacrifices, donation penance and "AUM TAT SAT" be uttered after it is done. (It will make it complete).

Purity in life and deeds will give excellence, perfection, sound health of managers and will lead to the emergence of an effective organisation.

THE CONCLUSION (THE YOGA OF RELEASE/ RENUNCIATION)

Contents

1. Renounce fruits, not work/duty
1. Work is function of nature
2. Knowledge and action
3. Three kinds of knowledge
4. Three kinds of work
5. Three kinds of doers
6. Three kinds of undertakings
7. Three kinds of steadiness
8. Three kinds of happiness
10. Duties based on attitudes
11. Karma yoga and perfection
12 Perfection and Brahma
13. The top devotion
14. Application of Teachings of Gita to Arjuna's case
15. Final appeal
16. Benefits and conditions of Gita janan a yajna
17. Arjuna accepts duty willingly
18. Master Key to effective Management.

1. Renounce fruits, not work/duty

arjuna uvaca
samny asaya mahabaho
tattvam icchami veditum
tyagasya ca hrsikesa
prthak kesinisudana (1)

अर्जुन उवाच
सन्न्यासस्य महाबाहो तत्त्वमिच्छामि वेदितुम् ।
त्यागस्य च हृषीकेश पृथक्केशिनिषूदन ॥ (१८।१)

shribhagavan uvaca
kamyanam karmanam nyasam
samnyasam kavayo viduh
sarvakarma phalatyagam
prahus tyagam vicaksanah (2)

श्रीभगवानुवाच
काम्यानां कर्मणां न्यासं सन्न्यासं कवयो विदु: ।
सर्वकर्मफलत्यागं प्राहुस्त्यागं विचक्षणा: ॥ (१८।२)

tyajyam doshavad ity eke
karma prahur manisinah
yajnadanatapahkarma
na tyajyam iti ca pare (3)

त्याज्यं दोषवदित्येके कर्म प्राहुर्मनीषिण: ।
यज्ञदानतप:कर्म न त्याज्यमिति चापरे ॥ (१८।३)

niscayam srnu me tatra
tyage bharatasattama
tyago hi purusavyghra
trividhah samprakirtitah (4)

निश्चयं शृणु मे तत्र त्यागे भरतसत्तम ।
त्यागो हि पुरुषव्याघ्र त्रिविध: सम्प्रकीर्तित: ॥ (१८।४)

yjnadanatapahkarma
na tyajyam karyam eva tat
yajno danam tapas cai va
pavanani manisinam (5)

यज्ञदानतप:कर्म न त्याज्यं कार्वमेव तत् ।
यज्ञो दानं तपश्चैव पावनानि मनीषिणाम् ॥ (१८।५)

etany api tu karmani
sangam tyaktva phalani ca
kartavyani ti me partha
niscitam matam uttamam (6)

एतान्यपि तु कर्माणि सङ्गं त्यक्त्वा फलानि च ।
कर्तव्यानिति मे पार्थ निश्चितं मतमुत्तमम् ॥ (१८।६)

niyatasya tu samnyasah
karmano no papadyate
mohat tasya parityagas
tamasah parikirtitah (7)

नियतस्य तु सन्न्यस: कर्मणो नोपपद्यते ।
मोहातस्य परित्यागस्तामस: परिकीर्तित:॥ (१८।७)

duhkham ity eva yat karma
kayaklesabhayat tyajet
sa krtva rajasam tyagam
nai va tyagaphalam labhet (8)

दु:खमित्येव यत्कर्म कायक्लेशभयात्त्यजेत् ।
स कृत्वा राजसं त्यागं नैव त्यागफलं लभेत् ॥ (१८।८)

karyam ity eva yat karma
niyatam kriyate rjuna
sangam tyaktva phalam cai va
sa tyagah sattviko matah. (9)

कार्यमित्येव यत्कर्म नियतं क्रियतेऽर्जुन ।
सङ्गंत्याक्त्वा फलं चैव स त्याग: सात्त्विको मत: ॥ (१८।९)

na dvesty akusalam karma
kusale na nusjjate
tyagi sattvasamavisto
medhavi chinnasamsayah (10)

न द्वेष्ट्यकुशलं कर्म कुशले नानुषज्जते ।
त्यागी सत्त्वसमाविष्टो मेधावी छिन्नसंशय: ॥ (१८।१०)

na hi dehabhrta sakyam
tyaktum karmany asesatah
yas tu karmaphalatyagi
sa tyagi ty abhidhiyate (11)

न हि देहभृता शक्यं त्यक्तुं कर्माण्यशेषत: ।
यस्तु कर्मफलत्यागी स त्यागीत्यभिधीयते ॥ (१८।११)

anistam istam misram ca
trividham karmanah phalam
bhavaty atyaginam pretya
na tu samnyasinam kvacit (12)

अनिष्टमिष्टं मिश्रं च त्रिविधं कर्मण फलम् ।
भवत्यत्यागिनां प्रेत्य न तु सन्न्यासिनां क्वचित् ॥ (१८।१२)

Arjuna said:

"O Mahabaho (Kṛsna), now I want to know the true nature of renunciation and relinquishment, severally.

Srikṛsna said:

"By renunciation the wise understand the giving up of works prompted by desire,the renouncement of the fruits of all works is relinquishment as per learned people.

(Gita supports *Niskarma Karma* and has no place for *"niskarma"* or renouncement of work/duty).

Action should be given up as an evil, say some learned men. Others say that acts of sacrifice, gift and penance should not be given up.

(Samkara holds this view that knowledge and work are incompatible which Gita does not accept). Now Srikṛsna declares his view emphatically. "O Arjuna, relinquishment has three aspects. Acts of sacrifice, gift and penance are not to be relinquished, but must be performed. These are purifiers of the wise. But even these works must be performed, giving up attachment and desire for fruits. (These acts be also done *Sattvik* or pure). O Arjuna, this is my decision and final view.

(This final view of Srikrsna is in conformity with *Brahadaranyaka Up.* IV,4,22. "It is the *Brahman*(God) whom the *Brahmins* (pure souls) wish to know by the study of *vedas*, and also by means of sacrifice, gift and austerities performed without attachment).

Verily the renunciation of any duty that ought to be done (as *Dharma*) is not right. It is "*tamasik*" to do so. He who gives up a duty because it is painful or from fear of physical suffering, does relinquishment of "*Rajasik*" (passionate) type. He will derive no gain from it. But he who performs a prescribed duty as "*Dharma*" renouncing all attachment and also the fruits (selfish benefits)– his relinquishment is *sattvik* (pure). Such a wise renouncer, whose doubts are dispelled, whose nature is pure *(sattvik)*, has no aversion to disagreeable action and no attachment to agreeable action (he has no preferences of work, action or duties).

It is impossible for any embodied being to abstain from work completely. But he who renounces the fruits of action, he is said to be the relinquisher.

Those who have not relinquished attachment to fruits of action, the fruit of action after death may be pleasant, unpleasant or mixed. But none for the relinquisher.

2. Work is function of Nature

pancai tani mahabaho
karanani nibodha me
samkhye krtante proktani
siddhaye sarvakarmanam (13)

पश्चैतानि महाबाहो कारणानि निबोध मे ।
साङ्‍ख्ये कृतान्ते प्रोक्तानि सिद्धये सर्वकर्मणाम् ॥ (१८ । १३)

adhisthanam tatha karta
karanam ca prthagvidham
vividhas ca prthakcesta
daivam cai va tra pancamam (14)

अधिष्ठानं तथा कर्ता करणं च पृथग्विधम् ।
विविधाश्च पृथक्चेष्टा दैवं चैवात्र पश्चमम् ॥ (१८ । १४)

sariravanmanobhir yat
karma prarabhate narah
nyayyam va viparitam va
pancai te tasya hetavah (15)

शरीरवाङ्मनोभिर्यत्कर्म प्रारभते नरः ।
न्याय्यं वा विपरीतं वा पञ्चैते तस्य हेतवः ॥ (१८ । १५)

tatrai vam sati kartaram
atmanam kevalam tu yah
pasyaty akrtabuddhitvan
na sa pasyati durmatih (16)

तत्रैवं सति कर्तारमात्मानं केवलं तु यः ।
पश्यत्यकृतबुद्धित्वान्न स पश्यति दुर्मतिः ॥ (१८ । १६)

yasya na hamkrto bhavo
buddhir yasya na lipyate
hatva pi sa imaml lokan
na hanti na nibadhyate (17)

यस्य नाहङ्कृतो भावो बुद्धिर्यस्य न लिप्यते ।
हत्वापि स इमाँल्लोकान्न हन्ति न निबध्यते ॥ (१८ । १७)

"O Arjuna, learn from Me, five factor theory of accomplishment of all actions, as stated in *samkhya (Vedanta)* doctrine.

Adhisthana (physical body), *Karta* (doer or agent), instruments, *cesta* (efforts), *daivam* (providence) are the five factors of action.

(In Management parlance, five causes or factors of action are –

1. Organisation, planning, control and motivation, i.e., Management (adhisthan). This includes the Leader (adhisthata) also.
2. Operating manpower (doers/agent), middle management.
3. Equipments or tools of action
   Physical resources/technology/finance, etc.
4. Efforts
   Start, progress, review, adjustment, compliance.
5. Destiny/Luck
   Unexplanied factors affecting final outcome–success or failure.

The weightage of each successive factor is higher than the preceding factors. Thus, destiny/luck, if strong, may bring succeess easily, whereas if it is not strong, then failure may arise in spite of best management, manpower, equipment and efforts.

Whatever action man undertakes by his body, speech or mind whether it is right or wrong, these five factors are behind it. Therefore, those who think self as sole doer are mistaken (soul is not a doer, it is only a witness. All acts are the products of nature. But all the five factors play their role in all actions).

One who is free from self–sense, who has clear/pure understanding, though he slays people (in a war), he does not slay nor he is bound (by his action of fighting war).

(Liberated man does his work as the instrument of God and for the maintenance of the cosmic order. Deeds may be terrific but if there is no selfish aim but it is done as duty, it becomes pure. Thus, what is significant is not nature of work but the spirit behind it. A session judge awards capital punishment and an executor executes it. No sin will come to them if it is done as duty without any selfish motive. But the same thing will be treated as a crime if X kills Y for some selfish purpose. For this, X will be punished by the court of law.)

3. Knowledge and Action

jnanam jneyam parijnata
trividha karmacodana
karanam karma karte ti
trividhah karmasamgrahah (18)

ज्ञानं ज्ञेयं परिज्ञाता त्रिविधा कर्मचोदना ।
करणं कर्म कर्तेति त्रिविधः कर्मसङ्ग्रहः ॥ (१८ । १८)

jnanam karma ca karta ca
tridhai va gunabhedatah
procyate gunasamkhyane
yathavac shrnu tanyapi (19)

ज्ञानं कर्म च कर्ता च त्रिधैव गुणभेदतः ।
प्रोच्यते गुणसङ्ख्याने यथावच्छृणु तान्यपि ॥ (१८ । १९)

Knowledge, the objects of knowledge and the knowing subject are the three–fold incitement to action. The instruments, the action and the agent are the three–fold composite of action.

Karmacodana: The mental planning for action

Karmasamgraha: The actual execution.

Each has three–fold aspects–knowledge, action and the agent are of three kinds in different modes of nature. Listen these now.

4. Three Kinds of Knowledge

sarvabhutesu yenai kam
bhavam avyayam iksate
avibhaktam vibhaktesu
taj jnanam viddhi sattvikam (20)

सर्वभूतेषु येनैकं भावमव्ययमीक्षते ।
अविभक्तं विभक्तेषु तज्ज्ञानं विद्धि सात्त्विकम् ॥ (१८ । २०)

prthaktvena tu yaj jnanam
nanabhavan prthagvidhan
vetti sarvesu bhutesu
taj jnanam viddhi rajasam (21)

पृथक्त्वेन तु यज्ज्ञानं नानाभावान्पृथग्विधान् ।
वेत्ति सर्वेषु भूतेषु तज्ज्ञानं विद्धि राजसम् ॥ (१८ । २१)

yat tu krtsnavad ekasmin
karye saktam ahetukam
atattvarthavad alpam ca
tat tamasam udahrtam (22)

यत्तु कृत्स्नवदेकस्मिन्कार्ये सक्तमहैतुकम् ।
अतत्त्वार्थवदल्पं च तत्तामसमुदाहृतम् ॥ (१८ । २२)

"*Sattvik*" or pure knowledge is holistic knowledge. The imperishable God is seen in all existences, undivided in the divided, "*Rajasik*" or passionate knowledge is segmented knowledge. It sees multiplicity of beings in the different creatures by reason of that separatedness.

" *Tamasik*" or dark/ dull knowledge is attachment to single effect as if it were the whole without any concern for the cause and without grasping the real.

(*Sattvik* knowledge leads to harmony, peace and excellent performance of the whole organisation. Segmented/departmented *Rajasi* knowledge leads to passions, conflicts, stress and strain, sickness, etc., inter–group, inter–deptt and inter–personal conflicts, leg pulling, back biting resistance to change, etc. Departments start working at cross purposes resulting into loss of harmony and loss of over all performance of the organisation. *Tamasik* knowledge leads to dullness and loss of opportunities, delayed and wrong decisions, indecision and procrastination, dissatisfaction,decline in production/productivity/profitability etc. Managers should stress on holistic knowledge and harmony in order to attain organisational effectiveness.)

5. Three kinds of work

nyatam sangarahitam
aragadvesatah krtam
aphalaprepsuna karma
yat tat sattvikam ucyate (23)

नियतं सङ्गरहितमरागद्वेषत: कृतम् ।
अफलप्रेप्सुना कर्म यत्तत्तामसमुच्यते ॥ (१८ । २३)

yt tu kamepsuna karma
sahamkarena va punah
kriyate bahulayasam
tad tajasam udahrtam (24)

यत्तु कामेप्सुना कर्म साहङ्कारेण वा पुन: ।
क्रियते बहुलायासं तद्राजसमुदाहृतम् ॥ (१८ ।२४)

anubandham ksayam himsam
had arabhyate karma
yat tat tamasam ucyate (25)

अनुबन्धं क्षयं हिंसामनवेक्ष्य च पौरुषम् ।
मोहादारभ्यते कर्म यत्तत्तामसमुच्यते ॥ (१८ । २५)

"*Sattvik*" work is obligatory and performed without love or hate. The work undertaken or done in great strain by one who seeks to satisfy selfish desires or is impelled by self–sense (*ahmkara*) is called "*rajasik* work" or passionate work. The action undertaken through ignorance, without regard to consequences (loss or injury to others) and without regard to one's human capacity is called *tamasik* work.

Bahulayasam: with great strain.

(This classification of work can be illustrated by an example:

(a) Work is tough and unpleasant. It is being done reluctantly or with aversion. Great strain and poor performance will arise.

(b) Work is tough and unpleasant but it is being done with a feeling of great sacrifice being made, it is failure of sacrifice itself. Doing tough and unpleasant work as duty but constantly feeling it as burden is *rajasik* work. It may result into performance with stress and strain. Failure can't be digested.

(c) Work is tough and unpleasant but it is undertaken as duty gladly, with a smile on lips, it makes the work "*sattvik*". Everyone minds own work. No conflicts stress and strain.

(This is the difference between an act of law and an act of love.)

Promote *Sattvik* work culture in order to make an effective organization.

6. Three kinds of Doers

kuktasango nahamvadi
dhrtyutsahasamanvitah
siddhyasiddhyor nirvikarah
karta sattvika ucyate (26)

कुक्तसङ्गोऽनहंवादी धृत्युत्साहसमन्वित: ।
सिद्ध्यसिद्ध्योर्निर्विकार: कर्ता सात्त्विक उच्यते ॥ (१८ । २६)

ragi karmaphalaprepsur
lubdho himsatmako such
harsasokanvitah karta
rajasah parikiritah (27)

रागी कर्मफलप्रेप्सुर्लुब्धो हिंसात्मकोऽशुचि: ।
हर्षशोकान्वित: कर्ता राजस: परिकीर्तित: ॥ (१८ । २७)

ayuktah prakrtah stabdhah
satho naikrtiko lasah
visdai dirghasutri ca
karta tamasa ucyate (28)

अयुक्त: प्राकृत: स्तब्ध: शठोऽनैष्कृतिकोऽलस: ।
विषादी दीर्घसूत्री च कर्ता तामस उच्यते ॥ (१८ । २८)

One who does work without any attachment, ego but with full resolution and zeal, without any worry about success or failure, he is called, "*sattvik*" or pure doer.

One who is swayed by passion, who eagerly seeks the fruits of his works, who is greedy, of harmful nature, impure, who is moved by joy and sorrow, he is called "*rajasik*" (passionate) doer.

One who is imbalanced, vulgar, obstinate, deceitful, malicious, indolent, despondent and procrastinating, he is called "*tamasik*" (dull,ignorant) doer.

Prakratah: raw, uncultured.

7. Three Kinds of Understanding

buddher bhedam dhrtes cai va
gunatas trividham srnu
procyamanam asesena
prthaktvena dhanamjaya (29)

बुध्देर्भेदं धृतेश्चैव गुणतस्त्रिविधं शृणु।
प्रोच्यमानमशेषेण पृथक्त्वेन धनञ्जय ॥ (१८।२९)

pravrttim ca nivrttim ca
karyakarye bhayabhaye
bandham moksam ca ya vetti
buddhih sa partha sattviki (30)

प्रवृत्तिं च निवृत्तिंच कार्याकार्ये भयाभये।
बन्धं मोक्षंच या वेत्ति बुद्धि: सा पार्थ सात्त्विकी ॥ (१८।३०)

yaya dharmam adharmam ca
karyam ca karyam eva ca
ayathavat prajanati
buddhih sa partha rajasi (31)

यया धर्ममधर्मं च कार्यं चाकार्यमेव च।
अयथावत्प्रजानाति बुद्धि: सा पार्थ राजसी ॥ (१८।३१)

adharmam dharmam iti ya
manyate tamasa vrta
sarvarthan viparitams ca
buddhih sa partha tamasi (32)

अधर्मं धर्ममिति या मन्यते तमसावृता।
सर्वार्थान्विपरीतांश्च बुद्धिः सा पार्थ तामसी॥ (१८। ३२)

"O Arjuna, now you listen the three–fold distinction of understanding and also of steadiness, according to the modes of nature."

The understanding which knows action and nonaction, what should be done and what should not be done, what is to be feared and what is not to be feared, what binds and what frees the soul, it is called *"sattvik"* (pure) understanding.

The understanding which one knows in a mistaken way the right and wrong, what should be done and what should not be done, it is called, O Arjuna, *"Rajasik"* (passionate) understanding.

The understanding which is enveloped in darkness (ignorance), conceives as right what is wrong and sees all things in a perverted way (contrary to truth), it is called *"tamasik"* (dull, ignorant) understanding.

8. Three Kinds of Steadiness

dhrtya yaya dharayate
manahpranendriyakriyah
yogena vyabhicarinya
dhrtih sa partha sattviki (33)

धृत्यायया धारयते मनःप्राणेन्द्रियक्रियाः।
योगेनेव्यभिचारिण्या धृतिः सा पार्थसात्त्विकी॥ (१८। ३३)

yaya tu dharmakamarthan
dhrtya dharayate rjuna
prasangena phalakanksi
dhrtih sa partha rajasi (34)

यया तु धर्मकामार्थान्धृत्या धारयतेऽर्जुन।
प्रसङ्गेन फलाकाङ्क्षी धृतिः सा पार्थ राजसी॥ (१८। ३४)

yaya svapnam bhayam sokam
visadam madam eva ca
na vimuncati durmedha
dhrtih sa parha tamasi (35)

यया स्वप्नं भयं शोकं विषादं मदमेव च ।
न विमुञ्चति दुर्मेधा धृतिः सा पार्थ तामसी ॥ (१८ । ३५)

"*Sattvik*" or pure steadiness is one by which, through concentration, one controls the mental activities, life breath and the senses.

Dhrtih: Steadiness of attention which makes us aware of much that our ordinary vision is not able to observe. It increases proportionally to our detachment from past regrets and future anxieties. Those who live in the present have higher level of steadiness.

The steadiness which enables one to hold fast to duty, pleasure and wealth, desire of fruits of action, O Arjuna, it is called *"Rajasi* (passionate) steadiness.

The steadiness which makes a fool to cling to sleep, fear, grief, depression, arrogance, etc; O Partha (Arjuna), it is called "*tamasik* (dull, ignorant) steadiness.

9. Three kinds of Happiness

sukham tu idanim trividham
srnu me bharatarsabha
abhyasad ramate yatra
duhkhantam ca nigacchati (36)

सुखं त्विदानीं त्रिविधं शृणु मे भरतवर्षभ ।
अभ्यासाद्रमते यत्र दुःखान्तं च निगच्छति ॥ (१८ । ३६)

yat tad agre visam iva
pariname mrtopamam
tat sukham sattvikam proktam
atmabuddhiprasadajam (37)

यत्तदग्रे विषमिव परिणामेऽमृतोपमम् ।
तत्सुखं सात्त्विकं प्रोक्तमात्मबुद्धिप्रसादजम् ॥ (१८ । ३७)

visayendriyasamyogad
yat tad agre mrtopamam
pariname visam iva
tat sukham rajasam smrtam (38)

विषयेन्द्रियसंयोगाद्यत्तदग्रेऽमृतोनमम् ।
परिणामे विषमिव तत्सुखं राजसं स्मृतम् ॥ (१८ । ३८)

yad agre ca nubandhe ca
sukham mohanam atmanah
nidralasyapramadottham
tat tamasam udahtram (39)

यदग्रे चानुबन्धे च सुखं मोहनमात्मनः ।
निदआलस्यप्रमादोत्थं तत्तामसमुदाहृतम् ॥ (१८ । ३९)

"O Bharata (Arjuna), now you listen from Me the three kinds of happiness (*sukham*).

The happiness in which a man comes to rejoice by long practise (of *yoga* and concentration) and in which he attains to end of his sorrow is "*sattvik*" (pure) happiness. It is like poison in the beginning but like nectar at the end. It springs from a clear understanding of 'self' (self-realisation).

The happiness which arises from the contact of the senses and their objects, which is like nectar in the beginning and like poison at the end, it is called "*Rajasik*" (passionate) happiness (in fact it is pleasure-sensuary pleasure).

The happiness which deludes the soul in the beginning as well as in the end and which arises from sleep, sloth and negligence is called "*tamasik*" (dull, ignorant) happiness. (in fact it is neither happiness nor pleasure but it appears so to an idle/ignorant person).

(Happiness is the universal aim. Ignorant seeks it in action, sleep, negligence, etc., passionate seeks it in action for wealth and power, name and fame. The pure soul will seek it in excellent performance of duty without attachment and ego. First, creates a mirage of happiness. The second, is pleasant when we gain but unpleasant when we loose. The third, is difficult in the beginning but it is nectar–like in the end.)

10. Duties Based on Aptitudes

na tad asti prthivyam va
divi devesu va punah
sattvam prakrtijair muktam
yad ebhih syat tribhir gunaih (40)

न तदस्ति पृथिव्यां वा दिवि देवाशु वा पुनः ।
सत्त्वं प्रकृतिजैर्मुक्तं यदेभिः स्यात्त्रिभिर्गुणैः ॥ (१८ । ४०)

brahmanaksatriyavisam
sudranam ca paramtapa

karmani pravibhaktani
svabhavaprabhavair gunaih (41)

ब्राह्मणक्षत्रियविशां शूद्राणां च परन्तप ।
कर्माणि प्रविभक्तानि स्वभावप्रभवैर्गुणै: ॥ (१८ । ४१)

samo damas tapah saucam
ksantir arjavam eva ca
jnanam vijnanam astikyam
brahmakarma svabhavajam (42)

शमो दमस्तप: शौचं क्षान्तिरार्जवमेव च ।
ज्ञानं विज्ञानमास्तिक्यं ब्रह्मकर्म स्वभावजम् ॥ (१८ । ४२)

sauryam tejo dhrtir daksyam
yuddhe ca py apatayanam
danam isvarabhavas ca
ksatram karma svabhavajam (43)

शौर्यं तेजो धृतिर्दाक्ष्यं युद्धे चाप्यपलायनम् ।
दानमीश्वरभावश्च क्षात्रं कर्म स्वभावजम् ॥ (१८ । ४३)

krsigauraksyavanijyam
vaisyakarma svabhavajam
paricaryatmakam karma
sudrasya pi svabhavajam (44)

कृषिगौरक्ष्यवाणिज्यं वैश्यकर्म स्वभावजम् ।
परिचर्यात्मकं कर्म शूद्रस्यापि स्वभावजम् ॥ (१८ । ४४)

sve sve karmany abhiratah
samsiddhim labhate narah
svakarmaniratah siddhim
yatha vindati tac chrnu (45)

स्वे स्वे कर्मण्यभिरत: संसिद्धिं लभते नर: ।
स्वकर्मनिरत: सिद्धिं यथा विन्दति तच्छृणु ॥ (१८ । ४५)

yatah pravrttir bhutanam
yena sarvam idam tatam
svakarmana tam abhyarcya
siddhim vindati manavah (46)

यत: प्रवृत्तिर्भूतानां येन सर्वमिदं ततम् ।
स्वकर्मणा तमभ्यर्च्य सिद्धिं विन्दति मानव: ॥ (१८। ४६)

sreyan svadharmo vigunah
paradharmat svanusthitat
svabhavaniyatam karma
kurvan na pnoti kilbisam (47)

श्रेयान्स्वधर्मो विगुण: परधर्मात्स्वनुष्ठितात् ।
स्वभावनियतं कर्म कुर्वन्नाप्नोति किल्बिषम् ॥ (१८। ४७)

sahajam karma kaunteya
sadosam api na tyajet
sarvarambha hi dosena
dhumena gnir iva vrtah (48)

सहजं कर्म कौन्तेय सदोषमपि न त्यजेत ।
सर्वारम्भा हि दोषेण धूमेनाग्निरिवावृता: ॥ (१८। ४८)

Nobody is free from three modes born of nature. The classification of four *varnas* is based on attitude (qualities born of nature).

(There is link between nature or *svabhava* or attitude and the duty or *svadharma*. It is not based on birth).

Serenity, self-control, austerity, purity, forbearance, uprightness, wisdom, knowledge, faith in religion are the natural aptitude elements of a *Brahmin*. (person of knowledge and good conduct).

Heroism, vigour, steadiness, resourcefulness, not fleeing from battlefield, generosity and leadership are the natural qualities of an administrator (*Ks'atriya*).

Agriculture (cultivation), tending cattle (generating resources by value addition), trade (generating profit/surplus by exchange or barter) are the born traits of businessman. *(Vais'yas)*.

Rendering service to others is the natural trait of *sudra* or employees.

(People have freedom to move from one category to other on the basis of aptitude. But once this is done, they must perform '*Svadharma*' or own duty, with full devotion and detachment.)

Devoted each to his own duty man attains perfection (excellence). How this happens now you listen from Me.

Man attains perfection by performing duty as a worship to the God from whom all–beings arise and by whom all this is pervaded.

(Work is worship to the God).

It is always better to perform own duty even imperfectly rather than to carry out others duty perfectly. No sin is incurred when one does his own duty ordained by one's nature.

(This is a question of democratic choice and deduction. But aping others' duty for which own nature has not made us is of no use. Nobody should be discouraged/depressed by making unwarranted comparisons with others performance for which one has no natural aptitude.)

One should not give–up the work suited to one's nature, O Arjuna, though it may be defective, for there is no enterprise which has no defect as fire is clouded by smoke.

(No work should be left on the ground that it has some defect. It should be given up only when it does not suit one's aptitude).

11. Karma Yoga and Perfection

asaktabuddhih sarvatra
jitatma vigatasprhah
naiskarmyasiddhim paramam
samnyasena dhigacchati (49)

असक्तबुद्धि: सर्वत्र जितात्मा विगतस्पृह: ।
नैष्कर्म्यसिद्धिं परमां सन्यासेनाधिगच्छति ॥ (१८ । ४९)

He attains to the supreme state through renunciation transcending all work. His understanding is unattached everywhere, who has subdued his self and from whom desires have fled. (He is a *Karma yogi*).

(Freedom from desire and nonattachment to sense objects are essential for spiritual perfection. Work is not to be renounced but only desires and attachments are to be renounced).

12. Perfection and Brahmam

siddhim prapto yatha brahma
tatha pnoti nibodha me
samasenai va kaunteya
nistha jnanasya ya para (50)

सिद्धिं प्राप्तो यथा ब्रह्म तथाप्नोति निबोध मे।
समासेनैव कौन्तेय निष्ठा ज्ञानस्य या परा॥ (१८।५०)

buddhya visuddhaya yukto
dhrya tmanam niyamya ca
sabdadin visayams tyaktva
ragadvesau vyudasya ca (51)

बुद्ध्या विशुद्धया युक्तो धृत्यात्मानं नियम्य च।
शब्दादीन्विषयांस्त्यक्त्वा रागद्वेषौ व्युदस्य च॥ (१८।५१)

viviktasevi laghvasi
yatavakkayamanasah
dhyanayogaparo nityam
vairagyam samupasritah (52)

विविक्तसेवी लघ्वीशी यतवाक्कायमानस:।
ध्यानयोगपरो नित्यं वैराग्यं समुपाश्रित:॥ (१८।५२)

ahamkarma balam darpam
kamam krodham parigraham
vimucya nirmamah santo
brahmabhuyaya kalpate (53)

अहङ्कारं बलं दर्पं कामं क्रोधं परिग्रहम्।
विमुच्य निर्मम: शान्तो ब्रह्मभूयाय कल्पते॥ (१८।५३)

"O Arjuna, now listen from Me, in brief how (*Karma yogi*) having attained perfection will attain to the *Brahman*, the supreme consummation of wisdom. Endowed with a pure understanding, firmly restraining one self, turning away from objects of sense and casting aside attraction and aversion, dwelling in solitude, eating very little, controlling speech, body and mind, ever engaged in meditation and concentration, taking refuge in dispassion, casting aside self–sense, force, arrogance, desire, anger, possession and egoless and tranquil in mind, he becomes fit to become one with *Brahma* (the Supreme God).

Dhyana yoga: Meditation on the nature of self and the mental concentration on it.

13. The Top Devotion

brahmabhutah prasannatma
na socati na kanksati
samah sarvesu bhutesu
madbhaktim labhate param (54)

ब्रह्मभूत: प्रसन्नात्मा न शोचति न काङ्क्षति ।
समः सर्वेषु भूतेषु मद्भक्तिं लभते पराम् ॥ (१८।५४)

bhaktya mam abhijanati
yavan yas ca smi tattvatah
tato mam tattvato jnatva
visate tadanantaram (55)

भक्त्या मामभिजानाति यावान्यश्चास्मि तत्त्वत: ।
ततो मां तत्त्वतो ज्ञात्वा विशते तदनन्तरम् ॥ (१८।५५)

Having become one with *Brahma*, and being tranquil in spirit, he has no grieves and desires. He regards all–beings are the same (equal). He attains Supreme devotion to Me. Through devotion (bhakti) he comes to know Me, what My measure is and who I am in truth. Having known Me in truth, he immediately enters into Me. (*advaita* state is attained).

(Thus, the supreme wisdom and supreme devotion both have common goal entering into the God/ liberation/emancipation).

14. Application of Teachings of Gita to Arjuna's case

sarvakarmany api sada
kurvano madvyapasrayah
matprasadad avapnoti
sasvatam padam avyayam (56)

सर्वकर्माण्यपि सदा कुर्वाणो मद्व्यपाश्रयः ।
मत्प्रसादादवाप्नोति शाश्वतं पदमव्ययम् ॥ (१८।५६)

cetasa sarvakarmani
mayi samnyasya matparah
buddhiyogam upasritya
maccittah satatam bhava (57)

चेतसा सर्वकर्माणि मयि सन्न्यस्य मत्परः ।
बुद्धियोगमुपाश्रित्य मच्चित्तः सततं भव ॥ (१८।५७)

maccittah sarvadurgani
matprasadat tarisyasi
atha cet tvam ahamkaran
na srosyasi vinanksyasi (58)

मच्चित्तः सर्वदुर्गाणि मत्प्रसादात्तरिष्यसि ।
अथ चेत्त्वमहङ्कारान्न श्रोष्यसि विनङ्क्ष्यसि ॥ (१८।५८)

yad ahamkarma asritya
na yotsya iti manyase
mithyai sa vyauasayas te
prakrtis tvam niyoksyati (59)

यदहङ्कारमाश्रित्य न योत्स्य इति मन्यसे ।
मिथ्यैष व्यवसायस्ते प्रकृतिस्त्वां नियोक्ष्याति ॥ (१८।५९)

suabhavajena kaunteya
nibaddhah svena karmana
kartuni necchasi yan mohat
karisyasy avaso pi tat (60)

स्वभावजेन कौन्तेय निबद्धः स्वेन कर्मणा ।
कर्तुं नेच्छसि यन्मोहात्करिष्यस्यवशोऽपि तत् ॥ (१८।६०)

isvarah sarvabhutanam
hrddese rjuna tisthati
bhramayan sarvabhutani
yantrardhani mayaya (61)

ईश्वर: सर्वभूताना हृद्देशेऽर्जुन तिष्ठति ।
भ्रामयन्सर्वभूतानि यन्तारूढानि मायया ॥ (१८ । ६१)

tam eva saranam gaccha
sarvabhavena bharata
tatprasadat param santim
sthanam prapsyasi sasvatam (62)

तमेव शरणं गच्छ सर्वभावेन भारत ।
तत्प्रसादात्परां शान्तिं स्थानं प्राप्स्यसि शाश्वतम् ॥ (१८ । ६२)

iti te jnanam akhyatam
gugyad guhyataram maya
vimrsyai tad asesena
yathe ecchasi tatha kuru (63)

इति ते ज्ञानमाख्यांतं गुह्याद्गुह्यतरं मया ।
विमृश्यैतदशेषेण यथेच्छसि तथा कुरु ॥ (१८ । ६३)

Doing continually own duty whatsoever, taking refuge in Me, he will reach My undying, eternal abode by My grace.

(There is no conflict between work, devotion and wisdom. All will lead to the same goal of excellence and freedom from bondage, God will be graceful to those who do their duties taking refuge in God).

(Therefore, O Arjunà, you should surrender in thought all actions to Me, considering Me as the Supreme and resorting to steadfastness in understanding, you fix your thoughts constantly on Me. Fixing your thought on Me, you shall by My grace, crossover all difficulties. If you will not listen to Me from self–conceit, you shall perish.)

(God invites man to be always with Him in heart, will, consciousness and action. Man is not forced. He is given free choice between salvation or prediction).

If indulging in self–conceit, you think "I will not fight" this resolve of yours will go in vain because your nature (of *ks'atriya*) will compel you to fight.

(Let us submit willingly to God's choice rather than falling victim of our desires/natural forces/forces of circumstances.)

Through delusion, you may wish not to fight, O Arjuna, you will do that even against your wish fettered by your own acts born of your nature.

The Lord (God) abides in the hearts of all–beings, O Arjuna, causing them to turn around by His power as if they were mounted on a machine. Run to take His shelter. By His grace, you will attain the Supreme peace and eternal abode.

(Saint Tulsidas has stated the same thing in *'man kram vacan chadi chaturai, bhajat krupa karihain Raghu rai."* God will shower His grace on you as soon as you leave cleverness (skill) of mind, speech and action and devote yourself to Him).

This is the wisdom secret of all secrets. Reflect on it fully and do as you like.

(Kṛsna is a democratic leader. He is not forcing Arjuna but advising him to make a proper choice after full reflection on His teachings. Gita teaching is not indoctrination or conversion).

·15. Final Appeal

sarvaguhyatamam bhuyah
srnu me paramam uacah
isto si me drdham iti
tato vaksyami te hitam (64)

सर्वगुह्यतमं भूय: शृणु मे परमं वच: ।
इष्टोऽसि मे दृढमिति ततो वक्ष्यामि ते हितम् ॥ (१८ । ६४)

manmana bhava madhakto
madyaji mam namaskuru
mam evai syasi satyam te
pratijane priyo si me (65)

मन्माना भव मद्भक्तो मद्याजी मां नमस्कुरु ।
मामेवैष्यसि सत्यं ते प्रतिजाने प्रियोऽसि मे ॥ (१८ । ६५)

sarvadharman parityajya
mam ekam saranam vraja
aham tva sarvapapebhyo
moksayisyami ma sucah (56)

सर्वधर्मान्परित्यज्य मामेतं शरणं व्रज ।
अहं त्वा सर्वपापेभ्यो मोक्षयिष्यामि मा शुच: ॥(१८ । ६६)

Listen again My Supreme word, the most secret of all. You are beloved to Me, therefore, I shall tell you what is good for you.

Fix your mind on Me;

Be devoted to Me;

Prostrate yourself before Me;

I promise you shall come to Me,

You are dear to Me.

(Verse 34 chapter IX of Gita is repeated here. It is the key verse of Gita. It has been repeated in final appeal by way of reiteration).

Abandoing all duties, clearing aside all controversial approaches,come to Me alone for shelter. Be not grieved, for I shall grant liberation/emancipation to you.

(This is *carma mantra* of *Ramanuj Sampradaya*. It does not give a call to renounce all duties. But it is a call to give up all controversies about what should be done and what should not be done and seek refuge of the God. Have full faith in His words and act with no attachment and desire as per the direction given by Him–the Supreme inner consciousness. He will make you free from all grief and grant emancipation).

Since Arjuna was confused about his duty due to various rituals, conventions and philsophies, Kṛsna uttered this *carma sloka* (ultimate *sloka*)

16. Benefits and conditions of Gita Janan a yajna

idam te na tapaskaya
na bhaktaya kadacana
na ca susrusave vacyam
na ca mam yo bhyasuyati (67)

इदं ते नातपस्काय नाभक्ताय कदाचन।
नचाशुश्रूषवे वाच्यं न च मां याऽभ्यसूयाति॥ (१८।६७)

ya idam paramam guhyam
madbhaktesu abhidhasyati
bhaktim mayi param krtva
mam evai syaty asamsayah (68)

य इमं परमं गुह्यं मद्भक्तेष्वभिधास्याति।
भक्तिं मयि परां कृत्वा मामेवैष्यत्यसंशय:॥ (१८।६८)

na ca tasman manusyesu
kascin me priyakrttamah
bhavita na ca me tasmad
anyah priyataro bhuvi (69)

न च तस्मान्मनुष्येषु कश्चिन्मे प्रियकृत्तमः ।
भविता न च मे तस्मादन्यः प्रियतरो भुवि ॥ (१८।६९)

adhyesyate ca ya imam
dharmyam samvadam avayoh
jnanayajnena tena ham
istah syam iti me matih (70)

अध्येष्यते च य इमं धर्म्यं संवादमावयोः ।
ज्ञानयज्ञेन तेनाहमिष्टः स्यामिति मे मतिः ॥ (१८।७०)

sraddhavan anasuyas ca
srnuyad api yonarah
so pi muktah subhaml lokan
prapnuyat punyakarmanam (71)

श्रद्धावाननसूयश्च शृणुयादपि यो नरः ।
सोऽपि मुक्तः शुभाँल्लोकान्प्राप्नुयात्पुण्यकर्मणाम् ॥ (१८।७१)

kaccid etac shrutam partha
tvayai kagrena cetasa
kaccid ajnanasammohah
pranastas te dhanamjaya (72)

कच्चिदेतच्छ्रुतं पार्थ त्वयैकाग्रेण चेतसा ।
कच्चिदज्ञानसम्मोहः प्रनष्टस्ते धनञ्जय ॥ (१८।७२)

This teaching of Gita should not be spoken to one who is not austere in life who has no devotion, who is not obedient or who speaks ill of Me (God).

(Gita teachings are not meant for non–devotees and non–believers in God. They may not understand correctly and may misuse them).

One who teaches this Supreme secret to My devotees, showing the highest devotion to Me, he shall no doubt come to Me. He is most dear to Me.

A teacher of Gita will attain to the God by spreading Gita message amongst devotees of God because he is most dear to the God.

One who studies this sacred dialogue of ours, I would be worshipped by him through *Gita Janana yajna*. He will also be liberated who listens this dialogue with faith and without scoffing. He will attain to My happy abode where righteous persons go.

"O Arjuna, have you heard this with pointed attention? Has your distraction (of thought) caused by ignorance has been dispelled?"

17. Arjuna Accepts Duty Willingly

arjuna uvaca
nasto mohah smrtir labdha.
tvatprasadan maya cyuta
sthito smi gatasamdehah
karisya vacanam tava (73)

अर्जुन उवाच
नष्टो मोह: स्मृतिर्लब्धा त्वत्प्रसादान्मयाच्युत।
स्थितोऽस्मि गतसन्देह: करिष्ये वचनं तव॥ (१८।७३)

Arjuna said:

My delusion is destroyed. I have gained memory through your grace, O Krsna, I stand firm with my doubts dispelled. I shall act according to your word (advice).

A person can make correct decision (choose correct alternative) when he is free from delusion and gains memory of what is he, where is he, why is he, and what is his final destination. He stands firm and is free from doubts. This happens through the grace of God. Then he declares that he will act as per the advice of God as against his own desires and attachments. That leads him to the realisation of God through excellent performance of God's work).

18. Master Key to Effective Management

samjay uvaca
ity aham vasudevasya
parthasya ca mahatmanah
samvadam imam asrausam
adbhutam romaharsanam (74)

सञ्जय उवाच
इत्याहं वासुदेवस्य पार्थस्य च महात्मनः ।
संवादमिममश्रौषमद्भुतं रोमहर्षणम् ॥ (१८।७४)

vyasaprasadac chrutavan
etad guhyam aham param
yogam yogesvarat krsnat
saksat kathayatah svayam (75)

व्यासप्रसादाच्छ्रुतवानेतद्गुह्यमहं परम् ।
योगं योगेश्वरात्कृष्णात्साक्षात्कथयतः स्वयम् ॥ (१८।७५)

tac ca samsmrtya samsmrtya
rupam atyadbhutam hareh
vismayo me mahan rajan
hrsyami carunah punah (77)

तच्च संस्मृत्य संस्मृत्य रूपमत्यद्भुतं हरेः ।
विस्मयो मे महान्राजन्हृष्यामि च पुनः पुनः ॥ (१८।७७)

yatra yogesvarah krsno
yatra partho dhanurdharah
tatra srir vijayo bhutir
dhruva nitir matir mama (78)

यत्र योगेश्वरः कृष्णो यत्र पार्थो धनुर्धरः ।
तत्र श्रीर्विजयो भूतिर्ध्रुवा नीतिर्मतिर्मम ॥ (१८।७८)

Samjaya said :

Thus, I have heard this wonderful dialogue between Vasudeva (Kṛsna) and Partha (Arjuna), causing my hair to stand on end. I heard this Supreme secret, this *yoga* taught by Kṛsna himself, the Lord of yoga in person (to Arjuna). It became possible by the grace of Vyạsa. (Vyasa granted to Samjaya power to see and hear from a distance what transpired on battlefield of Kurukshetra so that he may be able to report the events to king Dhritarastra who was blind).

O King, as I recall again and again this dialogue, wonderous and holy of Kesava (Kṛsna) and Arjuna, I thrill with joy, repeatedly. And as often as recall that most wondrous form of Hari (Kṛsna), great is my astonishment, O King, and I thrill with joy repeatedly. (The master key to effective management is revealed now in the end thus.)

yatra yogesvarah krsno
yatra partho dhanurdharah
tatra srir vijayo bhutir
dhruva nitir matir mama (78)

यत्र योगेश्वरः कृष्णो यत्र पार्थो धनुर्धरः ।
तत्र श्रीर्विजयो भूतिर्ध्रुवा नीतिर्मतिर्मम ॥ (१८।७८).

I think, wherever there is (leader like) Krsna, the Lord of yoga, and (executive like) Partha (Arjuna), the archer, there will surely be fortune, prosperity, victory, welfare and morality.

(A combination of wisdom leadership with devoted and detached executives is essential for prosperity (productivity) and well–beings in the society/organisation. Wrong leadership creates major crisis but wisdom leadership alone cannot make management effective unless it is accompanied by devoted expert executives who obey the orders of such leaders. Good executives led by unethical leaders would create ethical dilemmas and management would not be effective. Therefore, master key of effective management lies in a combination of widsom leadership (*Raj yogis)* with devoted expert executives. (*karma yogis*)

(a combination of knowledge, devotion and action)

(The picture of Krsna holding reins of five horses in his hands and advising Arjuna about his duty – *Karma yoga, Janan a yoga* and *bhakti yoga* depicts the great message to humanity. Handover control of your sensuary organs to the God and act as per His directions with full devotion and detached action. Never act as per force of your senses. Never sit idle on the pretext that God will take care of everything. Do your duty and take refuge in God. Thus, Gita is nectar which grants liberation/emancipation through performance of duty. Renounce attachment to selfish fruits and lower senses in order to perform your duty excellently. See the inner light, obey the inner voice and attain Supreme self-illumined abode of peace and eternal bliss through your excellent deeds.

Thus, chapter 18 entiled *moks karmasanayasayoga* (the yoga of release and renunciation) is over.

SUMMARY

Krsna told Arjuna that Niskarma karma is real renunciation. Work should never be given up because it is impossible for any embodied to abstain from work completely. Work is function of nature. It has five factors – Adhisthana, karta, instruments, cesta and daivam. Work be done for liberation. Perfection will take to Brahma and finally to liberation if all elements are pure (sattvik).

No work is small, big, good or bad. No work is without defects. Own duty must be performed with devotion and detachment. There must be matching of aptitude with work. One must concentrate on his own duty. Supreme wisdom and supreme devotion both lead to common goal of emancipation.

Leader should not compel or convert people to obey his orders. He should seek willing co-operation through open dialogue. When all doubts are dispelled and memory is regained through dialogue executives will be in a position to decide rationally.

Gita teachings are meant for devotees who have faith in God. Gita Janana yajna also grants liberation to teacher as well as listener. Krsna's final appeal to Arjuna reemphasises on concentration, devotion, sacrifice and surrender. Liberation is assured. He is advised to give up all controversies about ethics and take shelter of God. Liberation is guaranteed in this manner.

Master key to effective management is combination of wisdom leadership with devoted executives. This will guarantee prosperity (productivity) and well–beings in society/organisations. God may advise but you have to perform . Renounce fruits and attachments, and not work itself. This is main advice of Krsna.

APPENDICES

SELECTED BIBLIOGRAPHY

1. Telang K.T. the Bhagvadi Gita, 1882
2. Arnold Edwin: The song celestial, 1885
3. Sastri Mahadeva A: The Bhagvad Gita, 1901
4. Barneth L.D.: The Bhagvad Gita, 1905
5. Annie Besant *etal* : Bhagvad Gita, 1905
6. Sri Aurobindo: Essays on the Gita, 1928
7. W. Dougles P. Hill: The Bhagvad Gita, 1928
8. Tilak B.G: Gita Rahasya E.T., 1935
9. Sarma D.S.: The Bhagvad Gita, 1937
10. Franklin Edgerton: The Bhagvad Gita, 1944
11. Swami Prabhavananda : The Bhagvad Gita, 1945
12. Mahadev Desai: The Gita according to Gandhi, 1946
13. Dr. S. Radhakrishnan: The Bhagavad Gita, 1948
14. Farquhar J.N.: Permanent Lessons of the Gita. Madras, 1904
15. Gabre, R.: "Bhagvad Gita, in Hasings, J. (ed.), Encyclopedia of Religion and Ethics II (Edinburgh, 1909),
16. Garrett, J. (ed.): The Bhagvat Geeta, or Dialogues of Krishna and Arjoon. Bangalore, 1849
17. Hill, W.D.P.: The Bhagavad Gita. 2nd ed. Oxford, 1953
18. Vivekananda, Swami: Thoughts on the Gita. Calcutta, 1974

GLOSSARY OF SANSKRIT TECHNICAL WORDS

Dharamksetre: The field of ethic/ Righteouoness.

Kuruksetre: The field of action/ Duty Battlefield of Kaurava and Pandavas

Mamkah: My people

Acharya : Teacher one who has knowledge and practise of scriptures and preached it.

Dvijottama : Best of Twice–born most cultured born into world of nature and world of spirit.

Aparyaptam: Insufficient.

Acyuta: One name of Krsna/Visnu, immovable.

Swajanam : Own people, kinsmen.

Brahmavidya: The science of absolute.

Yoga sastra: The scriptures of Yoga (union).

Samvada: Dialogue.

Visada: Depression.

Anarya justam: Unaryan, devoid of courage, nobility and straight dealing.

Rudhiya pradigdham: Smeared with blood.

Niscitam: For certain.

Na yotsye: I will not fight.

Tusnim abhuva: Became silent.

Avidhya: Ignorance.

Niyata karma: Designated duty.

Tatam: Pervaded.

Svata siddha: Self–established.

Adhyaropana: Superposition.

Sariri : True self

Swadharma: Self–duty.

Brahman: The creator, the God.

Brahmana: Knowledge people of good conduct.

Ksatriya: Warrior, administrators.

Vaisyas: Businessmen.

Sudras: Service class.

Samkhya: Vedanta (in Gita).

Yoga: Union/skill in action/ meditation.

Buddhi: Intellect.

Manas: Mind

Cit: Concentrated mind.

Karma: Duty, action, work, creative force.

Sacrifice: Spending wealth and resources, life for some purpose.

Karmakanda: Rituals– vedic rituals.

Yogasthah: Steadfast in inner composure.

Samatvam: Inner poise/ self–control over lower level senses of anger, pride, desires etc.,

Buddhiyoga: Yoga of knowledge– union of intellect with spirit/ divine.

Samadhi: State of highest consciousness.

Srutivipratipanna: Confused by vedic texts.

Samnyasa: Abandoning rituals and social obligations. Last ashram in four ashrams/ renunciation.

Kama: Desires

Buddhinasa : Destruction of intellect.

Sthitaprajna: Who has no selfish aims or personal desires/ demands/undisturbed.

Carati: Acts.

Santim: Peace.

Brahmisthiti: Life eternal.

Nirvanam: Emancipation, liberation from rebirth moksham.

Naiskarmya: Unaffected by work.

Yajna: Work done in spirit of sacrifice

Kamadhuk: Kamdhenu cow of Indra which fulfilled all desires.

Loka samgraha: World maintenance.

Prakrteh: Power of Maya or the power of the supreme God.

Prakarati: Nature, aptitude.

Purusa : Soul.

Purushottama: The Supreme God, parabrahman.

Anicchanmapi: Agent his will.

Idam: This.

Janan: Knowledge of self/spiritual wisdom.

Vijanan: Personal experience based or experiment based knowledge/ logical knowledge.

Rajarsyah: Royal sages like king Janak, Ram, etc.

Kalena mahata: By the great efflux of time.

Yogah puratanah: Ancient yoga.

Bhakta: Devotee.

Sakha: Companion.

Avtara: Incarnation.

Dharma: Duty/ ethics.

Adharma: Violation of duty or ethics, unethical.

Sadhunam: Sages, righteous.

Duskrtam: Bad or wicked people.

Vinasaya: Destruction.

Yug:	Age, time period of 12 years.
Punarjanma:	Rebirth.
Moksha:	Emancipation/ freedom from re–birth.
Madbhavam:	Super natural being which I possess.
Mama vartma:	My path.
Sarvasah:	On all sides.
Sarvaprakarah:	In all ways.
Caturvarnyam:	Four fold classification on the basis of aptitude/ temperament.
Akartaram:	Non–doer.
Atma suddhiyartham:	For self–purification.
Loksamgrahartham:	For maintenance of world order.
Karma:	Action, work, duty.
Akarma :	Action/ work/duty without attachment.
Vikarmaa :	Prohibited action/work.
Saritam karma:	Work required to maintain body.
Prana:	The outgoing breath.
Sraddha:	Faith.
Narawsantim:	The supreme peace.
Yogasamnyastakarmanam:	Who has renounced all work by yoga.
Atmavantam :	Who possesssed his self.
Nityasamnyasi:	Who has ever the spirit of renunciation.
Yuktah:	United, disciplined in action.
Prabhuh:	The sovereign self.
Vibhuh:	All pervading.
Ajnanena:	By ignorance.
Parmartha tattvam:	The ultimate reality.
Vinaya:	Humility/ modesty (lack of pride).
Samadarsinah:	See all with equal eye.
Brahmani sthitah:	Established in God.
Brahmanirvana:	Attains to the God.
Sarvabhutatite ratah:	Engaged in the welfare of all beings.
Sadhanavastha:	Work done in the right spirit.
Siddhavastha:	Self-possession.
Samkalpa:	Purposes, resolve.
Jitatman:	Self-controlled.
Paramatma:	The supreme God/self.
Kutastha:	Set on a high place, firm, tranquil.

Ekagrena cetasa:	Mind fixed on one point, concentrated mind.
Satatam:	Constantly.
Ekaki:	Alone, solitude.
Yatacittatma:	Self-controlled
Nirasi:	Free from desires.
Aparigrahah:	Free from longing for possession.
Sampreksya:	Gaze fixed.
Nasikagram:	Tip of the nose.
Brahmacharya :	Celibacy/ being in the company of God.
Isvarah :	Personal God/ God in form.
Annirvinnacetasa:	No slackness of effort.
Brahmabhutam:	One with God
Brahmasamsparsam:	Contact with the eternal.
Atmaupamyena:	Equality of others with oneself.
Sucinam :	Righteous, Inward purity.
Sabdabrahma:	God in words (vedas).
Sahasranam :	Out of thousands.
Raga:	Passion.
Daivi:	Divine.
Sukrtinah :	Virtuous ones.
Udarah:	Noble kind.
Artah:	Sufferer.
Artharthi:	Seeker of gain.
Jnani :	Wise/knower of God.
Jijnasuh:	Seeker of intellectual satisfaction.
Bahunam:	Several.
Adhyatma :	Soul/phase of the divine which constitutes the individual self
Bhava:	Thought.
Anusmaran :	Remembering.
Prabhava:	Manifestation.
Pralaya :	Nonmanifestation.
Rajavidya :	The Supreme secret.
Avidya :	Ignorance, maya, darkness.
Raksasim :	Fendish, cruel, tamasik.
Asurim :	Demonaic, rajasik.
Daivam :	Divine, pure sattvik.
Anityam:	Perishable, impermanent.

Asukham: Sorrowful.
Lokam: World
Priyamanaya: Beloved.
Dama: Self-control.
Sama: Calmness of inner spirit.
Ahimsa: Non–violence.
Vibhuti: Glory.
Atmabhava : Inner sense of being.
Vibhutayah: Manifestations.
Amaratam: Nectar–like.
Gudakesa: A name of Arjuna, controller of sleep.
Adityas : 12 vedic Gods.
Kala: Time.
Ekamisena: By a single fraction.
Divya caksus: The divine or angelic eye.
Aneka: Several.
Vaktra: Mouth faces.
Nayanam: Eyes.
Aksaram: Imperishable soul.
Ksar: Perishable body.
Purushottam: The supreme person/God.
Sasvatadharmna : The eternal guardian of *sanatan dharma*
Gopta: (eternal ethics)/God.
Kalanala: Doomesday fire
Maya hatan: Doomed by Me.
Adikartr: Original creator/Creator of Brahma.
Jannivasa: The refuge of the universe/the God.
Saksatkara: The direct perception of the divine.
Samniyamya: Restraining of senses.
Aniketah: No fixed abode, homeless.
Prakarati: Unconscious activity.
Purusa: Inactive consciousness.
Ksetram: Field / body.
Ksetrajna: Knower of field or body /soul/God.
Mahabhuta: Five major elements–earth, water, fire, air, ether.
Anadimatparam: Beginningless supreme.
Bhutaprakriti: The material nature of being.

Trigunatita: Beyond or above three modes of nature sattva ṛajas and tamas.

Sattva : Pure good nature

Rajas : Passionate nature.

Tamas : Dullness, idle ignorant nature.

Prakasa: Illumination.

Aprakasa : Non–illumination.

Nistraigunya : The transcence of three gunas , emancipation.

Jivanmukta : Emancipated/ liberated.

Asvattham : Peepla tree.

Samsarvrksa : Cosmic tree.

Mamai vamisati : Fragment, fraction of mine.

Prakratisthani: In their natural placess.

Tej: Splendour.

Pacamy : Cook/digest.

Apohanam : Loss,destruction, rejection.

Aprvatistham : Without any (moral) basis.

Sastra : Scripture.

Sattva : Nature.

Aphalakanksi: O these who expect no reward.

Atmasamarpana : Complete self–giving.

Adhisthana : Seat physical body, organisation management.

Karta : Doer / agent.

Cesta : Efforts.

Daivam : Chance providence luck.

Karmacoderna : Mental planning.

Karma samgrtaha : Actual execution.

Bahulayasam : With great strain.

Prakrtah : Raw, uncultured.

Dhritih : Steadiness of attention.

Sukham : Happiness.

Abhiratah : Devoted busy.

Sarvabhavena : With all your being.

Bvimrsyaitad asesena: Reflect on it fully.

Yatha icchasitatha : Kuru Do as you wish.

Samsmrtya : Recall.

SUBJECT INDEX